Born in the Summer of his 27th Year

By Robert Hahn

Dedication

I dedicate this book to my dog Lazarus. My constant companion for the 12 years of his life, Lazarus was not only the most intelligent of all of my dogs, but he was the most human-like, as well. He thought like a human, he was competitive on a human level, and could do many things that the average dog was just unable to do, like opening locked windows, and the refrigerator, until I put a lock on it, or giving me canine CPR, and retrieving women for me. During the time span of this story alone we each saved each other's lives three times each! He was not only a special dog, but also a very special friend. He died in 1982, and yet he remains constantly in my thoughts to this day! I will always love you Laz, and one day we will be reunited, and I will throw the ball for you, forever!

Acknowledgements

I would like to thank Klaus for inspiring me to take off on this amazing, magical journey. I thank Little Bear (Father), and Holy Alex for imparting their great wisdom of what life is, and what our place in life should be in relation to ourselves and all other living things. I thank Josh, for being my friend and guide/teacher through almost all of this journey! I thank Brian and David for showing me that the impossible is always possible! And of course I need to thank all of the beautiful ladies that I met along the way, especially Chartreuse, Amber, Kathleen, Lucy Lou, Mary Lee, and Cassandra, who will always have a special place in my heart! And last but not least my buddy Ben, who is still one of my best friends to this day! I also thank my friends and members of the Topanga Writers Group, for all of your kindness, support, and guidance throughout the process of writing this book.

Text Copyright©2013 Robert Hahn

All Rights Reserved

Chapter 1

Beach livin', acid trips and my amazing dog, Lazarus

It was the spring of 1973. The war in Vietnam was just starting to wind down, as the Watergate scandal was starting to heat up. I was living in Marina Del Rey California; On the Marina Peninsula at the corner of Driftwood and Speedway about 50 feet from the beach in a small cottage.

There was no way that I could have known about the confluence of events both in my near past and future-- both fatal and near fatal-- which would propel me on a trip out of Los Angeles, north to Canada, on a crazy, funny, spiritual, magical, roller coaster ride of sex, drugs, and rock n' roll that would influence my life forever; a trip which will live in my memories, and my soul, until long after I shift off of this mortal coil.

The Peninsula consisted mostly of old cottages with only a few apartments. It looked very close to the way that it looked 15 years earlier in 1957-58 in Orson Welles classic film, "Touch of Evil," which was filmed almost entirely in Venice, California, and on what would eventually become the Marina Peninsula of Marina Del Rey in 1965. The film is a favorite of mine, not only because of the great cast and writing, but also because of the way Orson Welles shot it, giving it an amazingly dark noir quality.

I have heard more than one critic refer to it as, "The greatest B movie ever made."

I had moved in two years earlier with a girl named Andrea, who was a friend of a friend.

These cottages were small, two-bedroom houses apparently built in the '20s or '30s averaging about 900 square feet in size with no front yard to speak of, but a large concrete front porch. They did have a long fenced backyard, all sand of course.

I had my dog Lazarus, whom I had gotten from the SPCA in 1970. He was a black Labrador/Pharaoh Hound mix. Lazarus was a fetch junkie and the most intelligent dog that I've ever owned. He was addicted to fetching to the point that if I didn't have time to throw something for him, he would get his stick or whatever was handy and go to the nearest person that he could find and get them to throw it for him. He was so smart that if he saw two people talking, he would go to the one who was talking and nudge them with the stick, because he knew that they were involved with what they were saying and would just throw the stick over and over again to get rid of him, not realizing that he was just using them until they stopped talking.

    I was a singer-songwriter at this time playing in some of the local clubs like the Troubadour, the Whiskey-a-Go-Go, and the Bitter End West.

    I liked to sit on the porch and play my guitar and sing and write songs. I quickly learned that I could train Lazarus to bring home the girl of my choice.

    The way it worked was that a lot of people used Driftwood Street to walk to the beach. So when I saw a really pretty girl walking toward the beach with her beach stuff, I would get Laz and point her out aiming his head right at her so he would not miss her, and then I would say, "Go get her. Go get her, Laz." And he would run towards her, picking up something to throw on the way.

    Then he would go to the beach with her, her throwing the stick and him fetching it.

    I would sit on the porch singing and playing guitar for a couple of hours, or until their return.

    And then here would come, Lazarus with the pretty girl in tow on my side of Driftwood. And, when they were about 20 feet away, Laz would run up onto the porch and sit next to me. The girl would always ask, "Is that your dog? He's such a great dog. I really like that song you were singing. You wrote it? You're a songwriter? I love your voice." I almost always got the girl and Lazarus always got a nicely cooked chuck steak. It worked out well for both of us.

    I calculated that over the three or so years that I lived in the Marina, Lazarus retrieved around 25 to 30 women for me. It was a great partnership, I usually got the girl and Lazarus always got a nice juicy steak.

    Sadly, I could not keep Lazarus around the house and, when he would take off, he was really hard to find. Once, after finding him in Santa Monica, I had his picture and tag number and my contact info posted in every animal control office in a 60-mile radius, and put them up all over my neighborhood. I sprung him out of the Hermosa Beach pound twice and the Santa Monica pound four times. Between the numerous apparent fights and being run over four times, twice before my very eyes, I estimate that over the 12 years of his life, Laz racked up somewhere between 800 to 900 stitches.

While doing the music at night I started a furniture company in my backyard and did that during the day.

One bad incident with Lazarus occurred on July 4, 1972. Lazarus always hated loud noises. A car backfiring, a firecracker, even a champagne cork could set him off.

So knowing that I was going to a party a couple of blocks up the street on the 4th, I locked him in my bedroom.

But, as I said earlier, Lazarus was a very intelligent dog, and, apparently when the fireworks started going off around 7:30 pm on the beach while I was gone, Lazarus opened the snap latch on my bedroom window and got out.

Completely oblivious to the fact that he was running loose the whole time, I rolled back into my house about two o'clock in the morning with a girl, Cassie, that I had picked up from the party.

At about 4:00 a.m., while Cassie and I were in the midst of "flagrant delecto,"as Frank Macrae put it in the movie "Dillinger," Lazarus strolled through the open back door and into my bedroom doorway. And there he stood.

Suddenly my bedroom smelled like an old wet rug had been thrown onto a fire.

Startled, I turned on the light, and there was Lazarus. Burn marks around his mouth. Large spots of burnt flesh with no fur, some still smoking, covered his body. Cassie said, "Oh my God!" I jumped out of bed and put Lazarus immediately into the shower, soaping him down as he whimpered and cried. After drying him off, I coated his burns with vitamin E salve, after spraying them with Bactine. And then I wrapped his wounds with gauze.

Cassie helped and after we doctored him up I gave Lazarus a small bowl of wine. Wine always seemed to calm him down ever sense he knocked over half a bottle of wine and got drunk while I was gone, when he was a puppy. After we got him put to bed the dawn was just breaking, so Cassie and I climbed up on the roof and smoked a joint and watched the dawn break on the beach. After that and a cup of tea she took off.

About 9:00 am after breakfast, I went out on to the porch and started playing my guitar. I was too tired to do much of anything else. I had a big cushion that covered the top of the front porch landing that I would sit on while I played. Lazarus limped out and laid next to me on it.

Mike from across the street came running over to me. Excitedly he said, "You better get that fucking dog of yours in the house before somebody sees him."

I said, "What the hell are you talking about, Mike?"

Mike replied, "You don't know? You haven't heard?"

"Heard what?" I asked Mike.

Mike continued, "Your dog man, your dog. He terrorized the whole beach last night. I thought that he may have burned down a couple of places, and a car or two. "

It hit me like a slap in the face. I said to Mike, "Oh, God. It was the fireworks. He went after the fireworks, huh?"

Mike replied, "You're Goddamned right he did. Somebody would light a Roman candle and he would rip it out of the sand and run around with it in his mouth shooting balls of fire into the apartments, onto people's decks. He hit one guy in the middle of the back and set his shirt on fire. I tried to catch him, but he was too fast. At one point I thought that he was dead for sure. Some guy lit an M-100, and Lazarus picked it up, and I thought that it was going to blow his head off, but, at the last second, he spit it out, I think the fuse was burning his mouth. The worst part is that he spit it right next to a keg of beer, and it blew up the keg sending it about 12 feet into the air spraying the whole crowd with beer. The last thing I saw of Lazarus, he was running from the guys who brought the keg and they were chasing him down the beach. I heard that a black dog dragged a four-foot fireworks display through the middle of a crowd of people way down on Windward, but luckily nobody got hurt but the dog."

Mike continued, "The good news is that I made some calls this morning, and from what I can tell the only damage was that a dumpster caught fire, and a tree burned about four blocks down, and the guy whose shirt caught fire only has some minor burns. People quickly put out the small fires in the apartments. But make no mistake about it, animal control, and the cops are looking for your dog. So get him the fuck in the house."

I put down my guitar and put out my hand, and shaking Mike's hand I said, "Thanks a lot brother. I mean it, man. Thanks a lot."

I managed to keep Lazarus in the house, or took him with me if I had to leave for any reason over the next month, while he healed.

Most of my friends lived on the peninsula; including my good friend Ben who also was originally from Houston, Texas, like me. When I was in Houston, I was on the freeway and noticed that the new Buick Riviera in front of me had the license plate "EZ BEN." I remember thinking, "That's a cool license plate." And just then in the fast lane a Texas DPS (Highway Patrol) car came flying past us like we were standing still, followed closely by what seemed to be an endless number of cop cars obviously from many different jurisdictions going just as fast. I found out later that it was the infamous "Sugarland Express."

After coming to California later in 1969, I had lived with my parents for a few months and then moved down by LAX into a 3 Bedroom house with two buddies for a year.

And soon after that, I met Andrea, the girl who would eventually become my roommate in the Driftwood house in Marina del Rey; she invited me over to some friends' place on the other side of the Marina Peninsula; they were a couple, Ben and Georgia.

Georgia's nickname was Squirt. Ben was a handsome blonde guy and Georgia was a petite attractive blonde who was a Playboy Bunny. I hit it off with both of them. When I looked on their fireplace mantel and I saw the "EZ BEN" license plate, I yelled out, "Oh my God. You're EZ Ben." I recounted the Sugarland Express story, which he said that he recalled. And we both agreed that it is a very small world. He is one of my best friends still to this day.

I used to see George Carlin at the liquor store at Lincoln and Speedway all of the time, and we became friends. He even came to a couple of my parties. What a great guy, funnier than hell, and very intelligent. He used to call me Tex, because I wore a University of Texas letterman's jacket that a buddy gave me who went to UT. I went to the University of Houston. But for George, the name "Tex" always stuck.

My other friends were my new roommate, Richard, and Glenn, a crazy hippie who was also really funny and a great guy. Also there was Jim, who was a projectionist at the studios, plus Mike who lived across the street with his girlfriend Jane and her kid.

I had lost some friends. John White had fallen off of a Chinese junk in the marina harbor a few slips up from where Dennis Wilson of the Beach boys would die diving off of a 52-foot yawl, the "Emerald" 10 years later. John was loaded on downers; Dennis was very drunk, diving to the bottom and bringing up things that he had thrown off the "Emerald." The result was the same however, they both drowned.

Some months after Andrea and I moved into the Driftwood House on New Year's Eve of 1972 (my birthday is New Year's Day) Ben, Georgia, Andrea and I, and some other friends decided to go down town to the new Sports Arena to attend a New Year's Eve Party Concert featuring Canned Heat and Little Richard, among other bands. The posters said that there would be fire eaters, jugglers, stilt walkers, etc. Ben said that he had some acid, and when he asked if anyone else wanted to drop some with him. Only Andrea and I said yes.

The problem was that somehow Ben, Andrea and I wound up in my Buick with me driving, while everyone else went in another car. No one seemed to realize as we left, the problem of having all of the people on acid in one car, and everyone else in the other.

Somehow we got separated from the other car on the freeway and then got lost downtown as we were really starting to peak on the acid.

I was driving, and when everything started to melt, stoplights, buildings, etc. I saw a place to pull over with a man standing there. I pulled over and asked him for directions to the Sports Arena. I couldn't understand a word that he said, and seeing that as he spoke the bottom of his jaw seemed to extend out toward me, I started to freak out.

I turned to Ben and told him that I couldn't drive anymore.

He told me that he could take over. He came around to the driver's side of the car and led me back to the passenger side. Then, with Andrea in the middle, he took over the driving duties. It was amazing, he took the same amount of acid that Andrea and I did; however, he not only found the Sports Arena, but he eventually found the other car with Georgia and the rest of our friends. I remember that when we saw them in the parking lot we were so excited that we had finally found them.

Not realizing that we were over an hour late and that they had been waiting all of that time, as we drove up to them, I rolled down the passenger side window, and the three of us cheered. However they were so angry, and we were so loaded, that with all of their angry screaming and yelling, it was like seeing your long-lost friends, and rolling down the window to greet them, only to have them turn into a pack of snarling rabid dogs trying to tear off your flesh through the opened car window, which I immediately rolled up.

Well, Ben parked the car and we got everything sorted out with our friends, and started into the Sports Arena. Where we wound up entering was high up in the back of the arena so that we had to walk down through the stadium seats.

The stage seemed like a postage stamp with tiny little band members singing and moving about on it. As we walked down through the sparsely-populated stadium seats people on either side of the aisle would offer various drugs for sale. "Panama Red, Poppers, Coke. Thai stick, get your Thai stick right here." Most of the people seemed to be sitting down on the floor of the Sports Arena.

The whole scene down on the floor of the arena was really a trip. Guys walking around on stilts, jugglers, belly dancers and fire eaters.

Everyone, except the cops, was getting high openly. There was a uniformed LAPD officer stationed about every 50 feet around the arena floor. But they were obviously turning a blind eye to all of the drugs.

To this day I don't know if that was because they were outnumbered, or that they were there to do their real job of keeping everyone safe.

We moved around the Sports Arena until we got close to the stage.

At that point, somehow I got separated from the rest of the group. I searched for them, but could not find them. Finally I gave up and decided to explore my surroundings. I would walk up to people and say, "It's my birthday at midnight." I said this mostly to pretty girls who, nine times out of 10, would exclaim, "Oh, happy birthday," and then kiss me and hug me. I loved it. All of the guys would shake my hand and pat me on the back saying, "Cool dude," or, "Far out." I even went up to every cop I saw announcing that it was my birthday. Even they would all congratulate me as well. It was great.

Everything was fine until I announced that it was my birthday to one of the fire eaters, and he said, "Well then, I'll have to send up a birthday flame for you." He spat out this giant ball of flame, and everyone cheered in the vicinity, except me, because I saw the face of the devil in the flame. He said to me, "How did you like that?"

And I just ran into the crowd. I meandered through the huge crowd sitting on the floor of the arena until I wound up right behind the large podium occupied by the lighting guy.

Little Richard was just coming on stage. He was wearing a bright purple leisure suit, covered with small circular mirrors attached to it. This outfit would have probably seemed surreal to me if I had been straight, at the time. However, on acid, it was beyond surreal.

Suddenly I had an epiphany. It all made sense. It was my birthday, and therefore it was my birthday party. A party given for me by Little Richard, and the guy seated at the console in front of me in the middle of the arena floor manipulating all of the levers and dials was not the lighting guy, but the DEVIL, who was the one really running the show.

Now, in order to survive the night, and the devil's wrath; I would have to make my way up to the stage and thank Little Richard for my birthday party.

So, stoned out of my mind, I started my journey walking as the crow flies directly towards the stage, stepping on anyone or anything that was in my way. I fell down numerous times and made a lot of people angry, but I was oblivious to all of this. I was on a mission. It took me four songs to make it to the front of the stage where people were standing. I looked around, and I was surrounded by bikers and biker mamas. One of the bikers turned, and I could see the name on the back of his jacket, his colors if you will. It said, "Satan's Slaves."

This cinched it for me. I was surrounded by Satan's minions and I had to thank Little Richard for my birthday party if I was going to survive the night.

Just then, Little Richard started singing. "Good golly Miss Molly," the song that he would quite often close with. So for me it was now or never. As he sang, "Good golly Miss Molly sure likes the ball; good golly Miss Molly sure likes the ball, whoa. You're a rockin' and a rollin'; can't you hear your momma call?" I started screaming, "Thank you, Little Richard. Thank you for my birthday party!" I screamed it so many times, and so loudly that in the middle of the song, Little Richard called out, "Shadddup."

At the end of the song Little Richard jumped up to uproarious applause. Looking and pointing at me, he laughed, took off his mirror-laden purple jacket and threw it to me. The problem was that the bikers caught most of the jacket and all that I caught was one sleeve.

We immediately got into a tug-of-war over the jacket.

Finally, one of the bikers pulled out a large bowie knife and showed it to me.

I said, "I don't care. It's my birthday party, so it's my present." With that, the biker proceeded to cut off the sleeve that I had a grip on, releasing it to me. My eyes widened as I announced, "Cool. Thanks." The biker replied, "Happy birthday, man." and I wandered away, clutching my sparkling purple sleeve.

I walked about 40 feet to the right of the stage and saw my friends up in the stands, about 15 rows up. I walked up to Ben, smiling. I showed him the purple sleeve with mirrors and said, "See what I got?" Ben replied, "Yes, very nice. I'm just glad you're still alive." I looked back at him with my acid-glazed eyes and replied, "Me too." Yeah we were both glad that I was alive, but for very different reasons.

Another interesting adventure that I had with Ben was around the same time. Ben decided that it would be fun to drop acid and go see the movie, "The Hellstrom Chronicle," an amazing documentary about insects, it won the academy award for best documentary in 1972. We thought it would be cool, because we had heard about the footage of cascading butterflies, millions at a time. What we hadn't heard about was all the footage of ants battling, and multiple species of insects devouring each other.

I had a Sunbeam Tiger with a Cobra 289 motor at the time; and Ben had to take over driving, which he had the talent to do while loaded.

By the time we got inside of the theater, the movie had started. I was peaking. So the majority of the movie went like this. Me: "Ohhhhhhhhhhh, Oooooooohhhhh, Oh my Gooood, Far out, Woooooow."

The people around us: "Ssssssssshh, Shut up, Quiet, If you don't shut up, I am going to get the manager."

Well, that's the way it went until they threw us out of the theater. As we were leaving, I asked Ben," Was I really that loud? "

Ben said, "Yeah, but personally I thought your comments, made it a better movie." Ben is a cool guy, and will always be one of my best friends.

One of my favorite places both before I went to Canada, and after I returned and then moved to Venice, was always the Fox Venice Movie Theater.

I had more fun in that place; it was almost like a smaller version of that New Year's Eve party at the Sports Arena. People were always drinking, smoking weed, doing coke and what have you during the movies.

They would always run at least one and usually two different movies every night of the week.

And sometimes the combinations were fabulous.

One of my favorites was when they ran, "Beach Blanket Bingo," before running the newly released, "Super Fly." Everyone in the place was loaded, and it was a crowd comprised of roughly about a 50-50 mix of white and black.

About a third of the way into "Beach Blanket Bingo," a couple of the black guys fired up ghetto blasters and began blasting the soundtrack from "Super Fly" over the movie. A couple of white guys took exception and a small scuffle ensued. I didn't understand why the white guys had a problem with it. I always loved Curtis Mayfield's music, and never really cared much for "Beach Blanket Bingo".

Anyway, the scuffle was over real fast when one of the white guys pulled a gun, which cleared half of the theater, but not me and my friend, Jim. We just stayed there and smoked our joint; a few people ran into the lobby, and then filtered back in slowly.

However a lot of the people, and the guys in the fight went out of the back exits, and probably straight home.

"Super Fly" was great with black members of the audience jumping up at various times in the theatre, and screaming stuff like, "Don't do that nigga. What you crazy? Or, "Kill that motherfucka." Other times in the theater you would miss really important parts of the dialogue, because it would be drowned out by a wine bottle rolling under the seats from up high in the back of the theater down to the front, breaking loudly against the back of a seat at the bottom.

One night in the early '70s they ran, "I Am Curious Yellow," one of the earliest porn movies.

I realized early on that I should have brought a date. Every couple in the place was making out, or feeling each other up, and not even halfway into the movie heaving mounds could be seen interspersed throughout the audience, where guys had taken their jackets and thrown them over their girlfriends heads while getting blown.

I ran out of the place and raced home and called every girl I knew until I got one to come over and spend the night.

The theater also had some of the wildest movie combinations in history, combinations like, "Rosemary's Baby," and the Marx Brothers, "Duck Soup," or, "2001 a Space Odyssey" and "Moby Dick," and of course, my all-time favorite combination of "Little Big Man" and "Harold and Maude." Seeing "Little Big Man" at the Fox Venice, when it came out in 1970 is how I recognized Chief Dan George in Canada, in 1973, met him, and became friends with him. What an amazingly small world this can be at times.

1972 New Year's Eve Concert Poster

Chapter 2

From almost taking my life to completely changing my life and beginning the most magical journey of my life

It was at this time (Early in 1973) that my father died, my mother having died three months earlier. I believe the combination of their deaths coming so close to one another, and the fact that various people from my manager to club owners, etc. were shoving mountains of coke up my nose, and telling me that I was going to be a star, all culminated in my eventual nervous breakdown.

I remember it like it was yesterday. It was about 3 AM on a Friday night. I had just come home from an open mike night at a club in Hollywood.

I was home alone, my roommate Andrea had moved out the week before. I was drinking wine, snorting coke, and smoking Panama Red. I remember starting to laugh when Lazarus came over to me with one of my microphones in his mouth for me to throw for him.

Then out of nowhere I started to weep uncontrollably, I stood up and looked in the mirror and everything hit me at once. My parents were dead, a lot of my friends were dead from drug overdoses, and I felt lost, lonely, and alone. I smashed my face into the mirror. I remember looking into the mirror, or at least what was left of the mirror, and watching the blood run down my face. It seemed like life had lost all of its meaning.

I grabbed a bottle of brandy from the kitchen and started to drink it as I staggered toward the beach with Lazarus by my side. I started crossing Speedway; I noticed that I had stepped in something wet; because I had to wait for a car to pass. I looked down at my bare feet and realized that what I had stepped in was my own blood which had pooled at my feet while I was waiting for the car to pass.

I looked down at Lazarus, who was very anxious and starting to cry, as I walked across Speedway he grabbed a discarded beer can and brought it to me to throw for him, but I ignored him, trudging on toward the beach drinking the brandy as fast as I could, while wiping the blood and tears from my eyes as I walked toward the sound of the crashing waves.

By the time I reached the water I remember thinking, "Why am I so wet, I haven't even jumped in yet." And then I realized that I was soaked in my own blood. I know that as long as I live I will never be able to fully describe what was going through my mind at that time; I know that I felt alone, that life seemed so futile, and there seemed to be no real good reason to go on.

So with Lazarus running around me in the shallow water, crying,, I drank the last of the Remy Martin brandy and started to walk into the ocean. Lazarus was now swimming to keep up with me.
I looked up toward the star-filled sky and told my parents that I would see them soon. I opened my mouth wide, kicked my feet out from under me and went under the next oncoming wave. I drank in the brackish salty water. I remember how it burned, and the immediate sense of fear that gripped my body.

What had I done! I have heard people talk about near-death experiences, like having their life pass before them, or seeing a white light at the end of a tunnel.
Well, all I can tell you is that all I saw was black. All that was going through my mind was what have I done. I had so much to live for. I had so much to do. What have I done?
During my life I have felt a lot of regret at various points in my life. However never since have I experienced the regret that I experienced at that moment. I remember thinking I'm really dead? Fear was replaced with anger. Anger was replaced with resignation. Then a jolt hit me; and black turned to bright red.

And then a bright flash of light, and then I could hear myself vomiting what seemed like half of the ocean, and I felt a strange sensation on my face, it was Lazarus licking my face and crying.
I could hear and feel him run up and hit my back with his front paws, and then do the same thing to my chest. As I regained my vision, I could see that I was lying on my side in the surf.

To this day I don't know if he dragged me back to shore, or I washed back to shore on my own. I do know that he saved me, however, because of the redness and scratches from his paws on my back and chest, and the fact that he was still jumping against my body after I came to.

Canine CPR, it doesn't get much better than that. I'm not sure if it was the idea of losing me; or the steaks that I was giving him, that motivated Lazarus to save me. All I know is that over the next two years I would save his life three times, and he would save mine twice more.

After cleaning myself up and getting a few stitches in my eyebrow and lip, I realized that there aren't too many things worth killing yourself over.

A few days later, I met Klaus he was a tall blonde Nordic fellow who essentially moved from place to place living with different people while working on his guitar skills. He was quite a guitarist and a real lady-killer.

This is where my whole lifestyle began to change. I fired my manager, and essentially quit the music business.

I met a girl that I really liked. Her name was Shelley, and she moved in with me. I had a new roommate, Richard, so now with Shelley, me, Richard and Klaus in the living room, there were four of us, along with Lazarus, in a small two bedroom house.

Klaus told me that I needed to get out of LA. That LA was killing me. He suggested that I head with him up to British Columbia, to clear my head. I was really torn; I really cared for Shelley, who couldn't go with me because she was law review at USC, and supposedly had a job waiting with the Los Angeles District Attorney's office.

However deep down I knew that he was right. I needed to get out of Los Angeles right away. So I sold the old Buick that I had acquired from my father years earlier, and I sold my Sunbeam Tiger. And I bought a 1953 Willys Jeep pickup, and after totally restoring it, I started building a camper shell on the back.

The shell had a basic steel welded framework to which I

applied hand carved wood panel sides, which had pictures of everything from ocean scenes with seagulls, to Lazarus with a ball in his mouth, and mountain ranges etc. I put in stained glass windows, a skylight, and built compartments on either side of the rear fenders for storage, all with different scenes, either hand carved, or done in marquetry, or parquetry inlaid wood.

Without exception, wherever I stopped with the vehicle from the day that I finished it people would always ask the same thing. "Gee, did you build it yourself."

So, after a month or so of building the camper shell, and modifying the truck so that I could address any potential problem that might present itself in the middle of nowhere, which after all is where I was headed,

I was finally ready to jump into the deep end, and head to the wilderness. Around this same time I received a letter from the mayor of Homer, Alaska; offering me a job to build a bunch of custom furniture for her, which could help pay for the trip. So I accepted the offer, which sealed the deal on making the trip.

I gave Shelley the lease on the driftwood house; and I put all of my money into traveler's checks, and bought a pound of weed to take along, so we wouldn't run out.

I put Lazarus in the camper, because he could climb through the opening that I built between the shell and the cab of the truck, Klaus and I climbed in, I started the truck, and with a sad farewell to Shelley, we were on our way to British Columbia.

The moment that I knew that this was going to be an exceptional journey, was when just before Santa Barbara I turned on the radio. I looked over at Klaus who had the pound of Panama Red weed in his lap rolling up joints, and on the radio came the John Denver song "Rocky Mountain High". I remember the words like it happened yesterday.

"He was born in the summer of his 27th year, comin' home to a place he'd never been before, he left yesterday behind him, you might say he was born again, you might say he found a key for every door." With those words John Denver was describing my life at that moment. I was 27 years old. I was coming home to British

Columbia, a place I'd never been before. I was leaving yesterday behind me,
    I felt like I was born again, like I had found a key for every door.
    I remember looking at Klaus as the music played loudly over the whining of the overdrive, and saying, "Whoa!"
    Klaus looked back at me with a big broad smile, blew out a big puff of smoke handed me the joint and said, "I told you this is what you needed, and that this was going to be a magical trip, didn't I?" I took the joint, and took a hit, nodding with approval, exhaled, and while handing the joint back to Klaus noticed Lazarus in the window opening crawl through, with a glove in his mouth for somebody to throw.
    I recall thinking to myself this is going to be a trippy trip.

    John Denver was an amazing performer and songwriter! I have always felt that in the later stages of his career, he was treated very unfairly by comedians and others in the media, although he still had a loyal fan base right up until his untimely death in an Ultra-light accident, flying in the skies that he loved so much.
    Sadly it wasn't until his death that the country was reminded once again of what a great talent he was
    A man with a great voice, and a smiling face, who through his writing ability, proclaimed his love of life, and love, and all of the natural wonders that are a big part of what makes America great.
    And a man who certainly left an indelible imprint on my life forever!
    I have his *Greatest Hits* album, and listen to them as often as I listen to Sinatra, The Beatles, etc., which is a lot!
    The proof of his talent lies in the fact that his Greatest Hits are a multiple DVD set, and unlike some other performers, the songs are all hits. Rest in Peace John, you are missed!

    The overdrive on the truck only made it as far as San Luis Obispo. After getting that repaired, we headed to Point arena to see a lady I knew there. We decided to stop just outside of Point Arena to take a break from the road. We were on the side of the road, Klaus was playing guitar, and I was drinking some water and throwing the ball for Lazarus.
    All of a sudden, there was a loud crack, and a spark rose off

of the pavement a few feet from Lazarus, he ran toward the truck, and as he did another spark came off of the pavement behind him, and I heard another loud crack.

Looking up on the hill above the highway, I saw a man with a rifle aimed at the truck and gun smoke rising from the end of the rifle. Klaus took Lazarus behind the truck;

I grabbed my rifle from inside of the camper and fired back, and after only one shot the man ran away. We all got into my truck, and drove off.

We got within a couple of miles of Point Arena, when a cop pulled us over. Luckily Klaus had time to stuff the pound of weed up inside of the truck's dashboard.

The cop ordered us out of the truck, we complied, and he handcuffed us. I explained that we were the ones who had been shot at.

That's when I learned, to my chagrin, that in and around Point Arena farmers and ranchers were allowed to shoot any stray dogs' onsite, apparently because of a problem with feral dogs killing livestock.

After explaining to the officer that we were not from the area, and did not know about such a law, and pointing out that this man was firing onto an interstate highway, and that even though I fired back I had the right to have the rifle because of the Second Amendment, and I had the inherent right to defend myself, the cop let us go.

We only spent a couple of hours in Point Arena visiting my lady friend, because frankly we were pretty rattled and just wanted to get the hell out of there.

After some thought, we decided to check out the Mendocino National Forest. Klaus was more confident of this move farther inland then I was, seeing that we had had a bad incident earlier on in the trip, a couple of days before, when we decided to go inland before we hit San Francisco.

Somewhere along the way before we hit San Francisco, near Salinas, Klaus decided that we should get off of the coast highway and head inland for a while, and I agreed. So off we went. The countryside was beautiful, and we had only driven about 10 miles or so when there standing along the side of the road were two really cute hippie girls hitchhiking.

We pulled over and asked them where they were headed? The brunette, Carla, said that they were just checking out the countryside, and I said, "We are too".

So I climbed out of the passenger seat, and Carla jumped in with Klaus. And Karen the blonde, who liked calling herself "Star Child" and I jumped into the camper with Lazarus, and we were on our way.

It was getting late in the afternoon, so as we passed a joint back and forth between the camper shell and the truck cab, I told Klaus to look for a good place to camp for the night.

As darkness began to fall, the trees along the side of the road seemed to grow larger as we moved along the road winding deeper and deeper into the forest.

I asked Klaus, "Don't those trees seem to be getting bigger? Is it just me? Or is this Panama Red better weed than I thought it was?"

Carla replied, "No it's not the weed; the trees are getting bigger."

And Klaus said to Carla, "How do you know it's not the weed, we have all smoked three joints so far, I am surprised that we haven't seen a pink rhino." And we all laughed.

Klaus saw a dirt road on the left that looked like it led to more open ground, so we took it. We went for five or six miles and found a great campsite in the middle of a huge field.

Karen had a bottle of wine, I had a cooler with food and ice, we had some dinner with wine, and we played guitar and sang and smoked and drank under a three-quarter moon with a ceiling of stars.

And then Klaus and Carla started making out, and climbed into the camper. I was still playing guitar by the fire and singing, and then Karen leaned over and kissed me.

Oh, how I miss the days of free love!

I put away the guitar and we started kissing, one thing led to another and before we knew it, we were making love under the stars. Suddenly she pushed me over on my back, and climbed on top of me. This was not my first cowgirl episode, but it was definitely the first one that I had experienced out of doors.

I remember looking up at her, her beautiful body undulating as her wild blonde hair flailed against the star filled night sky and saying just before I climaxed, "Far out, you really are a star child."

We fell asleep in each other's arms, and just before I fell asleep I thought to myself, "Why didn't I leave LA sooner?"

And then I thought about Shelley.

And now I think that that is the first time that I realized deep down what I learned later on, that Shelley and I were never meant to be together anyway.

It was a cold night, and I had to get up to put more wood on the fire every couple of hours. So I was sound asleep, my naked body wrapped around Star Child's naked body when the ground began to shake, and I was awakened by the sound of distant explosions.

As I rose up slightly to see what was going on, the distant Booms, and Bangs got a lot louder. And the shaking that accompanied the explosions became so violent that they shook everybody out of bed.

Lazarus ran up to me barking an alert, and giving me a look like get in the truck and let's get the hell out of here NOW..

As we ran toward the truck trying to put our clothes on at the same time, I heard the *wup, wup* sound of a helicopter.

I turned to see what appeared to be an Army helicopter rapidly closing in on us. Behind it in the distance I saw what looked like a couple of artillery rounds going off, and this time the accompanying shock waves almost knocked us off of our feet.

We were all very scared.

And then, as fast as it had started, it all stopped. We were all just finishing getting dressed and loaded up when the helicopter landed. Two soldiers ran over to us, an officer and a young soldier with an M-16. The officer screamed at us, "You are in a restricted area. How did you get in here? You interrupted a live fire exercise. You could have been killed, all of you. I should detain all of you for arrest by proper civilian authorities. You are on the Fort Hunter Liggett military reserve in violation of federal law."

Now we were really scared.

Then two jeeps raced up behind us with guys with machine

guns in them. And I must admit that I thought everyone was as scared as I was. That is until,

Klaus spoke up. "Sir, you cannot detain us, or arrest us."

"What?" The officer replied.

"You heard me," said Klaus. "I drove this vehicle in here last night and there was not one sign posted anywhere declaring this as restricted government property. There were no locked gates, or gates of any kind. Also there were no warning signs anywhere declaring "Danger Live Fire Area Do Not Enter."

So go ahead and detain us, and have us arrested."

My heart sank. Shut up Klaus. I thought.

Then Klaus finished. "Yeah, have us arrested, so we can go to trial and our lawyer (who is very good, has many friends in Network News, and hates the Military) can show how the Army has a non - posted area, located a few miles off of the coast highway, with no gates or guards, where they randomly fire large ordinance.

And when four kids unsuspectingly drove in and camped for the night, and you almost killed them the next morning, and then failing to kill them you decided to have them arrested?

Let me know how that one works out for you Captain, or should I say private?"

The officer ran back to the chopper and got on the radio for a few minutes, and then he ran back to us and said, "You will be escorted off of government property, and back to the coast highway. You may go North or South on that highway. However, if you back track east from that point? You will be immediately arrested."

I was really proud of Klaus, he saved our asses.

That is when I first learned about how if you know what you're doing you can wield the News Media like a sword.

Sadly, the ladies were heading south, and we were heading North to Frisco, and Point Arena, and then, as it turned out to the Mendocino National Forest and Hammer Horn Lake where our story begins again.

Chapter 3

Cheap bongs and free love

We dropped off the girls on the coast highway, and headed north to Point Arena.

Since we have already covered that part of the story already, I'm going to take up the story where we left off, leaving Point Arena.

We were heading for Hammer Horn Lake in the Mendocino National Forest.

A ways outside of Point Arena, we pulled over for gas, and parked on the side of the gas station was a young guy in a 64 Ford station wagon with a trailer behind it.

He had put up a sign that read, "Everything for sale."

It turns out that he had gotten his draft notice, and had only two weeks before he had to report for induction. So he was selling all of his belongings just to make enough money to get across the Canadian border.

When I looked at all the things that he had displayed around the car and trailer, I suddenly realized why Klaus had wanted to stop for gas at this station so bad.

Because there in the middle of all of this stuff that he had for sale was a small guitar.

You see Klaus had been complaining since we had hit the road in LA that the cab of my Willy's pickup was too small for him to comfortably play his Martin guitar.

As I filled the truck with gas Klaus ran over and immediately picked up the small guitar. He looked inside the guitar and smiled. He surveyed the guitar from every angle and smiled, and then began his negotiations.

I finished filling the truck with gas and paid for it, and then pulled over next to the six wheeled Flea Market. I must say that the kid had some interesting things.

My eye went immediately to a bong, and what a bong. All clear glass, long stem, with a pistol grip, and a threaded chamber pipe for different kinds of interchangeable bowls.

Believe it or not at this time I had never owned a bong. I always smoked joints.

Klaus and I wound up trading the guy an ounce of weed and two packs of rolling papers and $20.00, for the bong the guitar and a pack of new strings for the guitar. And we got him to throw in an old-style kerosene cook stove, the kind you have to pump up, and six 8 track tapes. He seemed very happy with the deal, and of course so were we.

I went back to the gas station bought some ice, some food to cook on the stove, some wine, and a pint of ice cream, along with a small bottle of Crème de menthe.

I used to like to add it to the bong water; the marijuana smoke always seemed a lot smoother and less harsh with some Crème de Menthe, and ice added to the bong water.

We jumped in the truck and were on our way up Mountain View Road, toward Covelo, and then on to Hammer Horn Lake. I was driving and Klaus was restringing his new guitar.

Klaus asked me, "What did you buy the Crème de Menthe for?"

I replied "For the bong. I like to add Crème de Menthe, and ice to the water in a bong, to make it really taste good, and cool the smoke, so it's not so harsh."

He laughed and said "Where did you hear that crap?" I replied "I've tried it myself. And it works. Besides, if you don't like it, we can just go to ice and water, and drink the Crème de Menthe, and add to our Panama Red buzz."

The countryside was beautiful.

We went another eight miles or so and saw two kids hitch hiking; a guy and a girl.

We stopped and picked them up. We always picked up hitch hikers; it's amazing when I think back on it, that we never picked up the wrong people along the way and got robbed or murdered or the like.

They were always nice people, starting with the black bus driver in uniform that we picked up on our way out of Los Angeles at State beach on the coast highway.

The two kids were headed north as well; their names were Matt and Kylie.

They jumped into the camper with Lazarus. He greeted them

like he greeted most people, with licks and tail wags. I must say that Lazarus was a great judge of character; he always knew which people were cool, and which ones were assholes.

By this time Klaus had his new small guitar restrung and tuned. He started playing scale progressions, while I talked to the kids.

They had just left the Haight-Ashbury district of San Francisco; and they told me that it wasn't what they had expected. I told them that we had passed it by on the way up on purpose.

But then again, we had almost been blown up that morning, and had driven straight through Frisco up to Point Arena, only stopping to sleep, thinking that it would have to be safer there.

And then we got shot at in Point Arena.

Matt said, "That's why we're heading up North to the woods."

I replied, "No shit, us too. We're headed to the Mendocino National Forest and Hammer Horn Lake."

Kylie said. "That's still in California man. We're headed to Washington State. There is too much shit going on down in California for us."

Sadly, I was to find out soon enough that she was absolutely right. I asked them if they wanted to try out the bong. They did.

So Matt added ice, Crème de Menthe, water, and installed the biggest bowl.

So here we were, a motley crew, cruising down the highway smoking Panama Red from the newly christened bong; with Klaus playing his new guitar and alternately, steering the truck while they shoved the long stem bong from the camper into the cab so that I could turn around and take a hit. Then I would take over driving again. He would take a hit and then the bong would go back into the camper, and he would start playing the guitar again.

This ludicrous ritual continued for miles. It's amazing that we never got into a car wreck. However, we did manage to get wrecked, if you know what I mean.

And the whole time that the bong ritual was taking place, Lazarus was frantically trying to get Matt or Kylie to throw the ball for him inside of the camper shell.

When I think back on it the whole scene was crazy; a sort of super-high version of a Chinese fire drill, just, rolling down the road;

With people laughing, guitar music playing, my dog frantically whining, along with the fact that marijuana smoke was pouring out of both camper shell windows and both windows of the cab. I am sure that had a cop come up behind us at that point, we all would've gone to jail.

But we were all carefree and oblivious to any thought of getting busted at the time.

Ah, the good old days.

I wanted to throw in one of the eight track tapes, like big Brother and the Holding Company, or Cream, but Klaus wanted to play with his new guitar, so I just made up a song to the scales that he was playing on his guitar.

It went something like this as I remember. "Yes we're rolling down that open highway. Two new friends are by our side. Good weed and good companions. Oh Lord, what a ride. We've had to ride through hell just to get here; had lots of troubles along the way. But now it seems it's all been worth it. Cause we're getting closer each and every day. We all have different destinations. But deep down, they're all the same. Forget the past and find the future. That certain place without a name."

So, there we were, rolling down the road, not a care in the world, smoking weed, singing, laughing, our biggest worry was figuring out where to camp for the night. I of course suggested a campground that was just before Ukiah.

Klaus said, "Oh no. Let's go find a place in the woods. I reminded him of what had happened the last time that he suggested that. And he said "Do you really want to camp next to some fat slob in a motor home, with the TV and radio blasting, as his little fat grimy kids run around screaming?"

I replied "Okay, just try not to get us killed, this time."

He laughed, and I turned off of 253 onto the next road on the right. I must admit that the countryside was beautiful with a lot of open land and by this time I was starting to get pretty high. So I was glad to stop just about anywhere.

I had noticed while I was driving that Kylie was really giving Klaus the eye as he was playing the guitar. However, when I started singing, she seemed to cast her gaze upon me. I didn't quite know what to make of this?

We found a great place to camp by a stream with surprisingly, no mosquitoes. I wanted to try out the stove, however, Klaus wanted a fire, and it turned out that he was right, it was much better.

We ate a nice meal with wine, and passed the bong, played guitar and sang old songs and new ones into the wee hours of the night.

I saw Kylie whisper something to Matt, and then he grabbed his sleeping bag and started to walk off.

I said "Matt. Where the hell are you going?" He looked back with a casual smile, and said, "Kylie will explain." And then he continued walking away from the campsite.

I yelled, "Don't go too far man. You're better off by the fire. There are some serious critters out here."

Kylie came over and gave me a long kiss and then gave Klaus a long kiss? I didn't know what was going on? I looked over at Klaus and he seemed as baffled as me.

Kylie looked at both of us and said, "Don't worry about Matt, once the three of us are in the camper he'll come back to the fire, and he'll be fine."

I asked, "What are you talking about, Kylie?" I thought that you and Matt were a couple?"

Kylie replied "We are. But we are free lovers. I like both of you guys, and I want to make love to both of you guys.

It's a rule we have. If either of us is really attracted to someone else, then we can sleep with that person or persons as long as it doesn't affect our love for each other. In fact I think it makes our love stronger."

I looked at Klaus, he looked at me, we both looked at Kylie, who was very pretty I might add, and we both said almost in unison, "Sounds good to me."

I have to admit at this point in my life that this was my first ménage' a trios' ever, and frankly I was scared shitless.

However when we climbed into the camper and closed it up, Kylie took over like a general marshaling her troops.

I had put Lazarus in the truck cab, and he was up in the crawlspace watching what was going on intently.

I calmed down a little when I realized that she was going to have sex with us one at a time, for the most part. Klaus seemed perfectly at home with the whole deal. Obviously he had done this before.

However, I have to admit that the whole thing seemed a little strange to me at that time.

Well, to make a long story short, it was all quite exciting in a kind of seemingly perverse sort of way, and after we had all climaxed I said to Klaus, "I'll flip you for who gets to sleep with her for the night."

Kylie screamed out indignantly. "I'm not sleeping with either of you. I'm sleeping with Matt.

I replied, "Of course you are. In fact you and Matt sleep in here tonight, and Klaus and I will sleep outside." And then I apologized profusely; explaining that I would have to be a male chauvinist pig to say something like that about her in the first place.

She laughed and we all went to bed, with her and Matt in the camper, and me and Klaus outside on the ground around the fire. With Lazarus sleeping under the covers by the fire next to me, and luckily for us, it didn't rain at all that night.

Me, Laz and the pre-Camper Willys

Chapter 4

Bad times at Hammer Horn Lake

It was a chilly morning, the fire had gone out, and I had had the strangest dream.

I was in a movie theater and a huge fat man behind me was eating a huge tub of popcorn and the crunching sound was driving me crazy. Then suddenly with my eyes still closed I realized that the crunching sound that was so loud was not in my dream,

I slowly opened my eyes to see the head of a beautiful doe not two feet from me. Her eyes were like big soft pools of chocolate, and her coat was so perfect she seemed almost surreal.

I was about to say something when I noticed a large 10 point buck about five feet behind her, so I decided to keep quiet as we were just about into rutting season, and I didn't feel like getting gored or trampled to death. I remember lying there thinking about how beautiful she was and what quick work she was making of the grass. And even though my eyes were wide open she seemed to completely ignore me.

Then I heard Klaus say, "What the hell?"

And all six of the deer bolted. Lazarus started barking as they bounced away like their hooves had springs on them.

I looked down at Lazarus and said "Some watchdog. How could you not hear all of that crunching and chewing? Damn it, Lazarus, it even woke me up."

Klaus started laughing as Matt and Kylie stuck their heads out of the camper.

Matt said, "Deer huh". I replied, "Yeah, luckily the buck wasn't in a fighting mood."

We had some breakfast, and then drove back to the 253 and headed north. We dropped Matt and Kylie off in Ukiah, as they were heading north, and we were heading northeast to Covelo, California, and then Hammer Horn Lake.

The trip was fairly uneventful until we arrived in Covelo.

We stopped at a local diner for something to eat. and it was kind of like the scene from Easy Rider, the one at the end, where they go into the backwoods Louisiana diner, and all of the rednecks start making negative comments, even though there were no outright negative comments, but you could cut the vibe with a knife. So we ordered the food to go.

When I think back on it, I should have said to Klaus, "Forget Hammer Horn Lake, let's head back to the coast and head north". But I didn't. As we were headed out of Covelo,

I remember saying to Klaus, "That was a very strange vibe at that diner, and now we're traveling on Indian Dick Road?"

Klaus said, "What's the problem?"

I said, "I don't know man, but somehow this all seems wrong." Klaus laughed, and told me that I was just being paranoid, and that maybe I should lay off of the weed.

After we had gone about 8 miles north of Covelo we finally came to a Lake.

There was an old man with fishing tackle standing there, I asked, "Is this Hammer Horn Lake?

The old man laughed, and said, "Hell, no. This is Howard Lake. Hammer Horn is that little piss hole about 9 miles up the road."

So we drove another nine miles up the road and the old man was right it was about a 4 acre lake.

I looked at Klaus and asked, "This is Hammer Horn Lake? This is what you've been talking about for the last three months? Are you kidding me?" Klaus explained that it was not the size of the lake that mattered but its surroundings.

I said, "Well, we're here now". So we made camp had some dinner, and went to bed early.

We decided in the morning that Klaus was going to take a two-day hike, and that I would stay closer to camp. He said he'd be gone for a day and a half to two days.

I told him if he got back and the truck was gone it would mean that I was in town, and that I would be back shortly.

So he took off, and I did a little fishing, and then in the early afternoon Lazarus and I went for a short hike.

We were about a mile away from camp on a bluff in a huge field of yellow grass;

Lazarus was walking ahead of me when suddenly he dropped to his back and started crying looking up towards the sky.

As I turned I noticed the ground around us turning into a giant shadow; and then turning completely I saw the biggest bird that I have ever seen in my life, it was like a plane with feathers,

I didn't know what to do, because it was coming straight for us. I made up my mind that if it wanted Lazarus it was going to have to take me first.

I jumped up and down, waved my arms, screamed at the top of my lungs with the meanest look that I could put on my face.

At the last second this giant bird swerved away, the wind from its wings knocking me back on my feet.

A loud cascade of *wooooosh, woooooosh* filled the air, as it flapped its giant wings to gain altitude heading toward the mountains.

I was to learn later that this was my first encounter with a giant golden eagle.

These eagles have been documented on film taking 120 pound big horn sheep from the mountain sides. So I guess I'm lucky that the eagle didn't take me and Lazarus after all.

I was happy that at least in the knowledge that I could repay Lazarus again for saving me from drowning!

After this startling encounter I decided that it was time to head back to camp, and Lazarus was happy to be going back as well.

We got back to camp about 2:00 pm. I made some lunch, fed Lazarus and we climbed into my camper, and I started reading a book.

About a half an hour later Lazarus jumped up, his ears perked up, and he started his low guttural growl. I knew what that meant, and it wasn't good.

I put down the book, peeked through the crawl space and looking through the windshield of the truck I saw a man with a rifle and many different pistols and holsters draped across his chest, and around his waist sneaking up on the campsite.

I grabbed my Lee Enfield rifle, chambered a round and waited watching the man creeping along the side of my truck I knew just when he would stick his head around the right corner of my camper shell, when he did I stuck the barrel of the rifle in his face.

And I said very deliberately, "You move and I'll blow your head off".

At gunpoint I had the man remove all of the weapons and strip down to his underwear, and shoes, and while I had him at gunpoint, and face down on his belly, I picked through his five handguns and found a 357 magnum that I liked (it was loaded), I threw the rest of the weapons and his clothes into the camper,

I walked him out in front of my truck, after I had him tie a rope around his waist, which I tied to the front bumper, and then with Lazarus sitting in the passenger seat I proceeded to walk him at gunpoint in front of my truck back towards Covelo, the whole 17 miles, if need be,

Luckily for him I ran into a Ranger about 2 miles from camp. He was heading to Hammerhorn checking fishing permits.

When the Ranger saw me, and my prisoner he stopped his vehicle and came out with his gun drawn, and he was a little startled to say the least, to see me in my truck, holding a half-naked man at gunpoint.

As he drew his gun, I dropped mine.

I explained the story of what had happened to me and gave him the weapons as the man put his clothes back on.

I told him where I was camping and that if he needed any more information that he could find me there. He cuffed the man and took him and put him in his vehicle as the man tried to claim his innocence, and say that I had kidnapped him. The Ranger laughed, and told him to shut up,

And then the Ranger looked at me smiling and saying, "Yeah, you're the kidnapper, and yet you're walking him towards town on the main road, and he still has marks on his body from the multiple gun belts and holsters that he had draped on his body, just as you described, he has NO I.D. and you comply, and furnish me with all required paperwork, and I.D,

You are free to go sir! Are you going to be at you're campsite for a few days sir?"

I replied, "To be honest, ranger, I wouldn't even spend another night here, but I can't leave until my friend comes back from his hike tonight, or tomorrow morning, and then, after this episode, we are out of here tomorrow, why?'

He said," I have all of your information, but if we have any other questions, could you stop by the station on your way out tomorrow, I can give you directions.

I replied, "Of course, whatever you need." He thanked me, and I headed back to the campsite.

Klaus still hadn't arrived when I got there, so I got the fire going again and started making some food, about an hour after dark I heard a lot of crunching and breaking of branches, something big was coming my way I grabbed the Enfield, turned on the flashlight and thank God it was Klaus.

He was going to set up camp himself when he saw my large campfire. He asked, "What the hell are you doing with the gun?"

I told him the whole story. I remember saying, "Can we get the fuck out of here now? Before we are murdered in our sleep? Kylie was right; I say that if we survive the night, we stop at the ranger station in the morning. And then we head back to the coast and go straight through Oregon and Washington and into B.C."

Klaus agreed, and frankly by that point I didn't care if he agreed or not.

So the next morning, after stopping at the ranger station, we were on our way to British Columbia. And hopefully we were headed for much happier times.

Me in 1972

Chapter 5

Let's get out of here

As I mentioned we wanted to get out of the States bad. So we did just what we said we would do, we went back to the coast and drove straight through Grants Pass, Oregon, Eugene, Portland, Seattle Washington, and crossed the border at Bellingham, Washington.

About the only incident worth mentioning on the way to Bellingham was an encounter that we had with a mother moose and her calf.

That's when I learned what the most dangerous thing in the North American wilderness was.

It seemed like every time that we went off the highway we had some sort of strange and or dangerous encounter.

We had pulled off of the highway a couple of miles. I wanted to walk Lazarus and feed him, etc.

Klaus was hiding the weed in the truck for the border crossing, and I was walking Laz 40 feet or so down the road from the truck.

About 80 feet further down the road I noticed a moose calf, I remember saying, "What a cute little guy." Then I heard a loud thudding sound. That's when the calf's mother ran up and stopped in front of it.

Amazingly I thought nothing of this obviously protective behavior.

I yelled back to the truck, "Hey Klaus. Look at the mother moose and her baby."

Klaus bolted out of the truck frantically looking around he caught sight of the mother moose and calf.

He yelled back, while waving, "Slowly walk back to the truck. If the moose starts to run, then run for your life. If she catches you she will kill you."

I started to slowly walk back to the truck, I made it about 10 feet back towards the truck when I noticed that Laz wasn't with me, That's when I noticed that he hadn't moved and was intensely sniffing something on the ground.

When I called and he ran toward me the mother moose lunged and started to gallop toward us.

Klaus yelled, "Run." He ran around to the driver's side of the truck as Laz and I ran the last 40' feet to the open passenger side door. The moose was closing fast. As we reached the truck

Laz jumped in the cab, and I followed slamming the truck door.

As Klaus started the truck and popped the clutch we made it about 15' in low gear when there was a loud bang and the truck lurched forward like we had been violently rear ended by an eighteen wheeler.

The mother moose had caught us and taken her anger out on the truck.

A few months later I would see what happens to a person that gets caught by a mother moose, and it was quite grisly, I won't describe the whole scene, but they were only able to identify the man by his driver's license which they pulled from his wallet. For now I was just happy to be alive.

And relishing the idea of being able to tell people about how I got whiplash from a moose.

The border crossing was interesting in that on the American side they pulled me over just to check out the camper shell, it turns out that they weren't looking for anything in particular they just wanted to check out the craftsmanship.

This fact however did not help to soothe mine and Klaus's nervousness, because he had hidden what was left of the pound of weed in an airtight container wedged between the cowling and the transmission.

Luckily all they seemed to be interested in was the camper shell,

I opened all the side boxes for them and they asked me what all the power tools were for,

I showed them the letter from the mayor of Homer, Alaska explaining how I was going there to build furniture for the mayor.

Ironically they never did ask a thing about my rifle which was in plain sight in the camper.

One of the Border patrol officers asked about the broken plastic window in the rear camper shell door and the dented tailgate. He asked, "Did you get rear ended?"

I replied, "Yeah' by a Moose!"

He looked at me with a weird look, and then he started laughing. Probably because he knew that I wasn't kidding.

Then we crossed over to the Canadian side they also commented on the camper shell and had us pull over as well.

Klaus said, "You just had to put a fancy camper shell on this thing, didn't you.

"I replied "I'm sorry man, I've regretted putting the damn thing on since the third gas station we stopped at."

That was because almost every time that we stopped for gas, the attendant would always ask, "Gee. Did you make it yourself?" After a while I got to where I would repeat the question with them as they asked it.

The Canadians asked about the tools, I showed the letter, and then one of them brought out my rifle.

He said that I was not supposed to bring firearms into Canada.

I said that I was only passing through Canada going to Alaska. He asked, "What do you need a gun for in Alaska?" I asked, "You're kidding right? Have you ever heard of polar bears? You know they eat people too, don't you?"" He laughed, and put the rifle back in the truck, closed the camper shell door, and said we could be on our way.

We cruised into Vancouver, after the ferry ride, and with Klaus giving me directions, we wound up in a park, it was the main park called Stanley Park, and like a lot of Vancouver, it was an island. We drove around the wooded park until Klaus told me to pull over; he jumped out of the truck and ran over to a hippie guy with long braided hair and bells in his braids. While they talked, I gave Lazarus some water, and a short walk.

When we got back to the truck, Klaus was all excited, he said, "Jump in man."

I put Lazarus in the camper and climbed in. I said, "What are you so excited about."

He said, "I found out where Josh is, and he's at Michael's."

I replied, "Whose Michael?"

Klaus said, "Oh, you're gonna love Michael, and more importantly Michael's place".

I asked, "What's so special about Michael's place?"

Klaus smiled at me with that Cheshire cat grin of his and said, "Sex, drugs, and rock 'n roll, baby. Sex, drugs, and rock 'n roll." I smiled and said, "Sounds good to me."

I followed Klaus's directions and about 25 minutes, a few bridges and a ferry ride later, and after going through Victoria, we were driving down a road which appeared to have large estates; some of which were not visible from the road because of thick tall hedges and stone walls, Klaus said that we were on Vancouver Island.

Only the property's large entry gates spoke to you of what lay behind them.

Klaus told me "Turn into the cobblestone driveway ahead with the huge wrought iron gates."

We drove up to a keypad with a speaker; this was one of many firsts for me at Michael's house.

I asked Klaus, "Now what?" He told me to push the button.

A loud voice came out of the speaker, "Who the fuck is it?"

Klaus yelled back "It's Hippie Bob, and Guitar Klaus."

The voice yelled back, "Which Guitar Klaus, singing Klaus or Scales?" Klaus yelled back, "Scales."

The voice on the speaker said "Cool". And the giant two 15' x 8' high wrought iron gates started to swing open. We drove in.

Klaus told me to drive slow, and about 150 feet down the long driveway I realized why, when a zebra casually sauntered across the driveway in front of us.

Lazarus started barking and generally freaking out, I guess because he had never seen such a thing. I got him to shut up and we continued down the long cobblestone driveway.

About another 150 feet down the driveway we saw something that startled us so much that I stopped the truck.

It was a beautiful dark haired girl completely nude on horseback. She rode casually over to the truck, she said, "Nice truck.

I love the camper shell, amazing artwork."

I replied, "Nice horse. And you are beautiful. I've heard of riding bareback before, but don't you think that you're going a little overboard?"

She laughed and said, "Michael has a lot of property so we can do pretty much whatever we want, and riding naked is so liberating, you should try it. Maybe we can go for a ride later."

I said, "Sounds like a good idea except for the part where you have a vagina, and I have a nut sack."

She started to laugh, and said, "You're a funny guy, we will have to get together later." I replied, "Sounds good."

She rode off, and we drove up to the house.

The house was huge; I would guess somewhere between ten and 12,000 sq. ft., with lots of stone work, etc., English Tudor in style, you could tell from the age and craftsmanship that it had been there a while.. There was a huge cobblestone circular driveway with a giant fountain and pool in the middle, and around 30-40 cars and trucks filled about half of the parking area.

It was an unusual mix of vehicles, VW buses, new and old trucks, a Mercedes Gull wing, a couple of older Ferrari's, and miscellaneous cars, and sports cars.

I could see people going in and out of the 12 foot high leaded glass front doors which were wide open, some with clothing, and some without.

Jimi Hendrix's song "Purple Haze" could be heard blaring from inside the house.

I cracked the windows on the truck, and left Lazarus inside.

Klaus asked, "Why don't you bring Lazarus with us, Michael loves animals."

I replied, "I want to check this scene out first man, this guy has zebras running around loose, he may have a lion as well, for all I know."

Klaus said, "No way man, I heard he had a tiger once, but some asshole gave the poor thing acid, and it went ape shit, so once they brought it down with tranquilizers, he donated it to the zoo, or that's what I heard anyway."

We walked in, and the house was exquisite, a true mansion in every sense of the word. I saw what looked like a "Monet" hanging on the wall in a gold frame. Being that I was an art history major in college, I went over to check it out. I remember thinking it must be a copy. Upon closer inspection it looked very authentic,

I ran back and caught up with Klaus, I said, "That's a great copy of a "Monet". Klaus said, "That's not a copy".

We came into a massive fresco laden room with a high ceiling.

There were around 40 people in the huge room, with some nude, some with clothing on, and some half-dressed.

Some were getting high, some were having sex, and some were just sitting and talking.

One thing that I noticed was the graffiti on the walls, but not your average graffiti; it was different sayings and quotations done in Old English styled lettering.

I still remember some of them to this day. One was, "If love is joy, and joy is love, let's fuck." Another one was, "Happiness is not a warm gun; Happiness is a warm girl." And another one that I liked was, "Why be low, when you can get high." There had to be hundreds of these throughout the house.

I asked Klaus," What's with the graffiti?" He laughed and said, "Oh that's just Lay Low Eddie." I queried, "Lay low Eddie?" Klaus replied, "I'll explain later."

I asked Klaus why he had referred to me as Hippie Bob, and he told me that everybody that came to Michael's house had to have a moniker, and that if you didn't already have one, Michael, or sometimes Josh, if he was in town would give you one.

That's why he was called Guitar Klaus and Scales (which he didn't like) because it was a reference to him playing guitar scales all the time.

He pointed to the back of the room and said "There he is."

We started walking toward a dark curly haired bearded guy in a robe, holding the first camcorder that I had ever seen, it was large, and shot in black-and-white and I found it fascinating. He was filming a couple that was having sex on an expensive antique French provincial style settee, covered in elaborate tapestry.

Klaus came up, patted him on the back and Michael turned and said, "Good to see you Scales, who is your friend?"

Klaus replied, "This is Hippie Bob, a buddy of mine from LA". Michael asked, "Where in LA?" Klaus said, "Marina Del Rey". Michael said, "Far out." "Josh is here."

Klaus asked, "Where?" "In the peach room", said Michael. "Cool", said Klaus, "Come on Bob, I want you to meet Josh".

I could see why they called it the peach room. It wasn't peach in color; all the walls were a painted with a mural of a peach orchard, with the ceiling a blue sky with clouds.

And there, sitting at a large table with French provincial chairs covered in tapestries for upholstery was a small thin red haired man, with a red beard, wearing what appeared to be a robe and sandals looking kind of like a cross between Christ and Katherine Hepburn.

He was rolling joints from a huge pile of very strong smelling sensimilla buds.

This was my introduction to Josh, the guy who would be responsible for making my trip to British Columbia and Alaska the magical journey that it became.

Lay Low Eddie was a kid that had arrived at Michael's house a couple years earlier, and decided to stay.

He spent most of his time hiding during the day somewhere on the property, and then would come out late at night after everyone was asleep and scrounge food and do the graffiti.

It said a lot about Michael that instead of throwing the kid out for destroying the walls of his mansion, he adopted him for the reluctant, shy, scrounging scribe that he was.

Just another addition to "Master Michael's Flying Circus" as Josh called them.

We stayed with Michael for a little over a week. I always thought that an English Tudor exterior and a French Provincial interior was a strange choice, but it was what it was, and you never look a gift horse in the mouth.

The night before we left I actually saw and talked briefly to Lay Low Eddie.

Everyone was partying inside, and I had gone out to the huge heated pool with a new girl, and we were skinny dipping and kissing in the pool all by ourselves.

I was about to make my move when over her shoulder I saw someone in the bushes. It was a young kid maybe 15 or 16 years old. He was watching us. He was about 20 feet away.

I said loudly, "It must be lonely in there?

He started to run away when I said, "I love the sayings that you put on the walls. Did you make all of those up yourself?"

That's when he stopped and came back. He said, "Most of them." "You're one hell of a poet." I said. "Thanks" he said. And then he was gone.

I called out, "Hey. Where are you going? Come back. Let's talk some more."

The girl I was with, kissed me and asked, "Do you want to talk to that kid, or make it with me?" I said, "You don't understand. That was Lay Low Eddie."

Forgetting that she had just arrived, and so of course she asked, "Who's Lay Low Eddie?"

I replied, "You don't understand. Seeing Lay Low Eddie is like seeing a Unicorn. Talking to Lay Low Eddie is like; well nobody gets to talk to him."

I told her that I would be right back. I climbed out of the pool naked, grabbed my jeans too cover my erection. And ran into the main room of the house where Josh and Klaus were.

Michael was on the other side of the room. I ran over to Klaus and said, "I just saw Lay Low Eddie and I talked too him." Klaus said, "Are you sure that it was Lay Low Eddie?"

Josh interrupted, "What did he look like?" I said, "A scruffy-looking kid, 15 or 16, with red hair." "That sounds like Eddie? But he doesn't let anybody see him, much less talk to him. You need to tell Michael. Come on." said Josh.

So there I was, following Josh through this huge room filled with people, soaking wet, stark naked, except for my folded jeans which were barely covering my crotch.

When we reached Michael I could tell that he was really wasted.

Josh said, "Michael. Bob Just saw Eddie, and says that he talked to him.

Michael looked at me, and cracked that grin that he grinned when he was going to get a laugh at someone else's expense.

I recall saying to myself, "Oh Shit. I'm screwed now."

Michael said, "Bob. Loosen up man. What's with the jeans? Everybody knows your covering up your hard on. Be proud of your body man. Drop the jeans and let your hard cock proudly breathe. Nobody here will be offended; on the contrary around here it will probably get you laid.

So I dropped the jeans, rapidly turning red from embarrassment.

"That's more like it, very nice; good man. Be proud of your body." Michael said. "Now what's this shit about talking to Eddie."

I told Michael the story, and raced back to the pool.

Michael was an amazing character. Virtually everybody that I ran into while we were there had their own theory about Michael.

How old he was, where he got all of his money. Whether or not he was Bi-Sexual?

I had asked Josh about the Bi-Sexual thing. Josh laughed and said, "That rumor started a couple of years back after the Mazola oil incident."

I asked, "The Mazola Oil Incident?"

"Yeah", he said, "A couple years back Michael had a big party consisting of the whole Flying Circus, plus 100 or so other guests. I was there. And by midnight everybody was so wasted that the thing turned into a giant orgy.

So Michael, being Michael, leads a whole bunch of naked people into the kitchen, and breaks out all of these gallons of Mazola oil and starts covering all these naked people with it; and everybody gets in a pile on the kitchen floor. Imagine all of these naked people rubbing against each other on the floor and moaning, and fucking, with Michael in the middle of the pile.

By the time I got to the kitchen it looked like a big eel catch, with all of the naked bodies writhing on the floor together.

But I watched for a while as more people came in and jumped in the pile, and I never saw any homo shit or anything.

I mean one guys cock may have touched another guy's body, but the sex was all girls on guys.

After all it was not about the sex as much as the overall sensation.

That was some killer acid, little blue tabs called, "Sky Rider." I might add. Michael was getting 5,000 hits at time. Wow, that was really fun," Josh lamented.

But after that, the rumor started that Michael was bi-sexual. I asked him last year if the rumor bothered him. And he said, "Are you kidding?" I am convinced that it's getting me more pussy." "Typical Michael" Josh said.

"As for his age I would guess him to be in his mid- to late thirties, although While I was there I heard people claim that he was in everything from his late twenties, too his early fifties; that was just another part of the enigma that was Michael."

Josh told me that he asked Michael once about his age.

And Michael replied, "Who cares," and walked away laughing.

As for the matter of where Michael got all of his money, some said that he was a drug dealer and others claimed that he was selling the porn movies that he was shooting around the house on a daily basis.

Still others claimed that his father was a big international industrialist, and that both his parents had died in a plane crash, leaving him hundreds of millions of dollars. I believe that none of us personally had any idea of what the truth was.

However, Josh claimed that Michael had flown him and 10 or so different members of the Flying Circus at different times to locations like the Bahamas and Key West, on a private jet.

And all that I ever saw Michael do was buy drugs not sell them. And his huge Master bedroom was filled with Sony U-Matic tapes and two U-Matic players, and three TV's.

His house was the first house that I ever saw with a TV and tape player in the master bathroom. I asked Michael why the TV on the wall in the bathroom was on a swiveling TV stand.

He explained, "So that I can watch TV on the crapper, but if I have a girl, or girls in the shower I can turn the TV toward the shower and put a hot recorded scene on and we can watch it while we fuck in the shower." He also had numerous TV's throughout the house, including the first rear projection big screen which had just come out, and more tape recording equipment and cameras, in the massive living room downstairs.

What a guy! When it really comes down to it, I never really cared where Michael got his money; however I loved the way that he spent it.

And if it hadn't been for Josh I might have stayed there for years. I heard that a lot of people did.

I did stay there many more times while up in Canada, and I did stop there before making my way back to California. But that part of the story comes much later.

My friend Ben in 1972

Chapter 6

The great Sandy Creek acid and Salt Spring Island mushroom experiments

We were still at Michael's when Josh decided that we should do some scouting. I still remember it like it was yesterday. Klaus and I had managed to get a couple of girls the night before. Everyone was doing something they called skiing,
I didn't learn till the next day what it was that we were all taking, I knew that we were snorting coke, and I thought that the shot of liquor afterwards was some sort of chaser.

However I learned the next morning that the shot of booze had a half of a Seconal dissolved in it. Supposedly six lines of coke and half a Seconal in a shot of whiskey was supposed to be some sort of aberrant aphrodisiac.

I must admit that it had that effect on the girls, and it had the effect of reducing my inhibitions and allowing me to last longer.

The next morning Josh came into the bedroom where Klaus and I were with the girls from the night before.

He was yelling, "Get up, get up. You have had enough sex already. It's time to get you two perverts out of this den of inequity, and into the wilderness where you belong.

Bob! You've been in Canada a week and a half and all you've seen is Michael's house and a lot of naked women, not that that's a bad thing, but it's time for you to see the real Canada. Get up. Get up, time for a scouting trip. Anyway I got my welfare check and I scored a sheet of some three-way captain cranberry acid, 300 hits, and an ounce of Alaskan Thunder Fuck."

I remember asking Josh, "I know what acid is but what is Alaskan Thunder Fuck?" Josh laughed and said, "It's the best weed you've ever smoked." I said, "Better than Maui Wowie? He nodded, "Yes." I asked, "Even better than Humboldt Sensimilla?"

He nodded again. And I continued, "Better than Thai stick?"

He said, "You're wasting your time, it's better than anything that you've ever smoked."

By this time Klaus and I were both out of bed and half

dressed, the two girls were still asleep on the beds. We pulled the covers over them; finished dressing and we were on our way.

Michael was just getting up. Josh took a pair of scissors and cut a third of the Crimson sheet of acid off and gave it to Michael along with eight fat buds of the Alaskan Thunder Fuck,

I commented that the Alaskan Thunder Fuck looked and smelled much stronger than the stuff that he was cutting up when we first met him. And Josh told us that that was from one of his own crops, and that it was good, but not in the same league.

We told Michael that we would see him in a day or two and we were on our way, after I gave Lazarus a good walk of course. I asked Josh which way we were headed, and he said, "Don't worry I'll ride shotgun, and show you the way, and Klaus can play his guitar in the camper."

We went north through Vancouver and up along the Indian reservation lands. I had no idea where we were at the time.

I noticed steep mountains on either side of us and suddenly noticed a creek running alongside of the highway on the left side of the road; the land on the left side of the highway sloped down about 200 feet to the creek.

Josh yelled, "Turn left at that next road." And I did. We went down the dirt road about 250 feet to the edge of the creek.

It was very strange. Sandy. Almost like a beach.

Josh said, " Here we are, welcome to Sandy Creek, or that's what I call it anyway".

We all piled out. It was beautiful. The air was so clean and crisp. The creek was also a rapidly flowing, babbling brook, when you would close your eyes it almost sounded like a cocktail party with people conversing and laughing. And that's when I knew where the expression babbling brook came from.

Lazarus loved it. He could finally really run free.

Although he scared the crap out of me when he jumped into the fast moving stream and swam across to the other side after a squirrel. I called him back and he swam back making it both times, but winding up about 20 feet further downstream than where he started each time. Amazingly the squirrel made it as well.

I scolded him and set about finding firewood with Josh. We made a fire, set up camp, and Josh asked, "How much acid do you want?" I said, "I don't know man? I haven't done any acid in a while"

Josh continued "Nonsense, this is really clean Shit, you'll love it, and everything's better with cranberry, trust me." I said, "Okay, you're the boss". He handed me the rest of the sheet of acid and some little round nose scissors that he carried with him, and said "Just cut yourself off one hit, it'll be a nice mellow trip for you.

I'm going to get some more firewood."

I looked down at the Crimson Red sheet, held it up to the sunlight, I looked at all the tiny little bumps that made up individual squares and cut one of the tiny squares off and swallowed it with a drink of water.

Josh came back a few minutes later with an arm load of firewood and dropped it by the fire. I walked over to him and handed him back the sheet.

He asked, "Did Klaus take a couple of hits too?" I said, "No. I just took the one hit."

Josh said, "No, you took three hits, this is three-way acid, remember, dummy."

Frightened I said, "Oh my God."

"You'll be fine." he said. This stuff is pretty mellow shit." You shouldn't be worried about anything, it's not like you took 10 hits or anything. "

I said frantically, "I'm not worried, I'm scared to death." Josh said, "Don't be ridiculous. Let's see, I know it's here somewhere."

He was rummaging around in the big leather bag that he carried everywhere with him.

I remember looking at him as he rummaged through his bag, this 5'6" redheaded Jesus in a robe and sandals rummaging through his bag of tricks for some miracle cure that would ease my suffering, and thinking what have I gotten myself into. I felt like I was riding a guided missile to hell, with Josh the redheaded Jesus straddling the Atomic Bomb in front of me, waving his arms and screaming YeeeeHah! YeeeeHa! Just like Slim Pickens in the movie "Dr. Strangelove" riding the atomic bomb down towards the ground.

And then Josh said, "Here it is."

He pulled out a small prescription bottle and shook a couple of pills out of it, and handed them to me. I said, "Now what the hell is this crap, you want me to take more pills."

He said they're Valium; they will mellow your rush. Trust me. You're gonna be fine, besides, Klaus will be here."

I screamed, "You're leaving?" "Yeah" he said, "There's something that I want to retrieve that I saw on the road, I'll only be a couple hundred feet away."

So I decided that I should try and calm down. I took the Valium, found a grassy spot, laid down a blanket, took out my paint and glue and started painting my straw cowboy hat that I had just purchased. I started painting the mountain range that I could see in front of me, on to the cowboy hat. I even glued tiny pine cones and real pine needle branches to the hat which gave the scene depth.

The sun was blazing, so I started by taking my shirt off. The acid was starting to come on strong.

But it was so peaceful, and I was so interested in painting the hat that I barely noticed that Klaus was downstream about 75 feet playing his guitar in his underwear, while sitting on a stump in the middle of the stream.

I recall calmly thinking to myself; yeah the acid must have kicked in. I kept painting, and removing clothing, and intermittently throwing a stick for Laz. This went on for what I would guess to be another couple of hours.

The scene was so peaceful, tranquil, and mellow.

Until the mellow scene was rudely interrupted by the loud guttural growl of a giant monster, which came roaring down the road; dust rose from behind the green behemoth. Then it came to a screeching halt about halfway up the road from me, clouds of dust filled the air, that's when these strange creatures jumped out of the thing.

I learned later that it was just a family from Vancouver out for a picnic. But in my acid addled mind these were only the minions of the monster; they were here only to do its bidding,

I might add that according to Josh my green monster was a green Jeep Wagoneer.

As they were 100 feet or so from me they didn't seem to notice me naked on my blanket.

I watched in sheer horror as the mother un-wrapped some

steaks and started a fire in a portable barbecue.

And then the father took out a chainsaw and started cutting a branch off of a nearby tree, and the two young boys started chopping away on smaller trees with hatchets.

However in my mind the steaks were human flesh, not cow flesh, human flesh that was cut from previous victims.

And this monster and its minions were out to destroy all that lay in their path, trees, humans, animals, everything.

And with Klaus occupied with his guitar in the creek, and Josh up on the road

I was the only thing between them and their destruction of ALL life as we know it.

I looked at Lazarus, and he looked frightened. I said to myself, "I am not going to let you destroy this beautiful place and all its creatures, and I'm sure as hell not going to let you kill my dog".

I put on my shoes, put on my newly painted cowboy hat, tied the blanket around my neck like a cloak, and naked as a jay bird, I ran toward these monsters, while flailing my arms and screaming at the top of my lungs.

Like some sort of cowboy nudist superhero, on a sacred quest to save nature and mankind from alien monsters, armed only with my nudity.

The mother saw me first and she started to scream. The two boys saw me next and they started to scream. The father hearing them screaming, turned off the chainsaw, and yelled for all of them to run to the car. As they all ran back to the car leaving the steaks and the grill behind, they jumped into the Jeep with their various implements in hand and rapidly turned around and raced up the hill.

By this time I had almost caught up to them. I remember feeling the dirt and rocks hitting my chest, legs and arms, as their tires spun, digging up, and destroying the earth in order to hasten their escape.

This angered me even more; they apparently wanted to kill the earth as well?

But being high on acid I ignored the stinging pain, hell-bent to drive these demons out of Eden.

That is, until an errant stone hit me in the testicles; a blinding flash of white pain hit me and I fell to my knees, cutting them up.

I grabbed my crotch and fell over on to my side, with Lazarus licking my face;
I laid there for what seemed to be an excruciating eternity.
When a shadow broke the sunlight, it was Josh standing over me.
He bent down and said to me, "Are you okay? I guess I should've given you more Valium.
You scared the shit of that family. I would suggest that we move down the road 20 miles or so, if any of us could drive. But seeing that that's not an option, I guess we'll just have to get a pan full of that 36 degree creek water for you to soak your balls in, make some tea, and think good thoughts, and hope for the best.
We'll hide the rest of the dope for now, and if the RCMP comes, we'll just tell them that you had a bad trip.

I soaked my balls, and put my clothes back on as it was getting dark, and Josh put on a pot of Red Zinger tea.
Klaus finally rolled in shivering and saying, "Man, it's cold".
"Of course you're cold" said Josh, You're in your underwear, and you've been sitting in the creek for hours. Come over by the fire and I'll give you a cup of Red Zinger.
We sat around the fire talking for most of the night.
One of the subjects of conversation was what Josh was doing while Klaus was playing guitar and I was chasing off the campers.
He pulled out what appeared to be the long steel end of a harpoon, a very old harpoon from the look of it.
And he explained that he had noticed it sticking out of the top of one of the telephone poles just before we turned onto the road from the highway.
He had taken what rope I had and then found pieces of string and whatever to add to it to make a lasso to retrieve the harpoon.
He said it took him a couple of hours of trying, to retrieve it, and that while he was trying to retrieve it a car load of old ladies had pulled over to the side of the road on the other side of the highway and had a picnic while watching him retrieve the harpoon.
He said that they had tea and crumpets, a nice blanket and everything.
And that when he finally managed to retrieve the harpoon they all stood up and cheered, and while applauding, they screamed,

"Well done young man. Well done." he said he waved to them and held the harpoon above his head in victory, and that it felt great.

After that the elderly trio left and he walked down the highway for a while, and then on his way back he saw the green Jeep come flying out onto the highway, he said the whole family looked terrified, and flew past him heading back toward Vancouver at a high rate of speed.

We got up around 1 PM the next day. We were still a little stoned, but I let Klaus drive back to Michael's.

We spent the night at Michael's, I just slept while everybody else partied, and the next day Josh took off with some people to Toronto, to look for Holy Alex, saying that he would be back in two or three weeks. As he had just told us a story about how Holy Alex had saved him and his family on Salt Spring Island, some years before.

As Josh put it, 5 or so years back, after doing much reading, and listening to various visiting gurus, he had decided that money was the essence, and root of all evil!

And even though he had a wife and a young daughter, he took all of their money and burned it in the fireplace, and what happened next was obvious, all except the part where his family initially didn't leave him!

They moved on to Salt Spring Island, which has a much milder climate than the mainland. As they had no money, they were forced to live in a cave just outside of town. That is when Josh began to wear sandals and a robe, which he still wore when I first met him.

He told us that he would have to walk into town and beg for money, and dumpster dive to feed his family, they were on welfare, and receiving food stamps, and free healthcare, but it just wasn't enough.

Then he told us about how he had met Holy Alex a couple of years before the family dilemma, on the street in Toronto, when times were still good, and he was making good money as a mechanic.

Alex explained that he was asking for donations, and for those kind souls who gave donations to him, his gift to them in return would be, that in their future whenever they were in need, no matter what the circumstance, he would be there for them, to help them out of whatever predicament they found themselves in.

The only codicil to the agreement was that they must keep the card with Holy Alex's name and picture on it with them at all times.

Josh told us that as Holy Alex spoke to him, people would walk by occasionally and drop some coins or a dollar in his cup and scurry off quickly taking one of his cards from him, and with each card that he handed out he would say, "When you need me, I'll be there!"

Josh said, that he had gotten back to work an hour late that day, because he found Holy Alex so fascinating, and had given him all of the money in his wallet $55.00, this happening well before he burned all of their money of course.

Apparently when Josh gave Alex such a large sum of money, Alex put down his donation can, and grabbed Josh's right hand with both hands, and looking deep into Josh's eyes he held Josh's right-hand tightly, and Josh said a bright multicolored aura began to brightly glow around Alex's body! At the same time Josh said he felt like he was on really good acid!

When Holy Alex released his grip on Josh's hand, suddenly all of the sensations were gone.

At this point Alex took a pen from the donation can, and wrote on the back of one of his cards, "You will face three trials, and achieve three triumphs! When you need me, I will always be there; your friend in life, and for life, Holy Alex!"

Josh asked Alex what it all meant.

And Alex replied "You will have three great trials in your life, two of them will take place in the next few years, the third will take place near the end of your life; and even though my physical body will be on another plane at the time of your last trial, I will still be there for you, and my spirit will help you triumph over your last trial, as with the first two! Be well my friend, we will speak again in the future, and not that long from now, for after I help you through your first two trials, you will seek me out, and we shall do great things together, you and me.

Josh said that Alex gave him a big hug, and he folded the

card, and kept it in his wallet for safekeeping. It would be only a few years before Josh would seek out Alex as he had foretold.

However only a year later, after burning all his money in the fireplace, and being forced to live in a cave on Salt Spring Island with the first snow of winter beginning to fall, Josh found himself trudging along the snow-covered road into town in sandals his bare feet wrapped in rags, and his olive drab robe the only thing between him and the cold.

Yet in his empty wallet which he carried in the large leather shoulder bag that he made himself, along with his driver's license, welfare card, and a few food stamps, and a pack of matches, was Holy Alex's card.

As he continued to stumble towards town, a Land Rover pulled up alongside of him, and the guy driving it waved him over to the car, when Josh opened the door, the guy asked, "Do you need a lift?"

Josh replied, "Sure, thanks a lot!" Josh said that the car was so warm inside that his hands and feet began to hurt, meaning that he had early-onset frostbite! The guy driving continued, "Man, what are you doing out in this weather dressed like that?"

Josh told him that he had to go into town to try and scavenge some food, and buy whatever he could with what food stamps he had left, and that his wife and daughter hadn't eaten in a couple of days, and were barely keeping warm in the cave that they had moved into a few miles back, and just off of the road!

Now seemingly in shock the man asked, "What are you and your family doing living in a cave?"

Josh said that he replied, "I did something very foolish, and now I and my family are paying for it!"

The guy driving the car came back with, "Well my friend, I think this is your lucky day! You seem like an honest man just down on his luck! And it happens that I was driving into town to try and find someone to watch my place, and caretake it through the winter.

You see every winter I have to spend all of my time in Vancouver, and only get back here to Salt Spring once during the whole winter, if at all.

So if you would be interested in caretaking the place for the winter, and promise to take good care of it, and feed my animals, there's a winter's full of firewood already cut, Do you drive?"

Josh replied, "Yes of course, I'm a mechanic by trade!"

The man continued, "That's great, I have an old Ford truck that runs great that you can use to go to town, and even though the fridge and freezer are stocked with food, after we go back and get your family out of that cave and into my place so they can clean up and eat; you and

I will run into town real quick, so that I can introduce you to the owners of the general store, gas station, feed and grain, etc. so they know that you can sign on my bill for anything that you need while I'm gone, and I'll leave you both of my numbers in Vancouver just in case!

Now let's go get that family of yours out of that hole that you've been using for a home!"

Josh said that he was completely overwhelmed, and as the man turned around the car in the snow to drive back and retrieve his family, he first took the man's right hand with both of his hands thanking him profusely, and then lunged over and hugged the man, startling the fellow momentarily!

Josh said that as he walked his family out of the woods and put his wife and daughter into the backseat of the warm Land Rover, and climbed into the front seat tears were still streaming down his face!

As they drove towards the man's home, the man inquired, "I hope those are tears of joy?"

And Josh replied that they were!

Then after getting his wife and daughter settled into the home, and going to town with the man to make arrangements, Josh said that the man drove him back to the house, and after showing him how to feed and care for the animals, etc.; he handed Josh the keys to the cabin / house, and the truck, and said I'll see you in the spring, if not before, I'm usually back by March,

I'll check on you every once in a while by leaving a message for you at the general store, and they will let you use their phone to call me back, just don't lose my numbers, have a good winter!" Josh thanked the man profusely again, and then he was gone!

Josh said that he went into the house and his wife and

daughter had already bathed, and found some clean clothes to wear, and his wife had made a big meal!

They ate, and drank tea, and smiled and laughed, when Josh said that he began to cry again, and when his wife asked him, "What's the matter honey?" Josh replied, "It's just been so long since we have had anything to smile or laugh about, and it's my entire fault!"

His wife tried to console him, saying, "Forget about all of that honey, that's the past, and now we will have a happy present for the whole winter, and we can start thinking about our future!"

Josh said that while he bathed, his wife cleaned up after the meal, and then after stoking the fire for the night, they put their daughter to bed in one of the lower bunk beds, and then climbed into the lower larger twin size bunk bed on the other side of the room.

And that's when to their amazement, as they lay back in the bed, and looked up at the bottom of the upper bunk, there it was, one of the 4 x 5" Holy Alex cards with his picture smiling down upon them, and the saying, "When you need me, I'll be there!"

Josh said that he looked at his wife in amazement, and jumping out of bed, he pulled out his wallet, and pulled the holy Alex card from it, and then unfolding it and handing it too his wife, he said, "You see honey! That's the best $55.00 that I ever spent!

That guy was for real, I knew it, I just knew it! I've got a go find that guy one day, like he said I would!

I wonder what my other two immediate trials in life are going to be."

Josh said that he learned that Alex was right about the next life trial coming soon after the first, when his wife took his daughter and left him the following year!

And even though they remained friends, and he would visit them whenever he could, he said that's when he knew that he was never really cut out to be a husband, or a father, and that in the meantime she had found a new man who wanted to play that role, as he put it!

At this point I said, "Now, I not only want to go to Salt Spring Island, but I have to meet Holy Alex as well!"

Josh replied, "And you shall, you and Klaus have to go to Salt Spring on your own, Klaus knows it well, but I promise you that before you go back to the states, I will personally see to it that you get to meet Holy Alex!"

Klaus suggested that he and I go over to Salt Spring Island for a couple of weeks while Josh was in Toronto. So that's what we did.
The following day we were on the ferry to Salt Spring Island, and I must admit that it's one of the most beautiful places I've ever seen.

The town was small and down by the water. But the community on the island had been growing as more people had started commuting from Salt Spring to Vancouver.
But we were not just sightseeing.
We were also there for the Amanita Muscaria and Amanita Pantherina mushrooms.
The Amanita Muscaria or (fly agaric) mushroom, as it is also known, is a powerful psychedelic mushroom.
However, it is also poisonous and can be lethal if consumed in large quantities.
The Amanita Pantherina, the Muscaria's brown cousin is much more potent and so we would only put two of them into a whole pot of soup.
The name fly agaric comes from its use in the late 19th and early 20th century in the manufacture of flypaper. It is a large red or brown capped mushroom with white warts, very distinctive in shape and color, and native to Salt Spring Island.
Klaus and I stocked up on provisions at the general store in town, and after driving around the island we made camp by the main road that lead down to the ferry.

We found numerous Amanitas our first afternoon there, and made a big pot of Amanita Muscaria soup.
Of course we only ate very small bowls testing from teaspoon amounts on up, until we determined that a small bowl in the morning would give you a really nice high for most of the day.
So every morning we would get up, have a nice veggie sandwich, some chips and a small bowl of Amanita soup.
And after breakfast we would sit by the side of the road and play our guitars and sing for all of the commuters waiting to get

onto the ferry. At first it was strange, we were so happy and they seemed so sad.

But then it seemed that we started cheering them up, because they started rolling their windows down and smiling, some even singing along.

And then on the second morning the strangest thing happened, they not only rolled down their windows, and sang along, but they also started throwing money to us.

At first we thought they were crazy, but when we picked up over $30 Canadian in change the first day, we changed our mind.

But by the end of the first week we were starting to think that we could make enough money playing and singing during the summer to rent a place during the winter.

The second week we noticed that one guy in a blue car was throwing us five dollar bills wrapped around $.50 pieces, and that he would always wave to us on his way home in the afternoon.

Finally a couple of days before we were supposed to go back to Vancouver Island and Michael's place, the guy pulled over on his way back home, came over to us, and we invited him back to our campsite and we all sat down.

He was a nice guy, after we talked a while; he asked if he could have some of our soup.

We explained what the soup was, and he said he'd still like to try it, so we gave him a small bowl of it, and a sandwich.

Klaus went out in search of more firewood. The guy said that the soup was delicious; I explained the special ingredients that we added to make it so tasty, like cheese, and basil, etc.

Just then Klaus started yelling from out in the woods that he needed help, his flashlight had gone dead, to hurry and bring the other flashlight, and batteries before he broke his neck.

I told the guy that I would be right back. He said, "Fine, go help your friend, I'm good."

I grabbed the flashlight and batteries, and put Lazarus in the truck, and went out in search of Klaus.

I had no idea how far away he was. I would call out to him, and he would call back. But every time that I seemed to get closer to the sound of his voice, suddenly he sounded like he was further away. After about 45 minutes I finally found him at the bottom of a small canyon. By the time we changed batteries in his flashlight and carried all the firewood back and found the campsite again it was over an hour and a half later.

When we got back I let Laz out of the truck.

I asked Klaus, "Where's that guy?" Klaus asked, "Was he here when you came to get me?" I said "Yeah. I told him that I would be right back."

We called to him, and then walked up to the road to see if he had left. His car was still there, all locked up.

We walked back to the camp site, I sat down with Laz, and then Klaus yelled, "Holy Shit." I turned to see him holding the lid to the soup pot. I asked "What?"

He said "It's almost gone. Why did you let him eat so much? He could die." I replied, "He was still eating from that little bowl we gave him when I left to find you"." We warned him. We warned him, Hell. We've got to find him. He could die." reiterated Klaus.

So we spent all night searching the woods for him, we finally gave up about dawn. Klaus wanted to pack up and leave on the morning ferry,

I wanted to get some sleep and then go to the local cops in the morning.

We finally agreed to sleep, then eat, then go looking again in the morning. We got up around 11am. I needed some coffee, and Klaus needed some caffeine tea, we were both really tired.

So we headed to town to the coffee and tea place in the small shopping center. When we walked into the little group of buildings we knew that something was up. There was a cop there questioning people. And across the little mini-mall there was a reporter questioning another group of people

Klaus said, "Let's get out of here." I said, "No. Let's have our tea and coffee and see if we can find out what happened."

When the waitress came to the table I asked, "What's going on?"

She said, "You haven't heard? It's all over the island." A couple of hours ago this fellow walked right into the center in his birthday suit. Right into the crowded farmer's market, over half the island was here."

That's when I realized, "Oh my God, it's Saturday morning. No wonder it's so crowded." So then what happened?" I asked.

She said, "Well sir, of course all of the women and kids started screamin', and runnin', except me, I thought it was funny.

Then the men started yellin' at him to get out. But he seemed dazed kind of like he was in some sort of trance.

He just kept on comin', holdin' that big red mushroom in his right hand kind of like a torch, and sayin' something like, "I am you, and you are me, and we are we, and we are all together." Isn't that from that Beatles song? Well, anyway they called the cops, and the island newspaper, and of course the reporter got here first. He took a bunch of good photos, but I am sure that they will have to block out the good parts if you know what I mean. The gentleman was quite well endowed you know.

Then when the cop arrived, he made short work of the poor man. Handcuffed him, and threw a coat over him, and took him off to jail. I hope that he's all right. He was all scratched, and cut, and bruised when he walked in. Poor thing looked like he'd been walking around in a briar patch for days."

"That's amazing." I said. Klaus and I finished our coffee and tea, and then we were on the next ferry back to Vancouver.

Back to Michael's and safety, and bidding Salt Spring Island a fond farewell.

Richer in experience, richer in spirit, richer in the pocket book, richer in the gift of another great story to tell at Michael's, but most importantly richer in the knowledge that we hadn't brought about the untimely demise of a poor innocent schnook, who just happened like our psychedelic soup.

Aminita Muscaria Mushooms

Chapter 7

Leaving the island of mushrooms to journey into the wilderness and live under the flag of Che Guevara

We came back from Salt Spring Island with two large duffel bags of mushrooms, a mixture of Amanita Muscaria and Amanita Pantherina. Michael was very pleased when we arrived back at his mansion.

Josh hadn't gotten back from his trip yet, so initially we decided to stay at Michael's and wait for Josh to return.

Klaus and I proceeded to explain to Michael and all those staying with him how to consume the mushrooms without dying, and to get the best high.

There were a bunch of new people at Michael's, which was usually the case.

There were five or six new girls, but one girl in particular caught my eye. She was very pretty but certainly not the prettiest of all the new girls. But there was something about her, she always seemed very happy and she had a very fresh innocent quality.

She had already garnered the nickname Bluebell because she always seemed to wear blue, her favorite color. Like everyone else she hated her nickname, so everyone started calling her Bell except me,

I referred to her by her real name, Kathleen.

For some reason this irked Michael, I think he felt that if you rejected your nickname that he had less control over you. Which was not the case, I might add.

Over the next few days Kathleen and I became very close. We became friends, then lovers, then something even more. I can't put my finger on it, but I have never been that close to a woman in that short of a time period again in my life.

She was easily as funny as me, always topping my one-liners with one of her own. She had beautiful blue eyes that I would stare into while we made love and then we would fall asleep in each other's arms. She was so warm and soft, and we seemed to make each other feel so safe and content.

But, sadly, soon she would be heading south to San Francisco and I would be heading north with Josh to above the Fraser River Valley.

Quite often I still think of what might have happened had I have headed south with her. I probably would have settled down with her in Frisco. Who knows?

After we had been back a couple of days, three guys with guitars arrived.

Klaus was in heaven. It rapidly became obvious that the trio was now a quartet, and Klaus and I said our good-byes, I thanked him for getting me out of LA and into a great new adventure, and he climbed into their VW bus, and the fearsome foursome were on their way to Montreal.

Kathleen and I had a wonderful time for about a week, and then she and her girlfriend were off to Frisco the same day that Josh came back to Michael's. If Josh had not come back I am pretty positive that I would've gone with her.

But Josh being Josh convinced me that my journey had just begun. And after all at some point I was still supposed to go to Homer Alaska and build furniture for the mayor. And as Josh put it "You are over halfway there, why would you backtrack now." He told me that we should head 240 miles up to the Fraser River Valley and Clinton, BC.

We would stock up on provisions in Clinton, and he would show me the Chain Lakes, the mountains, the wildlife, and how to live off of the land. Also he wanted to check in on one of the communes that he had formed about 35 miles northeast of Clinton.

So we said our good-byes, gave everybody at Michael's a big hug, thanked Michael, and were on our way.

The country was so beautiful, so clean, after coming from LA. We figured about four and a half hours to get to Clinton. And an hour to get supplies, along with another few more hours to go the 35 miles of logging roads to the commune. This would put us at the commune while it was still daylight.

Everything went like clockwork until we got off of The Caribou Highway north east of Clinton, and on to the logging roads, where a few hours became six, because of downed trees that we had to remove from the road, and getting lost after dark.

When we finally made it down to the end of the 9 mile road (if you want to call it that) that went to the commune from the logging road, it was well after dark.
We were within about 50 yards of the commune when what seemed like hundreds of dogs ran up to the truck, barking loudly. On either side of the truck more and more dogs came until we reached the commune compound, stopped the truck and there were dogs 10 to 12 deep all around the truck. Lazarus was going crazy.

That's when two guys came out of the main log cabin with long hair and beards dressed kind of like cowboys from the old West with chaps, cowboy hats, etc. I rolled down my window and Josh rolled down his. Each of the cowboys came to Josh's and my windows.

They both had handguns which made me very nervous. My cowboy spoke first. But I couldn't understand a word that he said. It sounded like gibberish, a series of guttural grunts and half words punctuated by intermittent growls.

I turned to Josh and said, "I can't understand this guy." Josh said, "Don't worry about it, I've got this." I remember saying, "I sure hope so." I looked back at my cowboy who was looking a bit angry and frustrated and said, "You can talk to Josh. "

That is when out of all of the gibberish my cowboy said something I understood, he said, "Josh?" He left my window and ran around to the other side of the truck, making his way through the herd of barking dogs, and yelled, "Josh?" Josh replied, "Yeah." My cowboy said, "The Josh?" Josh said, "Yeah."

At that point the two caveman cowboys proceeded to jump up and down and cheer amidst all of the barking dogs. The scene was bizarre to say the least, and extremely chaotic, however realizing that we were not going to die, did put a smile on my face.

Josh got out of the truck and he and the caveman cowboys did a group hug and he waved me over to them.

I left Laz in the truck, and waded through the throng of barking, snapping dogs over to the trio. The caveman cowboys seemed ecstatic, I had forgotten that Josh was the founder of this commune, and for these guys it was like being a Mormon and having Joseph Smith come to visit.

We went inside the huge log cabin. There were about 15 or 20 people inside, men, women, and children. Four or five cats were draped in various spots high and low. On one side was a kitchen with two large iron wood burning cook stoves, the walls were covered with hand hewn bunk beds some three bunks high. There were four or five large tables in the center of the room with miscellaneous chairs around them, a staircase led up to a second story, this huge structure was all log construction, I marveled at what a task it must have been to build.

Two of the women brought us over our dinner. I looked down at the plate and thought, "Oh my God".

Because what I was looking at was a combination of noodles, rice, and potatoes mixed in a weak tomato sauce. For dinner I was being served a tribute to starch.

I looked at Josh and he smiled and started to eat. I looked around the room at my hosts, and noticed that they were all watching me with a sense of anticipation.

At this point in time I had only been out of Los Angeles a little under a month, and Josh had me eating a tribute to starch for the amusement of the cast of "Deliverance".

I dug in and smiled a broad smile of approval. And my hosts grinned back. I remember thinking; maybe we will survive the night after all.

They all gathered around Josh and me, and were asking Josh many questions. As he began answering their questions I began to understand what they were saying.

I learned from living with these people that when you live as a tribe a long way from everyday society you kind of create your own language. You have to understand that these people only went into Clinton every 6 to 8 months, normally. The rest of the time they were their own little society.

Brian and David, the two caveman cowboys, were the current leaders of the commune.

The reason that they had so many dogs is that every stray feral dog that came along, the commune took in and fed. It was not only the right thing to do but had a very practical purpose as well.

You see that by taking in feral cats and dogs the commune was protected from rats and the disease that they bring, and the giant pack of dogs protected them from bear, wolves, coyotes, mountain lions etc. that would kill their chickens, ducks, geese, and goats, and yet they also warned of human predators.

I asked Brian how he fed them all. He said scraps/ because they killed a fair amount of deer, elk, and caribou throughout the year. And they augmented the dog's diets with Lay mash, which was a kind of stock feed that was cheap and high in nutrients that the dogs needed, and that could be fed to the livestock as well.

Then I knew why Josh had suggested that I buy 100 pounds of the stuff when we had been in Clinton.

Brian and David made their money catching wild horses; breaking them and selling them to neighbors and whoever were appropriate buyers.

That's why they looked like old West cowboys, they were real cowboys. They made us very comfortable that night, and David and Brian were kind enough to go with me when I walked Lazarus and introduced him to the pack.

The only frightening moment was when the leader of the dog pack, a big Irish wolfhound covered in battle scars came up to Lazarus who had a 'scorpion' tail,(which I had learned earlier in LA was like being a human, and walking around shooting the finger at everyone you saw.)

That is why Lazarus was in so many fights in Marina Del Rey.

But thank God Lazarus was so smart. He noticed that as this giant dog moved through the pack, all the other dogs gave way bowing their heads, so that by the time that the behemoth reached Lazarus, Laz was already down on the ground with his head bowed. I asked Brian, "He won't kill my dog will he?" Brian answered, "No. I won't let him."

I said, "That's a mighty big, mean looking dog. How would you stop him? "

He replied, "That's simple, I am the alpha male. Every man woman and child on this compound is the alpha male or alpha female to these dogs; that's the only way that it works. You just let them know that their boss works for you, and so they all work for you."

"That sounds great." I said "But how did you ever manage to

dominate that big son of a bitch?"

Brian laughed and said, "That's a funny story. When he arrived and was establishing his dominance over the pack, one day he decided to go after me." "What did you do?" I asked. Brian said, "I hit him in the head with an ax handle. He was out cold for about 10 seconds, and when he came to I was cradling him in my arms petting his head. I gave him a scrap of dried elk meat, and we have been fast friends ever since.

However, I am the boss." I said, "What do you call him?" Brian said, "At first we called him "Lobo" because he's a wolfhound, but he's such a crazy bastard that we changed his name to Reckless. Fitting don't you think?" I replied "Yeah."

The giant wolfhound sniffed Lazarus. Walked around him, draped his neck over Lazarus's neck, and then everything was fine. Lazarus jumped up, licked the giant dogs muzzle and proceeded to meander in and out of the pack unmolested. I exclaimed, "Amazing."

The next morning after an excellent night's sleep, (I say excellent, because I was so tired.) We awoke to eggs, venison steaks, toast and coffee for breakfast.

After breakfast I took Lazarus out of the truck for a walk, I must admit with some trepidation. But everything was fine the other dogs accepted him, and me, and we were accepted, just like that.

I started looking around this great compound; it was composed of eight buildings and 10 or so small outbuildings and barns. Two giant, and three medium sized corrals housed horses, goats, and sheep. I asked Josh why the goats had triangles around their necks.

He explained, "So they can't escape the corral. If they do they will eat everything in sight, and if they get into one of the buildings they will destroy everything. You don't understand goats are like garbage disposals with four legs. But I love goat's milk."

As I surveyed the property I noticed a huge red flag with the face of Che Guevara on it in black silhouette.

Brian came over and I asked, "What's with the Che Guevara flag?" Brian said, "That's simple. Why do you think we are in

Canada?" "You aren't Canadian?" I asked. "No," Brian continued, "I'm from Texas, David's from Oregon, Mike and Bill are from the East Coast, a couple of our ladies are from up here, but most of us are from the states."

"How did you all wind up here?" I asked. Brian said, "Duh. You ever heard of the Vietnam War? Some of us came up here to beat the draft, family and all. Some of us went AWOL after we saw how fucked up it was over there. And five or six others, we just took in because they heard about us, and they had nowhere else to go.

You see the Che Guevara flag represents resistance to us. It represents freedom, and never giving into authority.

The commune has gone through some changes since Josh founded it. We still believe in love, and peace, and we don't want to hurt anyone, but we don't want anyone hurting us either.

We are completely self-sufficient, and can protect ourselves from anything human or animal.

We haven't seen the RCMP in over a year, and the last time they came up here they were quite friendly, and impressed with what we had built. At first we were going to sculpt a giant hand shooting the finger. But then somebody rolled in with the Che Guevara flag and it seemed like it sent the same message without all the work." I laughed and said, "I love it."

We stayed at the commune for about a week, I got to know the people, and they were all very nice folks when you got to know them.

After about a week Josh was getting antsy, and said he wanted to go deeper into the Bush, and show me the chain Lakes and the huge wheat grass fields. And take me up a small mountain or two.

So off we went again, telling the folks in the commune that we would see them in two or three weeks.

After four and a half hours on logging roads, and switchbacks, all of a sudden we came out of the trees on the winding road looking over thousands of acres of wheat grass with small chain lakes interspersed in them. What an amazing site. These small chain lakes were supposedly tributaries formed by creeks that originated from Green Lake, a much larger lake just to the north of us.

We stopped sat in the truck, and just took it all in. What a sight. This golden carpet laid out before us with little silver lakes interspersed randomly in it like broken pieces of mirror strewn across a golden carpet.

I looked up, and jumped out of the truck. "Look", I said "Isn't that an eagle?" "No. That's an Osprey." said Josh "A smaller version of an eagle. They catch fish from the lakes. It's really fun to watch them hunt the lakes; I can watch them for hours.

Come on; let's find a campsite. We have a lot to do before dark." We found a great spot between two of the tiny lakes.

When dusk arrived I was really glad that I had brought all of the mosquito repellent along, because the sky went almost black with giant mosquitoes. I asked Josh if he wanted some.

He said no. That I could keep my poison, and that what he did was let them bite him for a couple of days and then they would leave him alone. I replied, "Good luck with that". And he replied, "Good luck with the poison". After dark they were not as bad, but I had to put repellent on Laz because they were biting him through his coat.

Josh had gone on a walk about, and came back after dark with mushrooms, cattail roots and a bunch of sage and eucalyptus. He proceeded to put some sage and eucalyptus on the fire and the mosquitoes virtually disappeared. I asked "Why didn't you put that shit on the fire an hour ago?" He said, "Because I had to find it, dumb ass."

As he leaned over the fire I noticed that his face was almost unrecognizable. I asked, "Did mosquitoes do that too your face." He said, "Do what to my face?"

I said, "Feel your face, man. You look like you just went 10 rounds with Ali." He said "Who's Ali?" "You're kidding right, the heavyweight champion?" I said sarcastically "Oh, he's a boxer?" He said continuing; "There is a fair amount of swelling for a few days but then it goes away." laughingly I replied "I hope so for your sake, because right now you could frighten small children."

Josh replied, "I doubt that I will run into any before the swelling goes down." Josh made some stew from mushrooms, cattail root, potatoes, and seasoning, and showed me how you can use a large flat rock in the middle of the fire, to make unleavened bread like chapattis on the rock with just wheat flour and water.

After a very good meal we were sitting around the fire smoking some weed from a chillum pipe.

And that is when Josh looked up at the gigantic 3/4 moon in the sky and began to howl. After a couple of howls I joined in, and then Laz joined in as well.

There we were, the three of us howling at the moon. And then out of the blue about 100 ft. away about 15 or 20 howls answered us from the darkness. I smiled and said to Josh, "What are those people doing way out here? Do you think that we should invite them over?"

Josh fell over onto his side laughing. So I asked, "What's so funny?" When he regained his composure he said, "You idiot, those are wolves." "What?" I said. I rapidly climbed into the camper shell, and retrieved my Enfield rifle, racking a round into the chamber.

"Put that away. You don't need that." Josh said. "Man, you really are green, aren't you? Wolves won't hurt you! They are scared shitless of humans. Hell, humans have almost wiped them off the face of the earth. They are just being friendly."

We smoked some more weed and then crashed. It got down into the mid to low thirties at night. So we made personal lean-tos in order to keep surrounded by the heat of the fire. I put Laz behind me in the lean-to to keep him warm and safe, and in front of me I kept my rifle ready to go with a gloved finger on the trigger guard.

A mosquito woke me up at the crack of dawn. So I got up and put more wood and sage and eucalyptus on the fire for heat, as well as some more bug repellent. When I turned from the fire I noticed that Josh was gone. I called out "Josh? Josh?"

And then Josh's voice came out of the camper shell, "I'm in here getting some acid." "Why are you getting it now?" I said. "Because this shit comes on slow, and I want to be peaking by the time I reach the foot of that small mountain over there." He pointed to the silhouette of a small mountain which could be seen in the background as the sun rose up behind it.

I said, "Are you kidding? It will take you three hours to get there." Josh replied, "I'll be there in less than an hour." "Bullshit." I replied. "How can you know that?"

He said "Because I have already walked from here to there."

"Fuck you." I said. "Why do you think I brought you here? It's one my favorite spots." Josh said. "Why would you pick a place filled with giant mosquitoes to come back to?" I asked. Josh replied, "The whole Frazer River Valley is loaded with giant mosquitoes this time of year. And aren't you the one who talked about how beautiful this place is yesterday? Look, why don't you go back to sleep, and I'll wake you up in a couple hours, we'll have some breakfast. And then I'll be on my way." "That sounds good to me." I replied.

Sure enough I woke up an hour and a half later to the smell of food cooking.

We ate breakfast and Josh was on his way to climb the mountain saying, "I'll see you in a couple of days". He gave me big hug and was on his way. I watched him as he walked through the large golden wheat grass fields between the lakes. And then I noticed what appeared to be the osprey from the day before circling about 400 ft. above Josh as he walked. I grabbed the binoculars out of the truck to look closer. I will never forget what I saw next as long as I live.

Josh stopped. He bowed his head, and put his arms out like a cross.

Slowly a visible aura formed around his body. First a yellow band then red, then green, then blue. I rubbed my eyes and then looked again I couldn't believe my eyes. I looked up and caught sight of the osprey circling down toward Josh. As the small eagle circled down closer the multi-colored aura which now began to appear to vibrate? I remember saying "What the fuck?" and thinking, "Should I break out my Beaulieu 16mm and film this. No, I don't have time. I could miss the whole thing."

I kept watching intently, completely sober I might add, as the osprey circled down and lit on Josh's extended right arm, Josh slowly raised his head. The bird seemed confused, its head moving side to side, and then suddenly the bird bowed its head, and Josh kissed it on the forehead.

Josh leaned back, and the aura disappeared, he waved his arm upward and the eagle flew away.

After Josh had walked out of sight, I crawled into the camper shell and took a nap. After all why not, I didn't have anything else that needed doing. Ah, what a great feeling that was.

When Josh came back three days later, I asked him how he had done it.

He replied, "Oh that. That's a trick that I learned from Holy Alex. I can only do it when I'm peaking, though. Alex can do it anytime. I thought to myself, "I really have to meet this Holy Alex Character."

And then I thought, As Klaus had said, "This was going to be a magical Trip." And as it would turn out, he was right.

Me and Glen under "No Hippies Allowed" sign

Chapter 8

The return of the prodigal son and climbing "Meltdown Mountain"

After Josh had walked out of sight and after I awoke from my short nap, suddenly a feeling of terror gripped me. I came to the realization that I was totally alone except for Lazarus for the first time in years.

You see I had always had a girlfriend or a roommate, or my family around me all my life, even though I did lead a very reclusive life as a child around the house.

But now just a month or so out of Los Angeles, I was in the middle of the wilderness by myself, just me and the dog.

Loneliness and fear rapidly turned into boredom. I recall thinking, well I've got the radio, and I've got the books and magazines, and I was smart enough to put two batteries on the truck with a stored spare, and an aircraft generator to keep them all charged, and do some welding if necessary.

So after I calmed down some, I turned the radio off and put down the book I was reading, "Black Elk Speaks" and took a nap with Lazarus laying beside to me in the camper.

My dreams immediately turned to memories of Kathleen.

At first I dreamed about us laughing and playing together, riding horses, swimming, walking through Michael's orchard leaning up against trees and kissing, and the time that Kathleen decided that we should get naked and paint our crotches and our faces bright blue and walk around the compound all day like that.

Just to as she put it, "Live up to the bullshit nickname of Bluebell", which Michael had given her.

I remember asking, "Why do I have to get dragged into your nightmare?" And her replying, "Are you enjoying the sex?" I told her that I would do it as long as we could fashion and attach some blue butterfly wings to our shoulders. She laughed and said, "That's what I'm looking for, motivation; and if you'll hang with me for the whole day, I promise you the best sex that you've ever had in your life tonight."

I asked, "Can we leave the blue paint and butterfly wings on?" She gave me a deep long kiss and said, "Oh my God, I finally found a guy who thinks like me."

Well, we did it. And surprisingly, not only did we not shock anyone, but by the end of the day virtually everyone at Michael's, including Michael, was completely nude and had painted their face and crotch in some way or another. And many people were very creative.

Michael for instance had one of the girls an artist, paint his crotch to look like the face of an old man with the penis being the nose and the balls being the chin, it was hilarious.

Another one of the guys had the Garden of Eden painted onto his crotch with his penis being the snake and his balls being two apples, or forbidden fruit. His stomach hips and thighs were the Apple tree, and his legs were painted to be the tree trunks, with Eve reaching up toward the apples in front of the trunk on his left thigh. It was very creative.

It went on and on all day. We really started something.

That night we all got stoned and drank champagne, and danced to the great paint God who had enlightened our day.

As I remember, when Kathleen and I hit the bed, that night at that particular point in my life, I don't believe that I've ever been any happier.

We laughed and kissed and rolled around on the bed, as our papier-mâché wings went flying to and fro. And then suddenly we stopped and looked deep into each other's eyes, and we kissed softly, slowly, and passionately.

I slowly ran my tongue all over her body then worked from her feet up both legs to her inner thighs; and then slowly, and lightly, I moved my tongue over the hair on her vagina, catching a hint of the taste of the blue water-based paint. By the time that I finally touched her labia with my tongue, she let out a loud moan and pressed my head into her vagina hard. I worked on her for about 15 minutes.

I was so excited about giving her head that when she came, I came with her, and I wasn't even masturbating. This is something that had never happened to me before.

We made love over and over again and each time we came simultaneously. It was magical. It was spiritual. It was definitely one of the greatest experiences, sexual or otherwise, that has occurred in my life.

So here I was out in the middle of nowhere in the camper shell dreaming about my memories of the girl that got away. And then I woke up to another recent first in my life. At the age of 27 I had just had my first wet dream since I was a kid.

I couldn't believe it. Then I got really bummed out. I could be in Frisco, With Kathleen right now, having the time of my life. But Noooo, I had to be a mountain man. What and asshole I am, I thought.

I decided that there were still at least four hours of sunlight left, and that I still had left over food, so why not go scouting?

So I grabbed my Enfield rifle, matches and lighter, flashlight, compass, knife, canteen, and jacket, and Lazarus and I were on our way.

After locking up the truck, and leaving Josh the hidden keys of course. I decided that we would head into the woods to the West of the wheatgrass fields where we were camping, and explore the many small connected chain lakes by the forest.

Lazarus wanted to run ahead and I wanted him to stay closer, scolding him over and over, after calling him back. After about a half an hour we got to a little rocky beach at the edge of the first small lake.

I was washing my face and putting some water on the back of my neck while Lazarus drank from the lake.

Then out of nowhere, Lazarus dove into the lake making the whimpering sound that he always made when he was excited about chasing something; that's when I saw it, 100 yards or so out in the lake there was a beaver, with Lazarus making a beeline for it.

I yelled and yelled for him to come back. But he was in hot pursuit; the fetch junkie in him had taken over again.

When he finally got within about 15 feet of the thing, it slapped its tail and dove under the water. When the beaver did this Lazarus almost dog paddled out of the water, he was so excited.

When the beaver resurfaced 20 feet behind him, he turned and gave chase again. I kept yelling for him to come back and he kept ignoring me and chasing the beaver, all the way to the other side of the lake.

I panicked and started running around the long way to the other side of the lake. However by the time I got there, they were swimming out of sight and into a connecting Lake.

I ran and yelled, and scratched myself up pretty bad running through the nettles and brush.

After dark, I finally dropped to my knees in exhaustion, and started to cry.

I had just lost my best friend, the friend who had recently saved my life. And now he was in the wild on his own, and the chances were that a 50 pound city dog wasn't going to last long on his own out here.

However, my weeping stopped immediately, when a loud roar pierced the darkness, and it wasn't very far away. I took my survival knife out and got some brush, and wood, and made a fire.

I used the light of the fire to gather more firewood. The more firewood that I gathered, the brighter that the fire got and the further I could go and search for more wood. Eventually I had a giant bonfire that I figured Lazarus could see for miles. I built a small leaned-to, to gather the heat, and built a stack stoke using the string from the survival knife. Josh had taught me how to build a stack stoke.

What you do is stack a lot of firewood angled toward the fire supported by a branch as close to the edge of the fire as you can, you tie a string to the bottom of the branch, and when the fire starts to go out in the early morning hours instead of having to get up in the cold, you just pull the string and the fire is re-stoked.

Clever guy Josh, after gathering enough pine fronds to use as a bed and a blanket, I finally managed to get some light sleep with one eye open and my finger on the trigger of my rifle.

The next morning I started out early and by the end of the day I had circled all three small connecting chain lakes, calling out for Lazarus so much that by the end of the day I had lost my voice almost entirely.

By this time I was getting quite hungry, and had to go back to the truck to get some food. I made some beans and flatbread, and ate.

I can only think of a few times in my life that I have been that sad. Because I couldn't yell anymore, I honked the horn on the truck, and played the radio as loud as I could;

But there was still no sign of Lazarus.

By the morning of the third day I was convinced that Lazarus was by now in the food chain.

I picked up my guitar and spent most of the day writing songs about my great friend and companion, I also wrote one about Kathleen.

About an hour before dusk all of a sudden Josh rolled in. The first thing he asked me was, "Where's Lazarus?" I hung my head and said, "I lost him."

Josh exclaimed. "He's dead? And you're not? What got him?"

I said, "I don't know? He went after a beaver in the lakes, and I had to chase them around the lakes, and they just went out of sight, and then it got dark.

And I went all around the lakes yelling for him all day yesterday until I lost my voice. And yesterday I honked the horn and played the radio so loud you could probably hear it at 70 mile house. And still no Lazarus.

And I heard some serious heavy duty growls out by that spot where I had to camp by the lake, night before last. So I don't think I'm ever going to see him again, and I really miss him, man."

Josh started laughing.

Angrily I asked, "What's so funny, asshole?"

Josh said, "Well he's coming back for sure now." I said "What the fuck are you talking about?"

Josh replied, "Why is it that I have to teach you everything twice?" I looked surprised, asking, "What?"

Josh replied, "What did I just teach you about finding mushrooms?" I replied, "That if you just look for them you will look for them all day long and you will never find them until they want to be found. So what you do is walk around for an hour or so and then you say, "Well I guess I'm not going to find any mushrooms today?"

And as soon as you do that you will see one and then another, and then another, but only because you said aloud that you were giving up."

"But what does that have to do with Lazarus?" I asked.

Now Josh laughed so hard he fell onto his side, and when he regained his composure again, he said "You dummy. That's what you just said about Lazarus. What an idiot."

I remember saying skeptically, "We'll see?"

Josh said, "Let's catch a buzz, and then start getting ready for dinner. Do we need any more firewood?" "Yeah, we do. I'll get some" I replied.

I stood up walking towards the fire, when Josh started laughing hysterically again.

I looked over at him, puzzled, but before I could say anything, something hit me in the back of the legs, almost knocking me down.

I turned around and there was Lazarus. Full of burrs, filthy, and dirty, and looking like hell.

And yet I've never seen anything more beautiful in my life.

I grabbed him, hugged him while he licked my face, licking off the tears of joy as I cried them. Life was good again. My friend was back. In fact both of my friends were back.

During dinner that night Josh told me of another small mountain that he had spotted from the one that he had just climbed. Using my light telescope, which he took along with him; He said that he had spotted a good-sized cave that we could stay in up at the high point of the mountain and watch the satellites, meteors, and maybe catch some of the aurora borealis?

He explained that we would have to fetch firewood up about 800 feet and stock it in the cave and that we would have to carry all of our food and water up there as well, so other than that we would have to travel light.

The next morning when he pointed out the mountain to me I said, "Damn Josh. That mountain has got to be at least 6 miles away." Josh replied, "I figure it's more like eight."

I looked at him angrily and said, "What are you nuts? We are supposed to carry at least 5 gallons of water, 5 pounds of food, 15 pounds of Enfield rifle and ammo, and another 5 pounds of incidentals for 8 miles, and then carry it up to the cave another 1500 or so feet, and then go back and forth up and down the mountain 800 feet to gather firewood? Are you out of your fucking mind?"

Josh casually replied, "Two gallons of water, no food, no gun, and no incidentals to speak of. Do you want to go or not? There's going to be some beautiful sites in the sky tonight, and from up there we can reach out and touch them. You carry the aluminum pot, I'll find the food and I guarantee you that tonight we will have a great meal in the cave on top of the mountain, and drop some acid, and you will have one of the best experiences of your life. Or you can just sit here in your truck listening to the radio, reading, and jerking off. But then again, you could do that in LA. So what'll it be? Are you a mountain man, or city boy? Just let me know in the next 15 min., because I'm going with or without you."

So we loaded up, locked the truck, put out the fire, and we were on our way. I thought that I was in pretty good shape, when I was down in the Marina. I ran on the beach, played volleyball, and had recently won both singles and doubles championships in the local paddle tennis tournaments at Venice Beach. But these 8 miles were tough.

I was pretty tired by the time we reached the base of the mountain. Josh wasn't even winded, this crazy little 5'6" redheaded Jesus, in his robes and sandals, walking ahead of me and setting the pace, where after a while Lazarus even dropped back with me.

I stopped momentarily to give the heavily panting Lazarus some water in my cupped hand, after lapping up three or four handfuls; he looked up at me as if to say, "What's with that little redheaded guy? Is he nuts?" And then we had to start running to catch up with Josh before he got out of sight. Losing him would not be good.

We caught up with Josh, and I suggested that we camp for the night at the base of the mountain as it would be dark in a little while, and it would take us that long to make camp. Josh said, "No, we've got to get up to the cave tonight, or we will miss all the action." "What action?" I asked do you know something that I don't know."

Anxiously Josh replied, "I'll give you 10 min., then we're going up this mountain, and I guarantee you that we will be in that cave, eating before dark." Luckily for me, Josh didn't carry a watch so I got to rest for 17 min. and Laz and I cherished every minute.

We started up the mountain, which when I think about it, was more like a large hill.

And it was actually a little easier than I thought it would be. Of course we weren't climbing the Eiger, or Mount Everest, or even the Cascades.

And sure enough when darkness fell, we were in the cave, the fire was going, we had stocked enough firewood for the night, and Josh was making a stew from things that he had gathered along the way.

He described every ingredient as he added it to the pot. "These are fried chicken mushrooms. Did you notice how I took them off the base of the trees? That's where they grow. They're very tasty, but you have to be careful. Check them out closely, there's another mushroom that looks like them. It is a little darker in color that will kill you deader than a rock.

These are stinging nettles, you have to be careful how you gather them or they will sting the shit out of you. However, when cooked, they taste just like fresh spinach.

These are wild onions, they grow everywhere, and they're delicious. I'll show you how to find them, it's really easy.

He went on and on, my redheaded Jesus looking version of Julia Childs. I must admit that the stew was delicious.

After dinner we fired up the chillum pipe, and I opened the bottle of red wine that I had carried all the way, with my Swiss Army knife corkscrew. Josh went on and on about how alcohol was poison. And I said, "Why don't you shut the fuck up, and give it a try before you bad mouth it? Besides, I've heard that wine is good for you, after all, it's made from grapes, like those damn raisins you're eating all the time."

Josh laughed, and took a swig from the bottle and said, "Ahhhh. Not bad." And then he proceeded to try and drink the whole thing. I had to grab it back from him, saying, "I should've kept my mouth shut."

I noticed him cutting something with a razor blade on a rock. I asked, "What are you doing?" He said, "How many hits of acid do you want, Daddy O?"

"Daddy O?" I asked, "Are we up so high that we hit a time warp? Are we back in the 50s? All of a sudden I feel like I'm in the cast of West Side Story."

It was just so strange hearing Josh use the expression daddy oh. Josh said, "How many hits do you want, hep cat?"

Now a little frustrated I replied, "Is this some sort of bizarre test to see if I need any acid? Or did you already put some in the wine? I wouldn't put it past you."

Josh chuckled and said, "I guess one hit is all you need." So, we dropped our acid, and sat at the edge of the cave entrance looking at the beautiful night sky.

There's something that you should know about the night skies in British Columbia and Alaska. They are not like the night sky is in Southern California.

You see, in Southern California a shooting star looks almost like a faint pencil mark going across the sky, and it's very hard to see a satellite with the naked eye. However, in British Columbia, especially at the top of even a small mountain, the stars are huge. And satellites are not only visible with the naked eye, but they appear large as well.

And the shooting stars? They're not shooting stars. They are meteors, which crackle across the sky with flames coming out from behind them in a gigantic trail or plume if you will.

I believe that the only time in my life that I ever OOOOOOhed, and AAAAAhed so much, other than this time, was when I dropped acid with my friend Ben, and we went and saw the film, "The Hellstrom Chronicle," which I mentioned in the first chapter.

What a strange trip that was.

I was fascinated by the night sky, Josh pointing to the left and then to the right. Saying," Look at that satellite. Wow. That's a big ass meteor. What a burner."

As we watched the night sky, sharing my binoculars the acid really started kicking in. And I made the mistake of looking down and of course at this point it appeared much steeper than it really was.

I thought to myself, "I am between heaven and hell. I am literally perched on the edge of the abyss. And if I'm not mistaken, I believe that that's the abyss calling to me?" It's funny how easy it is to flip out on acid, especially good acid. Of course my heart started to race, and I started to panic.

And as the fates would have it, right then, a giant meteor appeared to be heading right for us.

I freaked out, jumped up and ran as far back into the cave in the dark as I could. Tripping, and cutting my knee in the process. Josh grabbed a piece of wood from the fire, to use as a torch for light and went back looking for me.

When he found me he said, "I'm cutting you back to half a hit from now on. You're too much of a lightweight."

"Fuck you." I screamed, "That thing almost killed us." Josh laughingly said, "Are you kidding? That one wasn't even close, it went completely over the mountain, and impacted about 20 miles to the west. And you missed it all, lightweight!

It was close enough that you could really see it. And it was big.

Did you hear that bang that it made when it hit? That was loud. I hope it doesn't start a forest fire.

Oh, that's right. You were back here hiding like a little girl." Josh started to laugh.

Now I was pissed off, saying, "You know these mountains. I don't. You take this acid all the time. I don't. And frankly I am not just freaked out about the meteors. I'm also beginning to wonder how the fuck you plan on us being able to get back down this mountain, asshole?"

Josh grinned that wide grin of his and said, "Why, that's easy. We'll just melt down." Shockingly it all made perfect sense. How can you fall and kill yourself, if you're melting down the side of the mountain? It'll almost be like you're glued to it.

It's amazing how the mind works when you're on acid. How the stupidest comment can sound like such sage advice. Calming the acid fried brain. Instilling complete confidence in a person who just moments before was hysterical. We stayed up all night watching the stars and talking. And I learned a lot more about Josh.

Including a more in depth version about how years back he had given up everything including his family, a wife and child, and all of his money, to walk from one end of Canada to the other, planting marijuana, and networking with people all across Canada. He knew an awful lot about growing marijuana. And he grew a lot of it in the wild all over the country.

He told me how if you plant your seedlings in the right place you will never have to water them. He showed me how if you want to keep the deer from eating them. You just piss around the plants.

And that also urinating around the perimeter of your campsite can keep a lot of predators away.

I asked him how he was able to walk from one end of Canada to the other in the wilderness wearing nothing more than robes and sandals, and armed with nothing more than a fish cleaner's gutting knife and a razor blade?

He replied, "I understand the land; I understand and commune with nature. I have learned what to eat and what not to eat. I have learned when it's safe in the wild, and when it's not, and when to stay and when to go. When it's going to be wet, and when it's going to be dry.

You must understand your surroundings whatever they may be Bob. Or you can't survive anywhere. So I stay safe, and warm in the winter, and safe and cool in the summer.

I don't punch a time clock anymore. I am my own man. I plant my seeds. I gather my plants. I trade for money and other drugs that I like. And most importantly, I have really good friends like Michael all over this country in every major city and most small towns.

I'm sure that a lot of people look at me and think I'm crazy. But I am a very happy man. I still see my wife and daughter a couple times a year. More if I can. But I tell you Bob, there is nothing in this world that is more important than freedom. I really don't have a care in the world.

No mortgage. No job. No taxes. No car to break down. I do what I want and when I want. And it doesn't get any better than that.

Now let's go back down this mountain and head back to the commune and see what Brian and David are up to.

And then, if you want? I will ride with you, and show you the way up the Alcan Highway to Homer, Alaska. I still have a couple of friends up there. And I can catch up with them while you build your furniture, or if you want I can help you with that. I've built a fair amount of furniture myself.

Besides, you're going to need someone to help you prepare for, and navigate the Alcan Highway. It's not exactly like one of your LA freeways, if you know what I mean?"

So we went down the mountain and after a couple of days back to David and Brian's commune. Once again to live under the flag of Che Guevara for couple of weeks, while preparing for the big jump up to Homer, Alaska to build furniture for the Mayor, there.

When we got back to the campsite from the hike down the mountain, and back, I was pretty tired and even Josh seemed a little spent from being up all night, the acid, and the hike.
However as soon as we reached the campsite, Lazarus started barking loudly at the woods. Josh looked in the direction that Laz was barking with the binoculars. He shouted "It's a big brown bear, maybe a grizzly, hard to tell."
I shouted back "Let me get my 16MM camera, and let's go get some footage of him." Josh replied, "He's just gonna run. Let's just leave him alone."
I replied insistently, "No. I need more footage for my documentary." So I grabbed my camera, and the three of us were on our way, with Lazarus in the lead. We were starting to close in on the ambling bear, as I tried to film him as steady as I could while running, and Josh barked orders kind of like a director. Yelling things like, "Don't get too close, and keep your eye on the trail, or you're going to break your neck."

That is the way things went for a couple of hundred feet, until the bear finally tired of the ridiculous exercise, and stopping dead in his tracks, he turned and reared up on his hind legs, and let out one of the loudest and most ferocious roars that I have ever heard. He was frothing at the mouth, and it was obvious that this gigantic bear was easily 8-9 feet tall, and well over 1,000 lbs.
Josh and I stopped in our tracks, and poor Lazarus who was only 10 or 12 feet behind the bear when the bear stopped, was actually trying to furiously back pedal while his momentum was still carrying him toward the ferocious beast.(Kind of like in a cartoon.) He let out a loud cry as he finally stopped about 6 feet short of the bear, and immediately beat a hasty retreat back toward us about 45 or 50 feet to the rear of him and the bear.
Josh and I looked at each other panic stricken as the bear let out another loud roar. Josh yelled "That's a Grizzly, and he's pissed." And I replied, "This is my movie camera not my rifle."

That's when we both began to run as fast as humanly possible back to the camper. And as we ran for our lives with the bear in hot pursuit, Lazarus flew past both of us, his tail between his legs, crying, and whimpering all the way.

This is where I should explain that bears are a lot faster than humans; they've been known to do up to twenty five mph on land,

However we had two things in our favor. The forty-five foot plus lead, and the fact that from the blood around his mouth, the red bloody froth, and bloody paws, it was obvious that he had just finished a huge meal, which slowed him down a great deal. Still by the time we made it back to, and into the camper, he was only about 20 ft. behind us.

We all got into the camper, and I locked it from the inside. I didn't get more than a round racked into my Enfield rifle when the entire truck shook violently; knocking me to the floor of the camper, at this same time Lazarus shinnied from the camper up into the cab. (My guess was that he was trying to put as much distance between himself and the bear as he could.) I raised and aimed my rifle at the camper door, about to shoot, when Josh screamed, "NO. If you wound him you'll really piss him off. And we will both die deaf. Just open the side window and stick the barrel outside, and let off a round, and that should run him off!"

So I did just that, just as he pawed the camper shell once more, and sure enough it worked; because after the shot went off he slowly ambled away, and then we could finally be on our way.

As we navigated the logging roads back to David and Brian's commune, I recall thinking to myself, "This is going to be one hell of a trip, if I can just survive it." And it turns out that I was right.

Chapter 9

Bad day at Black Tree commune, back to the house of Che, and then back to Michael's to prepare for Alaska

We started back to Brian and David's but when we hit a four-way intersection on the Logging Rd., Josh yelled for me to stop the truck.

I stopped the truck and asked, "What's the matter?" Josh said, "It's not really that far." "What's not really that far?" I asked. "Black Tree commune." replied Josh. "How many communes have you started up here?" I asked.

"To be honest I don't really remember," said Josh. "You're kidding? Josh you really can't remember how many communes you helped start?" Josh replied, "Oh, I helped start around 6 or 7, but I actually only started 3 or 4 that I know of. You've got to remember, Bob, I've gone back and forth across Canada four times in the last six years, that's eight times if you count each way, and three times to Alaska.

Yeah, what the hell; let's go check out Black Tree. I haven't checked in on them since 1970. Yeah, make a left; in only about 15 miles and I can show you some really cool stuff on the way and the commune is another 30 miles on from there."

So we were off on another new adventure. He showed me a beautiful giant cascading waterfall that dumped into a small lake. We drove through a forest of giant pine trees which were so thick that it was dark then suddenly the truck would burst forth into bright sunlight in this section of the forest that had been clear-cut, and then back into the darkness.

We came to an area with a logging road that had tall green honey grass growing everywhere except where the vehicle tracks were laid perpendicularly through it.

We actually had to wait for around 25 minutes while a mother moose and her calf finished eating their fill of the honey grass before we could proceed. I was not about to upset her. Josh told me to stop the truck immediately and began to explain, when I cut him off with a reminder of why my tailgate was pushed in and the camper shell repair from our last mother moose encounter.

Josh was right, it was truly amazing country, and other than the mother moose encounter we made very good time, arriving at Black Tree commune about mid-afternoon.

Josh told me that the people that he started Black Tree with had come up from California in late 67.

A bad move, they apparently had been inspired in the summer of love to come north and form their own utopia, kind of like the hog farm in California. The problem was that they started too late, and by the time Josh found them they were stranded in the first snow, nine of them trying to survive in two VW buses. Freezing, starving, and, well you get the picture.

Josh took charge immediately, like he always did. I remember thinking how funny it must have looked all of these California kids right out of the city with this little redheaded Jesus in robes with his feet bound up and attached to handmade snowshoes taking charge putting them all to work, each with a task that meant life or death for all of them.

They fashioned lean-tos opposite the two VW buses which were facing each other and put branches over the back of the buses so they would hold in the heat from the fire and left a large enough area for a good-sized fire in the middle.

Josh got a fire going so they could warm themselves and then took one of the fellows with him about a half-mile through the snow to the closest lake, where they broke through the ice at the edge of the lake where the ice is thinnest with a tire iron, and he proceeded to catch enough fish for everybody with a small piece of line and lure that he carried in his bag of tricks.

He kept them alive through the winter, and in the spring showed the men how to build three good sized log cabins, and the women how to live off the land. He showed them how to make a still, and with different types of local flora and fauna how to make two different grades and types of alcohol.

As Josh put it "One was for drinking, and one was for driving."

By the way in case you're wondering the name Black Tree for the commune came from a giant oak that had been struck by lightning and badly burned.

I found out that the oak was kind of revered by the members of the commune, because it had come back to life as the commune had come to life.

By the time that I got there with Josh in 1973 the only signs that it had ever been struck by lightning at all, were some large jagged scars and blackened bark, but you had to look close to see them.

I don't know what it was; but I got a strange vibe off of the leader of the commune, Terry. Terry was one of the original nine that Josh had helped back in '67. There were only three original members left. But the commune had grown to 24 people; men, women, and children. They only had four or five dogs so I let Lazarus out of the truck, and he seemed to do fine with the other dogs.

Initially it was all hugs and handshakes. Everybody was glad to see Josh, or "The Josh" as most of the people referred to him. And as for me, any friend of Josh's, right?

As we all walked towards the main house I heard guitar music coming from a teepee on the right, and a woman's voice singing.

I asked, "Who's that?" "Oh that's Angie." said one of the girls. "Hey Josh, I think that I'll go back to the truck and get my guitar and join her okay?" Josh said, "Sure man, go do your thing, we will be up at the main house."

"Cool" I said. I ran back and got my guitar, and leaning into the teepee I said "Would you mind some company, Angie?"

She had a neat look about her, very natural, kind of the mountain momma look that I liked so much, and still do. "Cool song. Did you write it yourself? I really like your voice."

Angie cut me off, saying, "Whoa. Slow down cowboy, one question at a time. I bet you've been out in the woods for a while without a lady, huh."

This really rattled me. This woman can read my mind, oh my God, what if she's a witch? I thought.

I must have looked rattled because she began to laugh. "I'm just messing with you. And thanks for the compliments." I rolled a joint and we smoked it, and started playing guitar and singing.

First we each played a couple of our own songs, and then we started writing and singing a song together. Our voices blended really well and the song was very nice. What a lot of fun.

We finished, and we both laughed and I said "That was fucking awesome." She agreed, and before she could say anything else I kissed her.

We were having quite a hot make out session; that's when a girl ran into the teepee. She screamed, "That black dog killed Thunder."

I asked, "Who is Thunder?" And Angie started to cry saying, "Thunder is my cat." I said, "It can't be Lazarus, he's never killed a cat. He's a fetch junkie; he only chases balls and sticks."

The girl screamed, "Well this time he fetched and killed Angie's cat."

Just then Lazarus ran in to the teepee. He had blood on his mouth and was very excited. He looked at me like "I fucked up bad this time, dad." I told Angie that I was so sorry, and I didn't understand how this could've happened.

She became hysterical screaming at me "Just get out, Get out."

I told Laz to come, and guitar in hand we both ran back to my truck. I put Lazarus in the truck, and grabbed my Enfield rifle and the two spare magazines that I had, closing the camper shell door, I waited, and not for long.

Members of the commune were heading toward the truck from all directions.

The leader slash dictator Terry was leading a large group of the men down the hill from the main house the man to the left of him was carrying Angie's cat, dead in his arms. On Terry's right was Josh, attempting apparently to reason with him. They were about 80 feet away and closing in on me fast. Terry was carrying a pump shotgun; and a bunch of the other guys had rifles, and pistols.

This did not look good at all, so I immediately raised and pointed my rifle at Terry's chest.

By the time the group of men reached my truck most of the commune had the truck surrounded. I still had my Enfield rifle pointed at Terry's chest.

Terry screamed, "That God damn dog of yours killed Thunder. And now we are going to kill him. And don't try to stop us."

I yelled, "I'm terribly sorry about Angie's cat, Thunder. But Lazarus has never killed anything but a stick before. I don't understand this? But nobody is killing my dog unless they can kill me first." I heard some guy in the back say, "That can be arranged."

Josh chimed in, "It's not Bob's fault, and it's not his dog's fault. I'm sorry Bob, I should've told you. I caught Klaus teaching Lazarus to chase cats and rabbits when you weren't around. He thought it was funny."

"What! What the fuck Josh? You didn't think that that was worth mentioning to me? That's fucking wrong, man." Josh looked down at the ground and said, "I'm really sorry, man, I should've told you."

Terry screamed, "Fuck this shit. No more talk. Let's get the dog."

With my rifle still raised to my shoulder, and screaming loudly, I said, "Let me explain to you how this is going to play out, Shithead."

Everyone stopped; it was almost like time stopped.

"You move one fraction of an inch in my direction, Terry, and I am going to put a .303 round through your heart and it's going to kill two or three of the guys standing behind you before it winds up going through that shack of yours on the hill. (The two guys standing right behind Terry immediately stepped to one side, and out of the line of fire. This seemed to rattle Terry quite a bit.)

Continuing I said, "Then seeing that these other clowns have most likely never shot anybody they're going to freeze and I'm going to take them out. Hell I'll take this whole camp out if I have to. Before I let you kill my dog. You ever killed anybody Terry? Any of you other guys ever killed anybody? I have.

I had to shoot two guys, two different times in Houston in self-defense, like now, or I wouldn't be talking too you. So if you don't believe me, come on, try me. This dog saved my life and I am not going to let you or anybody else harm him.

Josh screamed, "Everybody calm down. Everybody please, calm, down.

Terry, we are going to leave. But for god's sake don't take this any further; because I know Bob, and he means it. He will kill you. So just back off and let us be on our way."

The whole group slowly started to back up as Josh ran over to me saying "Come on, man, let's get out of here."

Keeping my bead on Terry I said loudly, "Not until every one of them is out of sight. I saw Angie run up and grab Thunder's body from the guy who was holding him. I yelled, "I'm so sorry Angie. I'm so sorry." Angie screamed, "Fuck you." And she shot me the finger. Crying as she cradled Thunder's body and ran into the approaching darkness of dusk.

We drove most of the night, and finally stopped off the road just at the 9 mile entrance to David and Brian's place. I drove up into the brush where we couldn't be spotted from the road, just in case. Josh had gone to sleep while I drove, I told him to.

When I finally turned the truck off, Lazarus leaned through the crawl space into the cab and began to lick my face. I could tell he still had some of Thunder's blood on him.

I don't know if it was exhaustion, or depression, or the realization that my dog was now a killer, but I began to cry.

Josh woke up, patted me on the shoulder, and said, "That's okay man. It's been a really hard day, and you've been through a lot. By the way Bob, that was one gutsy move back there. I was scared shitless, mostly because I was standing next to Terry at first, and then you.

But to take on seven guys with rifles and shotguns, and pistols, and 8 or 10 others with spears, and bows, etc., with nothing but a bolt action rifle. That's either legendary or fucking nuts, man."

I asked, "There were seven of them with guns?" Josh said, "There were probably more. You see I was focusing on the ones in the immediate area. There could've been 15 or more. They've got a lot of guns man."

Josh asked, "Would you really have killed Terry?" I looked at him wiping the tears from my eyes and said, "There was no question of ever having to kill Terry."

Josh looked puzzled and asked, "What the hell are you talking about. Everybody was threatening to kill everybody."

I replied, "You just made my point Josh. Terry and his band of thugs walked up to me with their guns aimed at the ground. If you remember my gun was pointed at Terry's heart when he was over 80 feet away.

You see Josh, what I learned about armed combat at the ripe old age of 20 was something that I really learned much earlier at the age of six. You see my grandfather owned a general store in Texas he had lost a leg to Polio as a child.

One day a very mean looking character walked into the store and started demanding this thing, and that thing, so my grandfather piled all of the man's requested items on the counter by the register and said, "That will be six dollars and six bits."

The large thug then proceeded to threaten my grandfather in great detail, telling him how he was going to rip off his good leg and shove it down his throat, etc., unless my grandfather gave him all of the goods for free.

However while he was threatening my grandfather, my grandfather was retrieving a large Louisville slugger bat with lead weights in the end of it, from under his counter.

With one swing of his right hand he caught the scarred tattooed thug in the side of the head, knocking him 15 or so feet through the swinging doors and into the dirt street.

My grandfather grabbed his crutch, casually limped out with the bat under one arm, took a ladle of water from the water bucket in front of the store, and threw it in the man's face, and nudged him with the bat.

As the man came to, my grandfather said something that I still remember to this day. He said, "Son, now I know how you got so God damned ugly. If you're gonna hurt a man, don't tell him about it, do it!"

"You see, Josh, if Terry had had any intention of really killing me, he would've started shooting long before he ever started talking.

His body language said everything, his gun was held by his side, hell, all of their guns were held by their sides, while my gun was aimed directly at the leaders' chest, the alpha male if you will.

All of the real talking was done with body language before anyone said a word.

All I did with my deliberate rhetoric was to emphasize the point, so that they would go away, which is what they did. So nobody got hurt.

Any fight, from a fistfight to a gunfight, is a lot like a dogfight.

All dogs growl, however all dogs don't bite. And dogs that don't bite always recognize the ones who do. And nine times out of 10 they back down. It's one of the inherent laws of nature."

Josh looked at me with kind of a dazed look, and said, "Wooow. Man, you are a fucking trip. I am just glad that you're on my side. Let's get some more sleep."

Lazarus woke me up about 9 AM. So I let him out, and we both took a leak. Josh came out and did likewise, saying, "Let's go see if David and Brian's clan had a better day than we did."

We drove the 9-mile path down to what I started referring to as "The House of Che."

When we arrived it was obvious that something was up, because the normal 100 or so dogs that greeted us weren't there. As we pulled up to the compound there was some sporadic barking, but no cluster of dogs.

As David ran up to the truck we began to survey all of the damage to the commune. There were broken corrals, dead animals, livestock, and dogs alike, and a huge mound of flesh, with a lot of dogs just lying around it, some appearing to be asleep, others just appearing to be lethargic.

I asked David, "What the fuck happened?" David shouted, "Big ass Grizzer. He came in about 1:00 am. Killed four of our dogs, injured eight, put a real hurt on Reckless, the Irish Wolfhound, but he's gonna make it. That crazy son of a bitch jumped on to that grizzly and was hanging on to his throat, the bear was swinging him to and fro so much that it was hard to get a good clean shot with my 45/70. I finally got the big bastard with a head shot, when he paused to grab Reckless."

I said, "Maybe you should change his name to Fearless?" David choked up. "The worst part is, he killed Nancy. She was our alpha female; you know the big good-natured golden retriever. She was the best damn bird-dog we ever had. She's put turkey on our table every holiday for the last three years. We're really going to miss her. The guys are digging graves for all the dogs and the goat right now. We are gonna have a funeral for them in an hour or so."

"Hey Bob, you guys need to go into Clinton for anything?" Josh and I said in unison "Yes."

I needed gas because I was down to 10 gallons, and Josh of course was craving ice cream.

Every time we went in to the city from the Bush, Josh would take out his spoon walk in to the market and pull a half gallon of ice cream out of the freezer and start eating it on the spot, and usually pay for the empty carton and another full one at the register.

David said, "Cool. Because the good news is that that bear, we measured him at over 9 feet; means that we've got enough meat for the whole commune for most of, if not all winter, and on the way in to town we can stop at our neighbor's farm, and trade 50 or so pounds of that bear meat for sweet corn, potatoes, and probably some pies. Then we will go into town, get your gas, some liquor and whatever else, and come back here and have us the damnedest party, and Grizzer steak barbecue that this valley has ever seen, to send the dogs, and the goat up to heaven in style."

I asked David what was wrong with the dogs. He said, "Hell man, they are full of bear scrap. We've been guttin' and dressin' that bear all mornin', and those dogs have been eaten the leavin's all mornin'."

I noticed that some new people had arrived. Especially a very cute dark haired girl, who with four other women was scraping the fat from the giant bear hide. The upper part of the gigantic bear's head was hollowed out and even though the pads of the paws had been cut away the gigantic claws were still attached to the pelt.

I walked over to the women, and introduced myself to the new girl whose name was Lucy. I started a conversation, and then David came over and interrupted.

He said loudly, "Is that fucker big or what\? I know that he has to be well over 1300 pounds. He is gonna make one conversation piece of a bear skin rug. I left the head on because it's so big that the kids can ride it like a hobby horse during the winter. And look at those claws, 5 to 6 inches easy. If you ladies are almost done scrapin' the fat off that hide? I want to take that hide and start salting and curing it in the sun. Look at that Bob, a full metal jacket round right into his open mouth, and out the back of his neck severing the spinal cord, I turned him off just like a light switch, and the nice thing about full metal jacket ammo, it doesn't damage the hide as much, look at the small exit wound. That's one of the best shots that I ever made."

And then he lowered his head and sadly lamented, "I just wish that I could have made it a lot sooner!"

We drove to the neighboring farm, and then into Clinton, fueled up, stocked up, and after leaving town, headed back to the commune. It was mid-afternoon by the time that we got back.

We could smell the barbecue when we were about 2 miles out. We strung up four cases of beer, and six bottles of champagne that I sprung for in Clinton, and dropped them in the creek to chill. With the spring water being 34-36° even in the summer, it took less than a half hour to chill, and then we were all getting drunk and loaded on weed, and what have you, and filling our bellies.

At one point we all danced with torches out to the gravesites and poured liquor on the graves and sang the praises, and bravery of Nancy, Nickels', Spot, and Stinky, the dogs, and of course Mandy the goat. Then we danced back to the main house and partied into the night.

I of course spent all of my time talking with Lucy. She was really sweet, and quite pretty, with beautiful blue eyes and a great smile. I asked her if she would like to go for a walk in the moonlight, and she said yes.

We wound up in the back of my camper which had a small light that ran off the truck's batteries. We sat in there, just Lucy, me, and Lazarus. As we talked I couldn't help staring into her beautiful blue eyes.

She finally said to me, "What's the matter?" I said, "I'm really sorry. It's your eyes, they're so beautiful, but I didn't mean to stare."

She leaned over and kissed me, but not a hard passionate kiss, a very soft gentle caressing kiss. As she slowly pulled back, I grabbed her, and gave her the kiss that I had been expecting. And we were off to the races.

The sex was great. She was a great lover. And she liked to talk during sex, which was even better. Because she said things that I hadn't heard other women say. Like, "You're so hard, and you're so deep inside me, it's like we're one person, don't ever take it out, just leave it inside of me forever."

Or "You taste so good, so sweet, like honey on watermelon."

They were all lies of course. But it sure made for some great sex. We made love over and over again into the wee hours of the morning, and then finally fell asleep, with me still inside her, as per her request.

The whole experience was wonderful, that is until the rude awakening early the next morning.

That's when the camper door flew open and Josh screamed, "Get the fuck up. Get the fuck up man. We've got to get out of here now."

I woke up in a daze and asked "What are you talking about? What's going on Josh? Why do we have to get out of here now?"

Josh said, "Because her old man could be here any minute." When Josh said that, Lucy jumped up and began to dress rapidly.

I screamed, "What? You've got an old man, Lucy? Why am I just finding that out now? We talked for hours last night."

Lucy started to speak "I, I didn't know." Josh interrupted, yelling, "Who cares! We don't have time for this shit. I know this guy. The rules are different up here, Bob, and an old lady is more than just an old lady up here.

She's your cook, warmth in the winter, she's your lover, and everything good. And you can't just fuck another guy's old lady and get away with it. It's not done, it's a code." "Just what are you saying Josh?" I asked.

Lucy jumped out of the truck, running towards the main house while finishing dressing.

Josh became extremely agitated and screamed, "I'm saying, get your shit on. And let's get the hell out of here right now, or you are going to have to kill this S.O.B. Because he is not gonna come at you talking once he finds out that you fucked his old lady."

I got dressed and started the truck.

Brian and David ran out and David said, "It was real, man. But get the fuck out of here. They're going East in a couple weeks, should be cool around here after that, they are moving to Montréal, and we will make sure that everyone here keeps quiet about this."

We told him that we were headed to Michael's in Vancouver and then up to Alaska so it would probably be more like at least a couple of months.

And with that conversation we were on our way back to Clinton and then into Vancouver and Michael's house, to prepare for the trip to Alaska. As we headed into Clinton a truck passed us, and the two guys in the truck waved at us. So we waved back.

After they passed by, I asked Josh who the two guys in the truck were. Josh smiled and said, "You know that big hairy mean looking bearded bastard driving the truck?" I replied, "Yeah"

Josh said laughingly, "That was Lucy's old man." I turned and stared at Josh with a blank look on my face and said, "Holy shit."

Holy shit was right. And if we had known what lay before us after our stay at Michael's we probably could've come up with something much better than Holy shit.

Chapter 10

Bathed in Chartreuse after being Abby rode, and then north to Alaska for nothing but adventure and pain

We hit Clinton just long enough to get gas and be on our way, on the off chance that Lucy's old man had found out about me and her, and was after us.

When we got back to Vancouver, Josh wanted to stop at Bellboys house. I asked, "Who is Bellboy?"

Josh said, "You'll like him. He's a good guy, and there are always a lot of cool people at his house. It's Stoner central with lots of freaks, musicians, artists, nudists and the like.

"Cool," I replied. I continued, "Does he have bells in the braids of his long hair?" And Josh replied, "Yes!" I continued, "That's the guy that told Klaus where you were, when we first arrived and went to Stanley Park."

We pulled up in front of an old Victorian two-story house that was at the end of a long overgrown gravel driveway. Loud stereo music could be heard wailing from inside the house.

It was country Joe and the Fish singing "For it's one, two, three, what are we fighting for. I don't know I don't give a damn, the next stop is Vietnam. Yes its five, six, seven, open up your pearly gates, now there ain't no time to wonder why– whoopee, we're all gonna die."

A very pretty topless blonde girl with pigtails and ragged blue jean shorts was watering plants on the front porch. I looked at the girl, and then looked at Josh, and grabbing Josh I pulled him toward me, while mussing his hair and said, "Josh. You are the man. You always know where the cool people are. I'm just happy that I'm along for the ride. Well let's go in and see what trouble we can get into here."

Josh knew the blonde. Her name was Abby, he introduced me to her and we went inside.

About eight people were in the living room smoking weed and watching television with no sound while listening to Country

Joe.

I couldn't figure out what they were watching, it looked like a cross between rodeo and car racing with people chasing animals in cars.

Josh loudly announced our presence and introduced me.

They were all stoners, five girls and three guys, I remember thinking I sure like these odds. They were all in various states of undress. The guys had long hair and beards, and the ladies were all nice looking. Two of the gals and one of the guys were completely naked.

They all had stoner names like Sunflower, Meadow, Moonbeam, and Janice? I thought to myself, "Where the hell did that come from." The guys had names like Jimbo, Cloudy and Slider.

I leaned down and yelled over the music asking Jimbo what they were watching on TV? He took a hit and handed me the bong, and holding in the hit, he said, "I don't know man. The mescaline and acid kicked in a while ago." Then he exhaled.

Hearing that, I realized that this was going to get boring really fast.

So I walked back outside looking for Abby, but she wasn't there.

So I walked around the side of the house and there she was sunning herself on an old mattress with a blanket on it in the backyard.

I walked over to her and asked if I could join her? She said I could. So seeing that she was completely naked now, I took off all of my clothes as well.

As I started to lie down beside her I asked her if she wanted to smoke a joint.

And she said, "No thanks, I'm already stoned. You don't have anything cold to drink do you?"

I said, "I've got some iced tea and a six pack of Molson's ale in the cooler in my truck.

She rose up with an enthusiastic smile on her face and shading her eyes with her left hand she said, "Awesome, my hero. Can you bring the whole cooler?"

"Sure," I said.

I started to put my pants back on to go out to the truck. But she said, "What are you doing? You don't need clothes around here."

So I dropped my pants and got the cooler, and let Laz out. We lay in the sun and talked, while drinking our beers, and throwing a stick for Laz.

I couldn't help looking at her beautiful body glistening in the sun; she had beautiful breasts and was a real blonde and natural, a real mountain mama

It was at that moment I looked back to realize in horror that I had a giant boner aiming straight at the sky like a meat flagpole. As she talked with her eyes closed I slowly turned on my side away from her, however I had to keep my head in the same place so my neck was in an awkward and somewhat painful position.

I had to keep up with the conversation and at the same time try to think of things that would make the boner go away. Car racing, sports scores, I even desperately tried to pretend that all of my relatives were watching. But every time that I would get my penis just about back to normal she would ask me something like, "What's your favorite sexual position", and—boing, there was my penis again, standing at attention, hard as a rock.

I thought that my neck was going to break when she turned towards me and shading her eyes again she said, "Why are you in that weird position? It's not because you have a boner is it? Hell, I don't care about that. The guys around here walk around with boners half of the time.

Let me get you off so you can be comfortable. Do you want to fuck? Or would you like a blowjob, or maybe a hand-job, whatever you want. You're cute, and nice, and I like your curly hair. So whatever you want."

I said, "Truthfully, what I'd like to do is kiss you all over, then slowly work up from your ankles to your vagina and give you head while you give me head sixty-nining until we come simultaneously.

At first she didn't say anything, then she pulled me onto my back and straddling me she said, "You are hard?" She leaned down and whispered in my ear, "I want to do that 69 thing; it's been a while since I've done that, but let's fuck first. You don't mind if I scream a little do you? I love it when the neighbors watch; it really gets me off.

Then we can lie in the sun and sleep a little while before we go up to my bedroom and do the 69 thing."

So she started bouncing up and down on me in the middle of the back yard screaming to high heaven while turning in all directions to see if anyone was watching.

I noticed her looking off to the left and smiling, so I glanced over in that direction and noticed about 50 feet away an old man appearing to be jerking off while watching us from the storm porch of a neighboring house. This seemed to really excite her.

I thought to myself, "Did I bite off more than I can chew"? But she was so beautiful and it felt so good I just went back to watching her as she rode me like a bucking bronco.

Then there was a loud commotion over on the storm porch, and she started to laugh.

I looked over to see an old woman hitting the old man who was jerking off with a broom, and screaming at him.

As the old woman chased the old man into the house Abby came, which made me come, she fell off of me onto the mattress, and then we both looked up at the house when we heard loud applause.

Josh and all of the stoners were either in the yard, or were hanging out of the windows upstairs and down applauding loudly and cheering. Abby and I waved and hugged each other.

As the applause died down, I heard the old woman next door screaming, "You're all sick, sick I say. Perverted drug addicts, and you better leave my husband alone. I will call the police on all of you. You perverted drug addicts!

The stoner crowd answered her with jeers while exposing themselves to her, both men and women.

We all went inside and I pulled Josh aside and said, "This girl is great, but don't you think we ought to get out of here before the RCMP come and bust the place.

Josh replied, "Yeah. That's probably a good idea. It won't be the RCMP, It'll be the Vancouver P.D., but let's get out of here. We need to get to Michael's anyway."

Abbey was upset that we didn't get to do the 69 thing, but I promised that we would stop by on the way back from Alaska.

So Josh and Lazarus and I climbed into the truck and headed across town to Michael's.

Things seemed a little stranger than normal at Michael's; at first I thought it was because I was so ripped when we arrived.

However I soon realized that there was a kind of power struggle going on within the ranks of the Flying Circus.

Chartreuse who was Michael's regular girl, which meant essentially that she was Michael's girlfriend whenever he wasn't fucking some other girl who just walked in the door, had been replaced.

And she wasn't any too happy about it.

Chartreuse, whose real name was Darla, had acquired her nick name by arriving at Michael's in a Chartreuse colored dress. She didn't like her nickname either, nobody really did, but it was Michael's thing, so everybody put up with it. In fact I think Josh picked some nick names for people just to piss them off.

Michael had a new regular girl, her nickname was Rose, or Rose Petal, and what a beauty.

She had a surreal beauty about her, she was so perfect. The only comparison that I can make is a year later in 1974 when I was working on Roger Smith's house with him, and couple of my Texas buddies, and his ex-wife Jaclyn Smith walked up to me with two black standard poodles on leashes, this was before "Charlie's Angels." She was so beautiful that she literally took my breath away,

I couldn't speak, and I just stood there with my mouth open, staring at her, and stammering, until I caught myself and apologized, saying, "I'm so sorry. It's just that you are the most beautiful woman that I have ever seen in my life."

And luckily she took it well, saying that I was so sweet. As I remember, I even got a kiss on the cheek.

That's the kind of beauty Rose had. Everyone wanted to be with Rose; man, woman and child; if there had ever been any children at Michael's, which there never were.

And it didn't hurt that she was very sweet and smart as well. So of course Michael had to have her. And what Michael wanted, Michael got.

The good news for me was that Chartreuse was now available and gorgeous herself. So I immediately began consoling her. After all we were friends and she was very good looking, and she was previously unattainable, and I never got to do the 69 thing with Abby. So why not go for it. I remember saying to her that I never would have traded her in for Rose no matter how pretty Rose was.

Because the thing about Chartreuse was that if she loved a guy, she would do anything for him. And that trumps "Super Pretty" all day long in my book.

Chartreuse thanked me for the words of encouragement. Then I continued, "Oh, I would've fucked her, don't get me wrong. However of course, I would've stayed with you."

She slapped me on the shoulder and then started to laugh. And I could tell that she really needed a laugh. She had been through a lot.

So we polished off a bottle of red wine underneath the peach tree on the back of Michael's property and made out for a while, and then I showed her the 69 thing. She really enjoyed it and we did it numerous times over the next couple of weeks while Josh and I prepared for Alaska.

Over those next couple of weeks there were three big parties at Michael's and almost 24-hours of sex, drugs, and rock 'n roll a day. That was the thing about staying with Michael. We would go there to rest up for some trip to somewhere, and then when we finally left on our trip we would be just as tired as when we arrived and usually a lot more stoned; it was weird that way. About the only time that I could get any real rest was when I went to the beach which was close by, and slept to the sound of the ocean.

But I have to say that Michael was a hell of a host, a friend indeed, and a really good guy for someone with that much money. Chartreuse wanted to come along with us to Alaska, but Josh and I, mostly Josh, convinced her that it was too dangerous and there would be no amenities. So she finally gave in and told us to be careful and stay safe and that she would see us when we got back.

We were on our way to Homer, Alaska. Finally! It was very pretty country up to Dawson Creek where the Alcan started, however it didn't take long before we had trouble.

We only got a about 30 miles up the Alcan Highway, and the overdrive started to act up again, like it had in California just before San Luis Obispo.

We pulled over in the first town, at the first filling station that had a mechanic sign, and when the mechanic got back from lunch he took a look.

The good news was it was a short in the wiring; the bad news was he couldn't fix it until the next day. He said that he could weld some chain-link and 1/2" fencing over the windshield, headlights, and radiator, and give us a deal on the whole thing.

I asked, "Why I would want to do that?" Josh chimed in, "You really should do that, Bob. The semi-trucks on the Alcan kick up some serious rocks, and gravel from time to time."

I said, "I don't want my truck looking like a tank." They told us about a local campsite, but the people there were all drunk and loud, so we left and camped in the woods.

The next morning the mechanic fixed the overdrive and we were on our way again.

I should've listened to the mechanic, and Josh because we weren't on the Alcan 10 miles when a screaming semi-truck came at us heading south and peppered the whole cab and camper shell with a lot of gravel and few rocks up to 3 inches in diameter, breaking both windshields, both headlights, puncturing the radiator and putting a 3 inch hole in the camper shell.

Even though Josh and I both tried to cover our faces with our arms, we were cut up pretty bad.

We had pulled over when an RCMP came by and called for an ambulance, but they were too far away, and covering a bad accident. So he cleaned us up the best he could, and we drove another 40 miles to a small town off the Alcan that had a small clinic, and they stitched us up, and bandaged us, etc.

The RCMP had told us about another mechanic welder 95 miles up the road that also did auto glass repair. Every time we saw a big truck coming towards us for those 95 miles, I would pull off the road so we wouldn't get peppered again.

The mechanic was a really nice guy, but it took two days to get the glass, headlights, etc. dropped off, ironically by a semi-truck similar to the one that had done all the damage in the first place. However the mechanic did a great job of welding crossbars and chain-link, and 1/2" fencing over everything including the radiator which he also repaired, and then replaced the glass from inside the cab. I used my tools, and repaired the camper shell myself.

I forgot to mention that Lazarus was unhurt. The mechanic was so cool that he let us stay on his property for the three days of repair necessary, even feeding us from time to time, and gave me a great deal on the repairs. We hit the road again and I quickly learned how to drive the Alcan Highway in 1973; which is, when you see a very large oncoming semi-truck, immediately slow down and get as far as you can over to the right side of the road.

It took a lot longer to drive the 2500 miles to Homer, Alaska than we thought, along with two flat tires, getting stuck four times, and after we got off of the Alcan to finish our journey to Homer, Alaska on the smaller roads.

And of course there was the occasional moose, and one polar bear I might add.

But we finally limped into Homer 16 days and 14 hours after leaving Vancouver.

We were battered, bruised, and cut, and so was the truck.

We parked on the outskirts of Homer until morning, and then drove in and stopped at a very small diner.

It was summer and it was cold.

After we ordered breakfast I told the waitress that I was in town to build furniture for the mayor, and showed her the letter that she (The Mayor) had sent me in Marina Del Rey.

Her face saddened, and she looked shocked, she said, "You came all the way up here from LA?"

I asked her, "Is the mayor at home now? Or does she have an office that I should go to?"

She looked even sadder and replied, "Oh honey. Bless your heart. The mayor's gone. She's out of town on trip for at least a couple of weeks."

"I can't wait for that long," I replied.

"I'm so sorry, darlin', all that way up here for nothin'. It's a shame. It's a gosh-darned shame. You fellows have a safe trip back.

The eggs and coffee are on the house."

As she walked away she kept muttering "It's a shame, what a shame." I sat there stunned and speechless.

A good job that was going to pay for a large portion of the trip was gone. Head in hands I stared at the plate of eggs on the table.

Josh said, "You can't be in this right now, man. You've gotta stand outside of this, and look in.

Everything happens for a reason. You weren't supposed to make furniture for this gal. You were supposed to come up here to find yourself."

I looked up from my eggs and asked, "What are you talking about?"

Josh replied, "Aren't you the guy who a week and a half ago said to me and I quote, "You're the man?"

Up until this Alcan Highway debacle, and other than the Black Tree commune incident, haven't you had a great time?" I halfheartedly replied, "Yeah."

"Well," Josh said, "Let's get back on the road. Head East, and then South, and get the fuck out of Alaska.

I know a place on the way back on the coast, where we can pay for this trip with one weeks' work on a tuna boat."

I replied, "I don't know anything about fishing."

Josh said, "You don't have to. You've got that rifle. You can be the Sharker." I asked, "What?" "That's the guy who shoots the sharks when they try and take the tuna off the line--the Sharker." Josh replied,"

What about Lazarus?" I asked.

Josh said, "I've got a really neat lady friend who will be happy to take care of him while we're on the boat. Or if you want you can bring him on the boat with us, you just have to clean up after him. Either way we can make a couple of grand a piece, and I'll give you 500 bucks of my money for gas and such. So that makes $2,500 for you for a week's work. That ought to take some of the sting out of this trip for you, right."

I said, "Let me eat these eggs, and drink this coffee the kind lady gave us and let's get back on the road.

We'll have more than enough time to discuss it on the way back South along the highway to Hell."

So we finished our eggs and coffee, jumped in the truck, and after driving over 2500 miles up to Homer Alaska and spending a few hours there, we began re-navigating the Alcan Highway South, to tuna fish on our way back to Michael's place.

We had NO idea that I would wind up being detained by the RCMP for shooting at sealers after our voyage out that week, almost costing me my week's pay and my freedom. What wild a ride!

Glen at the Beach

Chapter 11

Fishin', fightin', and Eskimo pussy

Heading back from Homer, Alaska to Vancouver by way of Prince Rupert Island, British Columbia, meant that we had to go out of our way about at least 900 miles to the coast, so this meant that just going to Prince Rupert from Homer, Alaska was approximately 2,400 miles.

We stopped in a little one horse town; on our way back to the Alcan, there was literally a single horse tied up in front of the café along with two pickup trucks.

We ate, stocked up on supplies at a general store, and I bought 350 rounds of ammo and an extra five 10 round magazines for my Lee Enfield rifle. 100 rounds of hollow point and 250 rounds of Indian Army full metal jacket ammo. The trip was fairly uneventful and only took five days and it was beautiful country.

We rolled into Prince Rupert in the late morning and Josh directed me down to the wharf area.

I pulled over and Josh jumped out and ran over to some local fisherman asking, "Is the "My Mary Jane" docked here, or are they out to sea fishing?"

One of the old fishermen replied, "Neither. The RCMP were hassling them about all of the weed smoking, so they moved to the old cannery wharf outside of town."

Josh thanked them and ran back to the truck saying, "I know where they are, let's go.

I drove through town on to a winding dirt road until we came to an old ramshackle building with some smaller outbuildings, and an old beat up wooden wharf with one boat docked on it.

Josh told me to stop the truck and we got out. The boat was about 30 yards away, and at first I thought it was on fire, as there was so much smoke coming off the deck.

But as Josh and I and Lazarus got closer we could see that the smoke was generated by a combination of a BBQ grill on the deck, and the fact that all five long-haired guys on deck were smoking weed.

As we closed in on the boat I could see the name spelled out prominently on the rear transom, it read "My Mary Jane."

"How appropriate," I thought. Josh shouted out, "Ted!" And

the older hippie guy yelled back, "Josh, how you doing, guy?" Josh introduced me to this odd group of hippie bedfellows.

There was Ted the Captain.

Who I learned from Josh was AWOL from Vietnam.

After his search and destroy platoon had almost been entirely wiped out, the army had put him in charge of a supply depot and he immediately started selling everything that wasn't nailed down on the side, on the black market. He apparently amassed just under $100 grand in a short period of time, and as the MP's were hot on his trail, he took the money and ran, after buying falsified orders for himself to go on leave in Thailand.

He disappeared in Bangkok, hooked up with one of his black market contacts, purchased fake documents, a passport, merchant marine papers, etc.

Then he bought two gallons of honey hash oil and smuggled the hash oil into Canada while working on a merchant marine vessel for his passage.

He had smuggled the hash oil by pouring the hash oil into the bottom half of two cases of jars of honey and re-filling the upper third of the jars with the honey, a thin layer of yellow wax separated the two so that if custom officials would open the jars and taste them, they would taste honey.

He was quite clever. The hash oil cost $8,000 in Thailand, and he sold it all in eight months in British Columbia, and made enough money to buy the fishing boat and stock it, and he still had enough left over to buy a section of land 640 acres on a small lake with two cabins.

He had also had purchased a brand-new irrefutable British Columbian identification too; as he put it, keep the Army off his back.

He and three of the other guys were ex-U.S. Army, or draft dodgers. Those three were Bear, Jimmy and Sailor. The fifth member of the bunch was a small older Eskimo fellow, named Charlie.

I shook hands with all of the guys and they all went back to what they were doing, which was repairing fishing tackle, barbecuing, cleaning, painting, loading supplies and firewood.

I turned and looking back to shore, and I saw an incredibly beautiful young girl.

I said, "Wow! Look at her. What a beauty."

That is when Charlie the Eskimo ran at me with a hand ax screaming, "That's my daughter. You don't talk about my daughter. Or I'll kill you."

Sailor grabbed him just before he got to me. I held up my arms and yelled, "I'm really sorry, Charlie, I didn't mean any disrespect."

Charlie stopped struggling and seemed to calm down a little. He looked at me with a mean stare and said, "Okay. But you don't talk about my daughter, or touch my daughter, or I'll kill you, get it."

I replied, "Yes sir. It won't happen again."

I put out my hand, and he gripped it so hard that I thought he was going to break it. And looking me deliberately in the eyes with that steely eyed look he said, "Okay, boy. As long as we are clear."

I replied in pain, "Yes sir."

The other guys on the boat began to laugh. And Ted said, "You dodged a bullet there, son, six months ago he almost killed Bear for talking about Flower." "Who is Flower?" I asked. He said, "That's Charlie's daughter."

Charlie was not an average Eskimo. He was not an Inuit. He was from the Yupik tribe.

The Yupik's were from Siberia originally, and one of the oldest Eskimo tribes, a taller, thinner people with thinner facial features generally. That's part of where Flower got her beauty.

The other half of her beauty, or maybe two thirds came from her mother who was full-blooded Cheyenne, a very handsome people in their own right.

Supposedly her mother was very beautiful. She had died eight years earlier in a car accident. Charlie and Flower had moved into one of the other outbuildings that surrounded the old cannery. Ted and the boys had fixed up to the buildings for themselves.

Ted told us that the RCMP came out to visit from time to time, but had stopped harassing them like they had done at the city wharfs, because there was no one to complain about their drinking, pot smoking and carousing out by the old abandoned cannery.

I had to make a decision about what to do with Lazarus and it was a tough one.

Josh and I decided that we should drive across town and meet his lady friend Pamela who could take Lazarus for the seven days we'd be out to sea.

So we told the guys that we would be back later and headed across town. Pamela was an older gal probably in her late 40s but very pretty, and who was a kind of independent animal rescue for local pets. She had 10 or 12 dogs, and 14 cats, and various other animals. Goats, horses, sheep, even a llama.

She had a little five-acre place on the outskirts of Prince Rupert.

I'll never forget our first meeting. We pulled up in the truck with dogs barking, and multiple animal sounds.

And out from this old Victorian house walks this tall, blonde, pretty gal with a big floppy hat, and a loose fitting paisley dress, obviously without a bra, wearing a large handgun in a holster with a gun belt filled with bullets. I recall thinking, what's wrong with this picture. The picture was so perfect at first, blonde, pretty, big breasts, no bra, paisley dress, barefoot; and then I saw the handgun and a giant siren went off in my head--ee ee ee eeh.

However she was very nice, and Lazarus seemed to fit in with the animals, and he took to her as well.

We stayed till almost dark, working things out for her to keep Lazarus. We told her that we would be back in a few days to leave Lazarus with her for a week, and then we headed back to the cannery.

The next few days were busy, as we stocked the "My Mary Jane" for the fishing trip which would take place mostly off the coast of Northern BC.

Before we set sail we had to take Lazarus back to Pamela's house. This was one of the toughest things that I had to do on the whole trip.

Lazarus just didn't want to stay. I tried over and over again, and each time he would follow me, one time almost a quarter of a mile down to the road.

I finally took him back and sat him down inside her place and talked with him for over an hour. As I said before Lazarus was the smartest dog I've ever owned. So using the same technique that I used in our game that we played that I called 20 (where if I bounced the ball against a wall, and if he couldn't catch it before we got to 20, I would win.)

I slowly and painstakingly explained that I would only be gone for seven days.

You must remember that for dogs if you're gone for an hour or a lifetime, to them it's essentially the same thing. But this dog was so intelligent that after an hour of petting, consoling, and explaining, he got it.

I finally got up, and said goodbye, patted him on the head and walked out the door, and he stayed behind.

When I came back a week later, he greeted me all the way down at the road, I stopped the truck as he ran up to it, and jumping out of the truck, Lazarus ran up and jumped into my arms.

We drove up to Pamela's and she told me that the day that I left Lazarus was sitting on the floor in her living room, and when he heard my truck start he jumped up looked at the door, looked at her, and then just calmly laid back down. What a dog!

Well, back to the fishing trip. Josh and I had purchased the proper fishing apparel, including boots, waterproof coveralls, heavy leather gloves, etc., the engines were serviced, storage lockers were filled with ice, the boat was full of diesel, and we were on our way.

Everything was fine until we hit some rough weather; neither Josh, nor I had any sea legs. But I couldn't figure it out; I puked my guts out, while he stared at me.

At one point I said to him, between throwing up, "How is it that you're not sick?" He just gave me a blank expression and said, "I don't know, man. It just doesn't seem to bother me like it does you."

The next day the seas calmed down and I felt better.

Ted slowed the boat down, and taking a mug he scooped some sea water and tasted it spitting it back into the ocean he said, "This looks good, you see the ice flow over there, and all the gulls and pelicans over there. This is it boys, let's start hard lining. Bob, get your rifle ready!"

"Let me get her up to 5 knots and then put your lines in the water!"

The guys began to bait their lines and put them into the water. Charlie and sailor on the starboard side, Josh and Jimmy on the Port side of the boat, and Bear in the aft seat at the rear of the boat.

All of the guys were in chairs with seatbelts which were bolted to the deck; this was for safety to ensure nobody went overboard. Also the seats had tackle locks, to lock your rod and reel into, like big sport fishing boats have.

I would walk around the deck looking for sharks and would help stowing the catch with Ted during the more frenzied moments of the catch. I learned quickly that it's easy to get cut even with gloves on when you're stowing tuna.

They were biting well and so far I only had to shoot one shark.

However, Bear the big guy kept complaining about a hammerhead that was taking pieces of his catch as he reeled them in.

But I argued that the hammerhead was only taking pieces of the tail, and that if he took a whole tuna then I'd shoot him.

Bear screamed, "You'll do what I tell you too, or i'll kick your ass."

I replied, "Fuck you! I know my job."

Bear slammed his tackle into the tackle lock, and locked it down. Then unbuckling himself and jumping up, he ran toward me screaming, "I'll kill you, you fucking punk!"

He was a big man but he came at me so fast that I couldn't point my rifle at him. However what I could do was to bring the butt of the rifle in an upward motion across his jaw, knocking him out cold.

Ted ran up yelling, "Oh great you just knocked out my best angler." He leaned down and took Bear's pulse "Well, he's going to live!" He said.

He looked at me and said, "Grab Bear's tackle and start fishing." I screamed, "I don't know how to fish." He looked at me angrily and said, "I am going to take Bear below decks and handcuff him to a bunk, and you better have learned how to fish by the time I get back up here, or I'll throw you overboard myself."

He started dragging the monstrous Bear down below decks while I picked up my rifle, strapped myself into Bears chair with my rifle by my side, I began to try fishing.

I watched what the other guys were doing and tried to mimic them while Josh shouted tips to me from his chair, almost instantly there was a great tug on my line and I began reeling in the catch furiously.

It was a tuna, and a big one. As I yanked it onto the deck it flew past my cheek grazing my cheek and leaving a small gash.

But I didn't care; I let out a cheer as the blood ran down my cheek. I had done it.

Ted came up from below decks just as I launched the giant tuna onto the deck.

He yelled, "Way to go kid! You're a quick study. I like that. I'll get the first aid kit for your face as soon as I've checked the helm, and our bearings, and then I will shark and stow, I assume that I can borrow your rifle."

He looked down and noticed the rifle next to me and said, "You must have taken me seriously about that throwing you overboard stuff. Good, I like that too."

Then he grabbed my rifle, and ran to the bridge. The five of us made over half of our catch that day.

That night about 9:00 p.m. when they quit biting, we went below decks to have some chow and hit the sack for the next day.

Bear was not a happy camper the whole left side of his jaw was black and blue and swollen, had it not been for the handcuffs he probably would've torn my head off.

But Ted talked to him, and I apologized profusely, and he finally started to calm down, even though he gave me the stink eye from then on until we finally got back to Prince Rupert Island.

That was okay, I never liked him either.

The next day we had the ice lockers full by 3:00 pm and were on our way back. Ted decided to hug the coast line on the way back because we were so heavy with the catch, and he hoped to avoid bad weather.

To this day I still do not know where exactly we were, somewhere in Northern BC waters, moving south.

But as we passed an ice flow with a lot of seals on it, we could hear the seals screaming. I looked over through my scope to see guys with clubs and knives, clubbing and skinning the seals alive.

Something in me snapped. The whole scene was so grotesque that I couldn't stand it.

I aimed my rifle and began firing at the maniacs slaughtering the seals, not trying to kill them, mind you, but definitely firing close enough to run them off the ice.

Everybody but Josh and sailor were below decks, but they came running up fast when they heard all of the shooting.

As I put another 10-round magazine into the rifle they all started shouting at me, "You can't shoot at them! What they're doing is legal."

I turned and replied, "That doesn't make it right. And then I began firing again as fast as I could reload.

They all stood and watched me until I finished the fourth 10-round magazine.

Then Bear ran over and put me in a bear hug, while Ted and Jimmy wrestled the rifle away from me.

"Let go of me! Let go of me, you big piece of shit!"

Bear finally let go of me.

We all looked at the icepack and the sealers were fleeing in one direction and the seals were fleeing in the other.

I let out a cheer, "Run, you mother fuckers. Run!"

Ted looked over at me ashen faced and said, "Well, you've done it now sonny. We are probably all going to jail for this one!"

Bear asked, "Can I throw him overboard, Boss?"

Ted looked at Bear and said angrily, "Bear, you stupid shit. Great idea! Let's add murder to attempted murder! What a dumb fuck!" He said as he shook his head walking away.

We made it back to Prince Rupert and off loaded the catch at the new cannery, and I remember Ted commenting that if we all didn't wind up in jail, there would be a healthy bonus for us all, because the catch netted him an extra 8 grand. Because it was a great haul and the price of tuna had gone up.

By the time we got back to the old cannery there were three RCMP vehicles waiting for us at the docks.

Ted spotted them first with the binoculars, yelling out, "Here we go boys... Bob unload your rifle and separate all the ammo, and magazines from it. As soon as we get close to the docks everybody put your hands in the air, we don't need anybody shot on this boat."

I thought, "Well, Ted is right, I've done it now!" A great catch, extra money, and I fucked the whole thing up. Great!" As we pulled up to the docks there were six RCMP officers with pistols and rifles drawn.

They let us tie off the boat and then ordered us off, placing everyone in handcuffs.

I said loudly, "It wasn't them, it was me. I did all of the shooting. They told me to stop and then physically stopped me from shooting anymore. You don't want them. You want me."

Two of the RCMP officers hustled me off, and put me into the back of one of the vehicles. I couldn't hear what they were saying, but I saw two of the officers talking to Ted, and he seemed to be motioning with his hands explaining to them what had happened, while the other RCMP questioned the rest of the guys.

I asked one officer when they all came back to the vehicles with my rifle, and ammunition, etc. if I could leave the keys to my pickup with Josh, and he said that I could.

As the three vehicle caravan headed toward the local RCMP barracks one of the officers asked me, "What were you thinking, son?"

I replied, "Obviously, I wasn't thinking, sir. It's just that I have never seen anything so horrible in my life. The only thing that I can compare it to is like seeing a bunch of guys swinging baseball bats, running through a hospital nursery, Sir. Could you stand by and watch something like that, Sir? Well, I couldn't, and to be honest with you I would probably do the same thing again."

The RCMP officer replied, "Well son, I must admit that it isn't a very pretty sight, but it's the only way that those folks have of making a living. And it's legal, and they have the right to do it, and shooting at them is illegal, and you don't have the right to do that. So according to your driver's license you're an American, right?"

"Yes sir" I replied. "Well, that explains a lot," he replied.

We arrived at the RCMP barracks and they put me into a cell.

A few hours later they brought Josh back to see me.

It was really good to see him. He told me that he got our money from Ted who thought we might need it for my bail.

I was thinking about how cool that was of Ted. Josh told me

that he would be outside in the truck waiting.

A little while later they came and got me and took me into an office and sat me down in front of the desk of the head honcho. It was cold and I was still sweating bullets. He looked across at me very sternly and said, "Son, we should lock you up and throw away the key, However it turns out that nobody was injured in the incident, and even though what you did technically was attempted murder, we don't need any international incidents.

So this is the way this is going to play out. The magistrate is dropping all charges. You are to leave Prince Rupert in the next 24 hours and not come back, ever.

If you are involved in any illegal activities in Canada in the next two years you will go immediately too jail, for most likely a very long time.

We will let you keep your rifle for now but we are confiscating all of your ammunition. Now get out of here while the getting is good."

"Thank you sir," I said, but I must point out that there were numerous injuries sustained in the incident, they were sustained by the seals and their pups; Sir."

He looked up from his paperwork and said sternly, "Don't press your luck son; and get out of here before I change my mind."

I said, "Yes sir, Thank you sir." And turned and rapidly walked out of the building.

I talked it over with Josh and seeing that we only had 24 hours we drove to Pamela's and I picked up Lazarus and we went back to spend the night at the old cannery.

When we got there it was just getting dark, we had picked up a bunch of hot food in town, so Josh took most of it over to the cabins for our fishing buddies, and being worn out from the ordeal I ate my food in the camper and fed Lazarus.

I was just getting ready to go to bed, when there was a faint knock on the camper shell door, Lazarus didn't even bark, and hadn't warned me of anything, so I thought it was Josh.

I opened up the camper shell door and there stood Flower.

She looked beautiful, I hadn't seen her this close before, her face framed by the fur-lined collar of her coat.

She asked if she could come in.

I said, "I don't know? I don't need your father taking an axe to me." She replied, "Don't worry, he's gone to town. We have at least a half an hour,"

She came over to me and laid a long kiss upon my lips. I felt myself begin to get erect.

Thoughts ran around in my brain crashing into one another "If you keep this up you're going to die tonight. You've got a rifle, and no ammo. If you're going to do this, you better do it in a hurry. In less than 10 seconds my mind was made up. Young, stupid, and horny, won out over smart, careful, and safe. We started taking our clothes off, and passionately kissing. I went down on her, she went down on me, we 69'd, and then she climbed on top of me. I wound up coming inside of her as we both let out a passionate scream.

She rolled off of me and laid beside me our hearts pounding as we breathed heavily.

We lay there for about five minutes until Lazarus perked his head up and then his ears and started to growl.

I know that that is the fastest that I have ever gotten dressed in my life, and she beat me.

As we both just finished dressing I threw open the camper shell door, locking it up and in place, and pulling my empty rifle onto my lap as she jumped up onto the seat on the other side of the camper, then we heard running and Charlie ran up to the camper shell door opening, hand-axe in hand.

Leaning into the camper, he screamed, "What the hell is going on here! I'll kill you, you son of a bitch."

I aimed the empty rifle at him and said, "Don't make me kill you, Charlie. Nothing is going on here. We're just talking."

Flower said, "Yeah, Dad. We're just talking. Calm down. Bob is a nice guy. I came to talk to him. God! You can be so embarrassing sometimes."

Charlie seemed to calm down some, and actually looked a little embarrassed, as Lazarus started to stop barking and growling. I guess that the combination of a snarling dog, a rifle, and a very embarrassed daughter was too much, even for old Charlie.

The next morning we were on our way back to Vancouver and Michael's, $3500, and $3,000 richer respectively, but I must admit that I let Josh drive in the morning while I slept, because I didn't sleep too well that night with Charlie in the immediate vicinity.

Chapter 12

Back to Michael's, then up to the commune, and then off to Williams Lake stampede, to party and fight wildfires. Then back to Michael's and then to Calgary stampede to find Josh.

We left Prince Rupert and headed back to Vancouver and Michael's place. Both Josh and I needed a good rest. I was worried about where to get more ammo for my rifle until I remembered that I had hidden two magazines and 100 rounds of ammo in the truck.

On the way back to Vancouver I asked Josh why he thought Flower had picked me, of all people to make love too. Josh said, "I could tell she liked you from the beginning, and I think you shooting at the sealers put you over the top.

You see she had a pet seal that some drunk killed, and even though Charlie beat him half to death she never really recovered from the experience. Besides, why overthink it. You had a beautiful young girl give herself to you, and you got away with it without her father killing you."

When we finally rolled into Michael's and a strange voice answered at the gates. I said, "It's Bob and Josh."

The voice replied, "Who?"

I replied, "Bob and Josh." The voice replied, "I never heard of you."

Now I was tired and pissed. I screamed, "Get Michael. You stupid fuck."

The voice replied, "Michael's gone. He and a bunch of the others flew down to the Bahamas last week; they will be back in three days."

Josh yelled, "Is anyone from the Flying Circus at the house?"

The voice came back, "What's the Flying Circus?" Josh said, "Well. We're fucked now."

I said, "Let's try it another way. Can you tell us who else is here?"

The voice started rattling off names. When he got to Chartreuse, I said, "Go get Chartreuse, she knows us."

We got in to Michael's and just stayed overnight. I spent the night with Chartreuse and we slept in the next day, heading up to the House of Che in the early afternoon.

It was dark when we reached the commune, but we were received like family, as always. That night we decided to Part Company. Josh wanted to head east and see if he could find Holy Alex, who he wanted me to meet. Brian and David wanted to head Northwest up to Williams Lake for the Stampede. They planned on entering the rodeo where they had done well the year before making $1500 and $1200 each respectively.

And if I drove them up there, they claimed we could go to work for B.C. forestry fighting fires. And they told me that they would kick in some money for gas.

It sounded good to me, so the next day, after removing all of the chain link and 1/2 inch fencing from the windshields, etc., on the truck, Brian, David, I, and Lazarus were on our way to Williams Lake, which is situated roughly between Prince George and Kamloops. It is a couple of hours and about a hundred miles north of Clinton, on highway 97; The Caribou Highway.

On the way we saw a little guy hitchhiking on the side of the road, Brian and David started yelling frantically for me to pull over for the guy. So I did.

They jumped out of the truck yelling, "Willie Joe, Willie Joe, you crazy son of a bitch. How are you man? Get in. You can ride up front with Bob. We'll get in the camper with the dog." Brian and David sat up front in the camper and talked to the little Indian fellow through the opening between the camper shell and the truck cab.

I must admit that even though this little guy was only about 5'2" tall and seemed very amiable, he had a crazy look in his eyes and a very unusual haircut, kind of a cross between a crew cut an a Mohawk..

However he had a real gift for gab. Claiming to be the only living descendent of the Mohican tribe, who were supposedly wiped out by the early 1800s, he talked with an accent that was almost Irish.

While driving toward Williams Lake I noticed as we talked, smoked weed, and drank that there was a noticeable bulge under his shirt at his waistband.

I asked, "What's that under your shirt?"

He calmly lifted his shirt exposing a .38 caliber snub nosed pistol and said, "Oh. That's my snubby, it's my best friend, and has saved me many a time."

As freaked out as I was, I calmly replied, "Cool, man."

When we rolled into Williams Lake I couldn't believe the scene. The guys hadn't told me that Williams Lake was a town of around 8000-10,000 people; but it grew to around 60-100,000 people for the Stampede. Around 45% Indians and the rest white, but all are drunk, stoned, and generally fucked up.

The place was a madhouse. Drunken Indians dressed like cowboys staggered around the streets. Of course there were some real Indians, and real cowboys in town for the rodeo, like Brian and David, but most were drunken Indians, drugstore cowboys.

And interspersed in this throng of insanity were people openly selling any drug that you wanted, including Dilaudid which I had never heard of before (an opium derivative), and methadone, a drug normally used to kick heroin.

After driving around for a while we finally found a place to park the truck by the rodeo grounds. Between them and what they referred to as the Indian nations (which is where the Indians camped with their campers and teepees).

I made friends with the people camping next to us and asked them to keep an eye on my truck, dog. And I left Lazarus inside locking the camper and leaving Lazarus up front with the windows cracked and doors unlocked.

The four of us headed to town and went into the first bar that we saw. Willie Joe said that he would be back in a few minutes, that he needed to go see a friend. So Brian, David, and I walked into the bar.

Now remember Brian and David are looking like real rodeo cowboys, dirty, chaps, cowboy boots with spurs, beat-up cowboy hats, and gloves. And as I mentioned before, David and Brian were real cowboys that's how they made their money at the commune breaking wild horses and selling them during the year.

I had a beard and long hair like they did. except I had on a gray jumpsuit, work boots, mirrored sunglasses, and the cowboy hat that I had painted the mountain scene on with full pinecones, and pine branches etc. when I was on acid.

So here we were walking into a bar filled with clean cut drugstore cowboys, looking like two rodeo cowboys and a stoner. We walked up to the bar and ordered three beers. The bartender brought them over to us with a frightened look on his face.
    I said to Brian, "That's not good."
But before Brian could reply a guy blasted into the bar through the swinging doors on a dirt bike doing a wheelie through the bar he slammed up against the far wall, and then turned around and blasted back out through the swinging doors and into the street, all of the drugstore cowboys jumped up and cheered.

Then a guy came through the swinging doors on horseback, the horse reared up and came down knocking over a table, and then he rode back out to the street, and the drugstore cowboys cheered again.

As we started to turn back toward the bar we noticed that as all of the drugstore cowboys sat back down, they were all giving us dirty looks.

That's when Brian replied, "I see what you mean. We should probably finish these beers and get the hell out of here."

David said, "Fuck 'em. We've got just as much right to drink in here as anybody else." He barely got that out of his mouth when someone started lifting his hat off of his head.

We all turned around, and noticed that the two biggest drugstore cowboys were standing there grinning, the bigger one was trying to take David's hat.

David knocked his hand away saying, "Don't touch the hat." David and Brian started putting their gloves back on.

I was thinking, "Oh shit, the last thing I want right now is to get into a fight". And then out of nowhere; there was little Willie Joe standing behind the two behemoths.

He tugged on the shirt of the larger thug and said, "You guys are going to have to leave my friends alone."

The two large drugstore cowboys started to laugh to each other, the larger one saying to Willie Joe "Or what?"

Willie Joe calmly replied as he pulled his .38 pistol from his waistband, cocking it, and pointing it at them, "Or I'm gonna have to kill ya."

The two monsters put up their hands, and began stumbling backwards away from him, knocking over tables and chairs and then they ran out of the bar along with most of the other patrons.

I said, "All right Willie Joe. Way to go!"

Brian said to the bartender, "A drink for our friend. What'll you have Willie Joe?"

Willie Joe replied, "What's the strongest thing you have?"

The bartender replied, "151 proof rum, and 151 Wild Turkey. And we are not supposed to serve Indians, but seeing I have an allergy to lead, what will you have, and it's on the house."

Willie Joe replied, "Wild Turkey and leave the bottle." The bartender groaned and mumbled something under his breath as he walked away. Willie Joe said, "What's that?"

The bartender replied, his voice nervously cracking, "Nothing sir, one bottle of Wild Turkey 151 coming up." I pointed out that since we had just cleared the bar, we might want to clear out ourselves before the RCMP arrived. My three companions began to laugh uproariously, saying, "Are you kidding? There are only six RCMP in this whole town. And unless you're shooting the town up or killing people all they do is drive around watching everybody. Trust us. This bar will be full again in less than five minutes. People are a lot thirstier than they are scared."

And they were right. People started rolling back into the bar as we got three more beers, and Willie grabbed his bottle and we went for a walk around the town. We saw many flyers for a concert at the rodeo grounds that night with a bunch of Indian rock bands along with some local white rock bands, so we decided to go that night.

After walking for a couple of blocks in amongst the throng of people I noticed a silver haired elderly Indian man with two beautiful young Indian girls walking arm in arm with him. He was signing autographs, and someone took his picture. I couldn't believe my eyes as we walked up to them I said to the old gentleman, "Excuse me sir, but aren't you Chief Dan George?"

I had seen him in the movie "Little Big Man" with Dustin Hoffman a few years earlier. He replied in that gentle whisper of a voice of his, "Yes I am. Do I know you, young man?" I replied, "No sir. But I know you sir. And if you don't mind me saying so you are one hell of an actor, and I can't think of a single soul other than you, who could have played your part in Little Big Man, as well as you did."

He replied, "You are very kind." This is Elk's Toe and Mary. They are friends and followers of the band that I am here to see perform. They are from my tribe, the Tsleil-Waututh Nation" but most people know us as "The Burrard Indian Band. I was Chief a while back." I asked, "How many are in the band?" And he asked, "Do you mean the rock band, or the whole tribe?" Embarrassed I replied, "The rock band." He said, "There are five of them, all good boys, with a lot of talent. You fellows should come, and see them perform. In fact why don't you fellas come with us now, because we are right by the bandstand and there are about four pretty girls to every guy there anyway. So you should do well for yourselves." Elk's Toe and Mary giggled. "We'll all have a grand old time," he continued softly.

As we walked back I talked to him about being in the music business myself. And playing a lot of the local venues in LA like the Troubadour, Bitter End West, etc. when I told him that I had a one-man act playing guitar and singing, he suggested that I get my guitar and jam a little with the band after the band did their set. I told him that that would be great. He was a very quiet spoken and intelligent man and very funny, and I could see why the women loved and admired him. Brian wanted to see if there was still time sign up for the rodeo events; however David and Willie Joe met girls immediately at the band's tent.

I had to go back to the truck to walk and feed Lazarus and grab my guitar.

By the time I got back from the truck, the band was on stage playing, and to my amazement, they were quite good, and they could sing. They played four originals and two cover songs, and the crowd loved them. They actually did an encore, which I found out was rare for rodeo bands.

After their set, and him signing autographs and taking pictures with people, I and my guys, and Chief Dan and the band members and the girls all sat around in their large tent, with a small fire in the middle, and we smoked and drank a little, and played guitar and sang and talked for hours.

It was one of the best nights of my life. What fun. I took a girl that I had met there back to the camper. Bryan, David and Willie Joe stayed out all night, and woke me and her up early the next morning.

Willie Joe was heading into the nations to meet up with friends, and Brian and David wanted to go to forestry headquarters and see about getting jobs right away, as we had arrived to late for them to enter the rodeo.

So off we went to forestry headquarters on the outskirts of town. It was a group of smaller buildings surrounded by plane hangars numerous trucks, a C-47 and a couple helicopters, and a runway.

I walked in with Brian and David to the main building. There was a guy typing on a typewriter behind the counter.
Brian said, "Hey Sam, you got any work?"
The man replied, "Hey Brian, hey David. You guys want to work ground? Or do you want to jump again?" David asked, "Does jumping still pay as good? And do you still get to keep all the spare gear, and food?" Sam replied, "Yup." Brian said to me, "You want to jump Bob? It pays $100 Canadian a day and you get to keep a lot of your gear and left over food and some equipment."
Before I could answer Brian said, "Sure Sam, Bob will jump too." Sam replied, "Is he jump qualified?" Brian said "Of course he is. Don't you remember he jumped with us last year?" Sam got up leaving his typewriter and saying, "Okay, all of you sign here. Print name, then the signature, address, phone number, and then complete contact information for next of kin. Oh hell, you know the drill. Be here tomorrow morning at 5:00 am."

As we got back into the truck I asked "Jump? Is he talking about jumping out of a plane?
Brian said, "It's the easiest money you'll ever make. We'll show you exactly what to do. It's as easy as falling off a log."
I screamed, "Are you fucking insane. I don't care how much money you get paid, or how much crap you get to keep. I am not jumping out of a plane into a forest fire." David said, "Don't be such

a pussy. Besides, what do you want to do? Just hang around the stampede getting high and screwing girls while we have all the fun, and make all of the money? Come on Bob. Be a man."

We arrived the next day at 10 minutes until five in the morning.

Standing outside of the CFS buildings and started receiving our drop gear, which consisted of a parachute, and backup chute, leg harnesses, mask, helmet, goggles, etc. Brian and David were putting my gear on me and then themselves,

I found out that the leg harnesses were for hooking extra gear onto, like chainsaws, and other things that you couldn't hold while you plummeted to earth. Once we geared up, 20 of us ran down to a C-47 with its engines revving.

We all climbed in and sat down, 10 of us on either side of the plane. As we took off, the chief firefighter /jumpmaster standing in the front of the plane told us that we were dropping into the flat ridges 12 miles north of The Caribou Hwy, and because of crosswinds we were dropping three miles east of the fire to avoid anyone being swept into the fire. He said that it should be an easy one, and that most of the work would be the mop up the next day.

Then he said as you are all jump qualified and have done this before, so I assume that you all know what you're doing, but are there any questions? I started to raise my hand;

Brian quickly pulled my hand back down and whispered, "What are you doing?"

I replied in a whisper, "I don't want to die."

He replied back in a whisper, "Just do exactly what I do. And when you get close to the ground bend your knees so you don't break your ankle."

I saw the red light on the bulkhead up front go yellow.

The chief yelled, "Line 'A' stand up." And everybody in my line stood up. He said, "Everyone hookup your rip cord to the static line".

Everyone attached the line from their parachute to the wire line above us which ran along the ceiling of the plane. I'd seen this in World War II paratrooper movies. My heart was about to jump out of my chest. I was scared shitless.

The jumpmaster said, "Row 'B,' stand up and attach your rip

cords". And the guys across the way from us did the same.

The chief said, "You guys know the drill when the light goes green first row A, and then row B exit the plane.

Suddenly the light went green and the chief screamed, "Go. Go. Go." And all of these maniacs started jumping out of the plane.

Brian and David were ahead of me in line and when they both jumped I stopped, and pulled back from the doorway.

The chief grabbed my arm and screamed, "Jump. What are you doing? Jump,"

I unhooked from the static line and ran to the back of the plane wrapping myself around a pole.

The chief instructed the rest of the guys in my row to jump and they did. He told row B. to start jumping.

As they jumped he ran back to me. He hooked my rip cord onto the end of Row B static line, and tried to pull me off of the pole to make me jump saying, "Come on son, you've done this before it's no big deal".

He had two of the guys in the back of the exiting row unhook and try to help him pull me off of the pole. But they couldn't do it, so he had them run up to the front and re-hook and jump so that they wouldn't miss the group and the LZ.

On the way back to Williams Lake he asked me what was wrong.

I told him that I had never jumped before, and he became very angry, but he wasn't angry with me, he was angry with Brian and David for lying and putting me in that situation.

When they got back from the fire at the end of the next day he chewed them a new one. In the interim he asked me if I minded flying in helicopters. I told him that I never had flown in a helicopter before. So he took me up for a short ride in a Bell jet Ranger helicopter and I really enjoyed it.

Once I had told him about my previous fire experience in LA, he asked if I would like to work in the helicopter firefighting division which paid the same.

And I said, "Yes, if I could work with David and Brian?" He begrudgingly agreed. And they were very happy, because it was a new experience, and easier, less dangerous work, and paid the same.

It was great for a few days. We would grab our gear, jump on the helicopter which would slowly lift off the ground, and smoothly deliver us to the fire, setting us gently down to go do our job.

However after the fire which we were on for a few days, we arrived the next morning to see the silhouette of a new helicopter against the dawn sky. I had never seen anything like this before, but David and Brian let out rebel yells, with whoops and hollers.

David screaming, "Huey has left the building. So now boys, we get to scream into hell on the back of the Cobra. Yeeeeehaaa."

And that, my friends, was my introduction to the Cobra Jet. It seems that B.C. forestry had purchased a few of the attack helicopter gunships from the US as surplus, and converted them to a fire suppression delivery role. By putting a jump seat in the front cockpit with the pilot, and expanding the rear gunner's cockpit to accommodate three men abreast, a Cobra jet could deliver four men to a fire in less than half the time it took for a Bell jet Ranger to do the same job. And just about as fast a C-47 without the danger that comes with jumping.

I was told later that this was a short lived experiment, however. And I was not prepared for the sheer terror of the experience.

We crammed ourselves and our basic gear into this thing,

David was upfront with the pilot. Brian and I and another hippie firefighter named Lou were sitting in the converted gunners pod above and behind David and the pilot.

When the pilot started the engine, and the two huge rotors began to turn, the whole body of the chopper would torque, what seemed to be about 7 to 10° with each rotation.

I learned later that this was because the thing was much lighter with all the armaments and war related electronics removed. When the thing was finally ready to take off the vibration was rattling my teeth, and the sound was deafening. When we lifted off it was nothing like the Bell jet Ranger.

The only thing that I can compare it to is the G. force that I experienced when I raced my B roadster dragster. You are literally pressed back into your seat so that you can't move, even if you want to. And the nose of the chopper tips towards the ground as the massive rotor blades tear at the air, snatching the chopper forward.

This sensation combined with the knowledge that you have no control over the experience, left me with the horrifying sensation of riding a deranged tilt-awhirl into Hell.

I noticed that when we reached altitude that we were really moving. The hills were whipping past us on either side. Like telephone poles along the highway when you're going over 100 miles an hour in a car. The faster you go, the closer the telephone poles appear to come together, until around somewhere between 150 and 170 MPH they appear to merge into one telephone pole.

I said to Brian, "We've got to be doing over 200 miles an hour." And he replied, "More like 225 is my guess."

Just then I looked down at the pilot's cockpit to see David lighting up a joint of Alaskan Thunder Fuck weed. Then he started to hand it to the pilot.

I frantically started waving my arms and screaming, "No. No. David, No." Brian just laughed knowing that there was nothing that I could do about it. I turned to him and screamed over the engine noise, "You are literally going to be laughing out your ass after we crash into
one of these hillsides, because that's where your mouth is going to be, you stupid fuck." He still thought that it was hilarious.

Landing in a Cobra jet is not any more fun than taking off. I have never been so glad to get on the ground in my life.

We managed to get the fire out in record time; literally. I heard that the record stood until 1979. However the mop up took another day, and they had to bring in more guys and equipment, but we were the last four to leave and got to keep tons of extra food and gear, and more importantly they brought us, and the extra gear back in two Bell Jet Ranger's.

We literally filled my camper shell, leaving only enough room for Brian and Lazarus, and David rode up front with me. And we rented a trailer that we could drop off in Clinton afterwards just to carry all of the rest of the free stuff back to the commune. I'm talking about two-way radios, chainsaws, parachutes, and tons of food, canned hams, and the like. And all three of us with solid overtime and hazard pay split $2,100 Canadian, so it was well worth it.

While we were fighting fires, Willy Joe killed a guy who walked in on him while Willy was screwing the guy's wife in their teepee, in the nations, and the RCMP took him to jail, or that's what we heard anyway.

I saw Dan again (he let me call him that), once more before he and the band left, and we had another great talk. I gave him one of my furniture company cards. The name of my furniture company was Old Time Livin' and he said that he really liked the name.

I told him that I would be back in LA the following spring, and he told me that when he went down to LA again, that he would give me a call. However when I did get back to LA, I only stayed in the Marina del Rey House for a few months anyway, and by then Shelley had already changed my phone number, and my old phone number was no longer available. So I have no idea if he ever tried to contact me. But what a great man he was.

When we got back to the commune we unloaded all of the goodies, and I spent the night.

There was a new single girl at the commune, an Irish redhead named Carmen, from Oregon, and we hit it off famously and spent the night together.

The sex was great and she did something that only one other girl in my life ever did to me, and ironically the other girl was a redhead and Irish as well.

What she did was, after sex she would jump up out of bed, and put a pot of water on the stove in the camper, and clean herself up, and then come back to bed with a pan of warm water and a washcloth and proceed to clean me. And it's the weirdest thing, but the sensation of that warm wet washcloth on my genitalia was so sensual that immediately after cleaning me, I would be so turned on that we would start making out and then have sex again.

So that night we had sex four times in a row. It was amazing. Three years later I would meet another redheaded Irish girl in Venice, California named Amy who did the same exact thing and it was just as wonderful and amazing.

The next day I had to bid farewell to Brian, David, and Carmen, and everyone else at the commune and head back to Michael's to find out where Josh was, as no one at the commune had heard from him since he decided to head east. So Lazarus and I headed back to Michael's and I dropped off the trailer in Clinton BC for the guys on the way.

When I got back to Michael's he was home, and as always I

was welcomed with open arms.

Michael said that he was glad to see me, but that I looked like hell. He told Big Jerry the giant resident caretaker/ bouncer who stood 6' 8" tall and about 400 pounds, to call Giovanni, his personal barber. "Hell," he said, "Call everybody this poor guy needs help.

Within half an hour everyone was there. Soon the barber, stylist, manicurist, pedicurist, facial and skin therapist, had all arrived. You see Michael had a huge master bathroom on the second floor of the mansion.

They went to work on me immediately. I was scrubbed from head to toe. The barber had to relax my curly hair to get the Matts and debris out. Then shampoo, cut and re-curl it. Then he did a hot oil job on it. It looked great when he was done.

While he had been doing all of this two beautiful women were doing my manicure and pedicure, while saying things like, "So you're a mountain firefighter? That really turns me on, or what a great tan."

Now Giovanni the barber said, "The beard has to go. Let's take it off. But leave a mustache.

All of a sudden he said, "YES. That's it. Wonderful."

He held up a mirror and asked, "What do you think?'

"Wow." I said. "Are we done?" "

"Yes, you are now human again, and ready to rejoin society," he said.

When I came downstairs Michael yelled out "Now that's more like it. The new and improved Hippie Bob. I may have some real competition now."

Michael told me that he wanted to hear all about all of my adventures. So after a great meal with the 30 or so visitors and 15 or so remnants of the Flying Circus, he invited me and Chartreuse to come up to his bedroom with him and his new girl Tess, so that I could regale them with details of the Stampede, meeting Chief Dan George, and fighting fires.

So after dinner, the four of us went up to Michael's huge bedroom, and he pulled out a bottle of really good champagne and started chopping up and making lines of coke on an ornate mirrored tray, while I began my tale.

As I was telling the story, while drinking champagne and snorting coke, he and Tess were on one side of his huge 12'x12' four poster canopy bed, and Chartreuse and I were lying together on the other side. As the glasses were refilled, and the tray of coke was handed back and forth, I regaled the trio with tales of Brian's, David's, Willy Joe's and my exploits.

Then Tess pulled out Michael's cock, and started to suck it.

This shocked me a little, and I stopped talking.

Michael smiled and said, "Go on man. Don't leave us hanging. This is fascinating."

So I went back to my story. And after a few more minutes of my story, Chartreuse pulled out my cock and started sucking it. I was startled a little, but the first thing that came to my mind was Michael's got a pretty big cock, I hope that Chartreuse can get mine hard enough and big enough, so that it doesn't look so puny, or this is going to be embarrassing.

Well, Chartreuse was getting me hard and making it grow to the point that I was having trouble finishing the story. And just when I felt like I was a couple of minutes away from coming, Michael interrupted saying, "Do you want to switch girls?" I said, "What? Isn't that up to the girls?"

Michael replied, "Oh, you're absolutely right. How arrogant of me. I'm sorry. Ladies would you like to switch?" Tess taking Michael's cock out of her mouth replied, "Okay."

Michael looked over at Chartreuse, who looked up at me and replied, "Well. I guess that it's okay is it all right with you Bob?" I replied, "You know me babe, I'm fine with what everybody else wants to do."

And with that the two girls slid off the side of the huge bed, took off the rest of their clothes, and proceeded to change partners.

Michael had that sly smirk of his, and a glint in his eye.

Now I knew what he was up to. I forgot to mention that Tess was incredibly beautiful like Chartreuse had been a few years earlier, not to say that Chartreuse wasn't still beautiful, it's just that she was now 26 and not 20 anymore.

Michael had been watching me tell the story, and he knew that Chartreuse was about to get me off, and he knew what would happen to me in my current condition when this beautiful young girl put my cock in her mouth.

So sure enough we change partners and Michael says, "So,

Bob. Get back to your story. We're all fascinated."

So I start telling my story again, while looking all around the room and trying to look at, and think of anything but Tess sucking my cock. And now I'm somewhere floating around in the ether between exhilaration, exaltation, Nirvana, and anguish, pain, and suffering, desperately trying to finish my story, I momentarily looked down and saw Tess's beautiful face, and suddenly I screamed out in the middle of my story, "And the hills were whipping by at 225 miles an hour, while our pilot was getting high on Alaskan Thunder Fuck. And then I let out a loud, "Yeah, Oh my God," as I came.

Michael started to laugh loudly exclaiming, "Well done Bob. Well done. What control. I don't think I could've done better myself.

Michael began to applaud, and the two girls began to applaud me with him. Michael said, "Let's switch back." And Chartreuse came back to me and Tess went back and finished off Michael. I began to finish the story but we all fell asleep before I ever completed it. What a night, and what a guy.

I truly have never met another man like Michael since, and I'm sure that I never will.

He was rich and arrogant; and yet he was kind and giving, ruthless, and yet caring, generous and yet paranoid; occasionally very serious, but always very funny, with a wicked sense of humor. He was literally a walking dichotomy.

The next day a car load of kids came in with a message from Josh.

Josh was with Holy Alex at the Calgary Stampede. The Calgary Stampede had started that day, so I left immediately.

Chartreuse starting crying because she wanted to go, so this time I took her along. I don't think that I ever saw her so happy. And it really made me happy to see her so happy.

So we were off on a new adventure, heading to another Stampede, and a chance to finally meet the famous Holy Alex.

I still remember the scene like it was yesterday. With us rolling down the highway, towards Calgary, Lazarus curled up on the floor of the passenger side of the cab.

Chartreuse curled up next to me with her head on my

shoulder, and her arm around me.

As the radio played, "I've got sunshine on a cloudy day. And when it's cold outside, I've got the month of May. Well, I guess you'll say. What can make me feel this way, my girl, my girl, I'm talkin' bout my girl, my girl."

Chartreuse gently kissed me on the cheek, giving me an adoring look, and for a small moment in time, all was right with the world.

One of the helicopter pilots

Chapter 13

On the road again to the Calgary stampede, and a meeting with Holy Alex

Well. Here we were the three of us off on a new adventure to Calgary. Luckily we would be arriving during the middle of the stampede. I say this because in that year 1973, the Queen of England opened the stampede, and was there at the beginning, with the entire royal family. This was because it was an anniversary for the stampede, and also the Centennial anniversary of the formation of the RCMP.

All the way there I kept thinking, why would Josh and Holy Alex be in a town filled with rodeo goers, and RCMP. And I was sure that the Royal family was not the draw for them. So why were they there? After four or five hours on the road we got into Kamloops, and stopped for food, provisions and gas. After getting provisions and gas we stopped at a restaurant to get some takeout food.

While waiting for our food we struck up a conversation with another couple that was waiting there for their food. They were a cute young couple the guy had a goatee and blond hair, was thin, and handsome. His name was Bryce. The girl was very pretty, slender with curly hair, pretty face, and crystal blue eyes. Her name was Layla.
We had a great conversation and seemed to hit it off right away.
Since Bryce was a singer who played mandolin, and said he knew a great place to camp outside of Kamloops that not many people knew about, which had a nice waterfall and large pond for swimming, Chartreuse and I decided to join them for the night. At that time of year it didn't get dark until later. So we had a lot of fun for hours before it got dark.
We got loaded, drank wine, swam, and lay out in the sun; Lazarus was in heaven, four people to throw the stick for him. When it started to get dark we all went into preparation mode.

After gathering firewood, we parked my truck and his Ford station wagon together just far enough away from the fire to hold in the heat. We ate the rest of the takeout for dinner, then drank wine, and smoked weed, and Bryce and I sang songs as the girls chimed in.

We talked for a little while, and then Chartreuse suggested that we play spin the bottle. I asked, "What is this kindergarten"? Chartreuse replied, "Oh, come on. It'll be fun." So we made a small circle with a wine bottle in the center.
    The first few times I tried to spin it Lazarus wanted to grab it and run with it. So I put him in the truck.
    The first spin pointed at Bryce who of course kissed Layla.
    On the second spin the bottle pointed at me and I kissed Chartreuse, at which point she said," This is gettin' boring really fast."
    I replied, "Thanks a lot". Everybody laughed and Chartreuse said," Come on Bob. You know what I mean." I replied, "Okay. You're right. Anybody have any suggestions?"
    Layla said, "How about strip spinning? That's always fun." Chartreuse replied, "That's a great idea." I looked at Bryce, and we both shrugged our shoulders, and said, "Okay."
    So we started spinning the bottle again. I thought that I would have a big advantage in that I had on two pairs of socks and long underwear and regular underwear under that. As well as shirt, pants, shoes, hat, etc.

    The rest of the group booed when I immediately took out my sunglasses and put them on before the spin, so I did put them back in my pocket.
    Then of course the bottle kept pointing at me. Four times in a row. Everyone was laughing louder on every spin as I removed pieces of clothing. By the time the fourth spin pointed at me the other three were chanting, "Karma, Karma, Karma."
    Finally the fifth spin pointed at Layla.
    The furious spinning of the bottle went on, and on, until Bryce was down to his tighty whiteys. Layla and Chartreuse were down to their panties, and I was completely naked. I have never been lucky.
    The only sport that I have ever won any real money at in my

life gambling was dog racing when I was drunk in Mexico, in my college days, and some boxing and football games. But obviously I sucked at spin the bottle.

Two more spins and Bryce and Layla were naked with me.

The third spin of the bottle pointed at me again. I announced, "Now what? Chartreuse answered, "That's easy. Everyone that is naked gets a pass until the bottle points at me."

So, five spins later, off came Chartreuses' panties and the game was on.

Chartreuse announced, "Now. There are a bunch of ways that we can play the game from here on out."

Layla asked, "Which way is the most fun."

Chartreuse replied, "That depends on how open you are sexually, and how willing you are to experiment." I said getting up, "I'm up for anything that you guys are up for. But right now I'm putting a lot of more wood on the fire so we don't freeze to death."

Keeping my right hand over my crotch, I walked daintily barefoot over to the fire and started putting smaller pieces of wood on the fire with my left hand.

Chartreuse yelled, "Put some big pieces on there."

I replied, "Then I'll have to use both hands".

Chartreuse yelled back laughingly, "Then use both hands. We are all going to see your stuff soon enough anyway." So with that I took my right hand from my crotch and began loading larger logs onto the fire.

We began to discuss where the game was going.

We all agreed that the most practical idea would be for the three people who were not victims of the bottle to decide what the other was going to have to do, and who they had to do it with.

At this point Bryce and I almost in unison yelled, "But no guy on guy bullshit."

The girls began to laugh uproariously.

Chartreuse added, "But of course you guys are fine with girl on girl shit, right."

Bryce and I nodded our heads in approval.

Chartreuse yelled, "Typical, the old double standard." Layla yelled, "Can you believe these guys Chartreuse, nothing but male chauvinist pigs. Unbelievable."

I looked over at Bryce and he looked back at me. And we thought that the night was over until both girls started to crack up, laughing their heads off at the two idiots whose little head was doing the thinking for the big one.

Well we spun the bottle again. And of course it landed on me. Immediately the other three started thinking of sexual acts that I could do at first only to Chartreuse. And then Chartreuse suggested that I suck on Layla's breasts.

And Layla and then Bryce agreed. So I did it. We spun again and the bottle landed on Chartreuse. So to get her back I suggested that she jerk off Bryce. And surprisingly Layla thought the idea was hilarious.

I remember laughing when Bryce looked at Layla surprised and said, "Really honey?" So Chartreuse went over and started jerking off Bryce.

This went on for a couple of minutes and I could see that Bryce was really getting turned on. So I said, "Okay stop. And all three of them turned and looked at me; with Bryce asking, "Now," Chartreuse asking, "Why;" and Layla asking, "What?"

I looked at them all and said, "Of course, stop now. We don't want any of us to get off right away. Do we? Or this is going to be a short game." Bryce replied, "Good thinking Bob." We spun the bottle again and Layla had to kiss Chartreuse, and fondle her breasts. It was very sexy they were both beautiful girls. I was watching them intently, when out of the corner of my eye I see Bryce jerking off. I yelled out, "Hey, Bryce, no cheating, brother. You don't want to knock yourself out of the game early."

Bryce laughed and stopped fondling himself. At this point Chartreuse suggested that we up the ante. I asked, "How?" She said, "Double spin." Michael came up with it." I asked how that worked.

And she said, "Simple, two people spin, and the other two determine what they have to do to each other". I said, "Okay. But no guy on guy shit." Bryce yelled, "Yeah, none of that."

Chartreuse started to laugh, saying, "You guys are too much. If I didn't know better I'd think that deep down you really want to try sucking each other's cock." She and Layla laughed and pointed at us.

I said, "Well. There goes my hard on. Bryce said, "Me too." Chartreuse said, "Well Layla, we can fix that, right." With that they both started blowing us.

I said, "Whoa. Whoa. Wait a minute. Let's go back to the game before you two get me and Bryce off, and the game is called on account of two sleeping men." That line got a laugh from everybody.

We went back to spinning the bottle. The first spin landed on me again, of course, and the second spin landed on Layla.

My heart started to pound, and my penis started to harden. Bryce yelled out, "Mutual masturbation." And Chartreuse yelled out, "69."

When she said that, my cock raised just like a 16 inch gun on a battleship.

I looked over at Bryce, he had a sad perplexed look on his face as he said, "I don't know about this?"

Chartreuse laughingly said, "Loosen up guy. We're all just having fun here. Your gal isn't going to fall for my man. And I am not going to fall for you. Trust your lady. She loves you. We're all just sampling something different. It's always great for any relationship, unless you don't trust her, and if you don't trust her, your relationship is already fucked up." She looked over at Layla and laughingly asked, "Right, darlin'?"

Layla, who had already stood up, turned and leaned down to Bryce, and kissing him said, "That's right, baby, you're the only man for me. We're just having some fun, playing a game, and trying a new experience." As she started to walk over to me, I said, "I'm just going with the flow Bryce. But if you're not cool with this, then we can stop right now." Before he could answer Chartreuse interrupted saying, "He doesn't want to stop anything, he trusts his lady. And besides you wait and see what I'm going to do to you, Bryce." At that point Layla had just walked up to me, close enough that her nipples were touching my lower chest. And even though it made my penis rise a little more causing it to touch her bush, we both turned and looked at Chartreuse, as if to say, "What the fuck?"

Chartreuse looked back at both of us, and smiling she said, "Are you two going to stand there like a couple of statues? Or are you going to show us how to 69?" I had never seen Chartreuse like this at Michael's. She was always so quiet and submissive, always kind of under Michael's thumb. But out here, away from Michael's domination, she was strong. A take charge kind of gal. Frankly, it turned me on a lot.

Well, Layla and I lay down on a sleeping bag; with me on the bottom, and we proceeded to 69 for two or three minutes with Chartreuse cheering us on, and Bryce looking on with this sort of sad acceptance. When Layla really got me going I stopped licking her vagina long enough to let out a short moan.

And suddenly Chartreuse stood up and yelled, "Stop. Stop. She ran over and pulled Layla's head off of my penis, and smiling at her she said, "Sorry, my dear. But nobody gets to taste my man's cum except me. At least when I'm around, that is."

Layla and I got up. I was thinking to myself, "I thought that this was a game, and we're supposed to have fun. I feel like my nuts are going to explode." Chartreuse was all animated she grabbed the bottle and said, "Everybody in your places; it's time to spin again". I remember saying to myself, "If that bottle points at me right now I'm probably going to cum all over myself."

The bottle landed on Bryce. I thought, "Thank God." On the next spin the weirdest thing happened. The bottle stopped right between Layla and Chartreuse. I checked it out and said, "It's exactly between the two of you, so we can either spin again or give Bryce his choice of ladies." Chartreuse chimed in, "Or; We could both give him some head. After all Bob, you and Layla had your fun, why shouldn't Bryce and I have our fun."

The evil voice in my head thought, "Oh great. Now I get to involuntarily cum while watching my girl and the hot new girl who was just blowing me blow the other guy and get him off. Fantastic."

However the other voice in my head actually did the talking and I said, "That's fair. Bryce, you showed so much self control, you deserve that. Show him your stuff ladies." And with that they both went down on Bryce. I only watched for about 20 or 30 seconds because I didn't want to cum.

So I grabbed a blanket and went over to the other vehicle and turned the other way. After what I would guess to be about a minute or so I heard Bryce moan, and Chartreuse said, "He's all yours Layla."

She ran over to me saying, "How's my man? How's my wonderful man? She went down on me immediately, and when I was just about to cum, she looked up at me saying, "Give me your love, baby, your sweet love. I want to taste your sweet warm love." With that I exploded into her mouth. She swallowed and began to kiss me all over. I thought to myself, "Wow. I think she really loves me. What a trip."

I heard Bryce let out a loud moan. And after that I let Lazarus out for a walk, and we stoked the fire and crawled into our respective vehicles and went to sleep.

Before we went to bed, I walked up to Bryce and put my hand out and asked, "Are we cool man?" With both of us standing there naked in the firelight. Bryce grabbed my hand with both hands and said strongly, "We're cool man." And with that he grabbed me and hugged me, which frankly shocked the crap out of me. I pulled back quickly and startled I said, "I appreciate the sentiment man, but I don't want to cross swords with you if you know what I mean? (An expression that I had heard at Michael's place.) He started to laugh uncontrollably, slapped me on the shoulder, and laughing he said, "You are a funny man. You are a fuck'in funny man." And walking away he said, "Crossing swords. What a trip. That guy is a crack up Layla."

So with that exchange we climbed into our respective vehicles for the night. Chartreuse and I climbed under the mountain of covers in the camper. Lazarus snuggled in by the camper shell door at our feet.

As Chartreuse and I cuddled and kissed, I told her how impressed and turned on I had been by her take charge attitude with the spin the bottle game.

She grabbed me and gave me a long passionate kiss. And then she said, "That's why I love you Bob, where any other guy would be giving me shit for being too bossy, instead you tell me that you thought that it was great to see me come out of my shell. And that it actually turned you on. You're a very special man, Bob. And I haven't been this happy in years."

I put my arm around her. And she laid her arm across my chest as her warm soft breasts pressed against my body, and her soft beautiful face pressed against mine. The sweet smell of lavender faintly drifted past my nose. The two of us laid there watching the stars and an occasional shooting star through the camper's skylight, until we drifted off to sleep.

I recall thinking just as my eyes started to close, "This sure feels good. Could Chartreuse be the one?" Then just as I started going into deeper REM sleep, the answer came back in my dream. "Naaaahh!"

Helicopter picking us up after fire

Chapter 14

On to Calgary stampede to meet with Josh and Holy Alex

We rose early the next morning to the sound of Lazarus barking in the camper, and a loud clattering of pots and pans outside.

I lifted up the curtain on the camper shell door window, only to realize that I was face-to-face with a black bear who was apparently attempting to look inside of the window just as I decided to look out of it. This startled me, to say the least.

I lunged backward inside the camper knocking Chartreuse down in the process. She yelled "What's the matter?"

Rattled, I said to her, "There's a black bear just outside of the camper." I grabbed my rifle, opened the side window of the camper and yelled to Bryce and Layla to stay in their car, because there was a bear outside. Bryce yelled back to me, "We can see him. Thanks."

I peeked out of the camper door window again, and could see why the bear was there. We had left a can of shortening out; the bear was looking for food, and was eating the shortening from the can with his paw.

I figured that I could crack open the camper shell door and fire a shot from my rifle to scare him off. So I cracked open the camper shell door with the rifle barrel just outside. However before I fired, I noticed that he seemed to be oblivious to the gun, so I opened the camper shell door a little wider, and then a little wider, until it was all the way opened.

At this point Lazarus started to bark. I shut him up right away, but his barking was enough to draw the Bear's attention. I raised my rifle and Chartreuse screamed.

This seemed to startle the bear. He dropped the can of shortening and jumped backwards. When I saw this,

I set down my rifle, and then I began to clap my hands and wave my arms. And all of this commotion seemed to really startle the bear, and he ran off. He ran about 75 feet, and then stopped.

So I came out of the camper, with my rifle, and fired a round into the air, which sent him scurrying out of sight.

It was early and we were all wide awake, so we decided to go back into Kamloops and get breakfast and coffee, and then head toward Calgary. We made good time and arrived in Calgary a little bit after 3:00 pm.

Bryce and Layla were going to go right to the rodeo grounds. However I wanted to go check out Victoria Park to look for Josh beforehand. So we decided where we would meet up at night and went our separate ways.

The park was crowded, as there were many people in town for stampede. I put Lazarus on his leash, and the three of us walked around the park. There was no sign of Josh, but we met a pretty blond hippie girl in the Park who was handing out Holy Alex cards, and asking for donations.

I asked if she knew where Josh and Holy Alex were.

She said that Josh was at the commune north of town, and Holy Alex was in town, but that she wasn't sure where?

Chartreuse and I told her that we were friends of Josh, and asked her for directions to the commune. She gave us directions, and drew us a small map.

So directions in hand, we were on our way to the commune. The commune was only about 35-40 min. north of Calgary, nestled in a beautiful valley. There was a large log cabin, surrounded by tents, lean-tos, and a few teepees.

We got out of the truck and started walking toward the large log cabin. On the way, two people emerged from one of the larger tents. They were hippies, a guy and a girl, completely nude.

They waved at us and the bearded guy said "Howdy brother."
And I asked him, "Do you know where Josh is?"
He replied "I think he's up at the long house?"
I asked, "Do you mean the big log cabin?"
And he said, "Yeah. Are you friends of Josh's?"
I replied, "Yes we are."
He continued, "Josh is an amazing fellow. It's like he knows everything about everything. He started this place with Alex about three years ago. I've heard that Holy Alex has five other communes, all over Canada. But he doesn't have his name associated with any of them.

I asked him "Why?" The bearded nudist replied, "That's

simple, the cops, they're always out after Holy Alex for everything under the sun, taxes, fraud, drugs; You name it, and they want to bust him for all of it. The problem for them is they've never caught him yet. And whenever he and Josh settle and improve some government land, the paperwork is always in one or more of Alex's followers' names, so the cops haven't been able to seize any of the properties either. I've been told that Josh helped Alex build two of the three communes." Surprised, I blurted out, "Wow I didn't know that."

Chartreuse said, "Now I know what Josh was doing when he would go away for months at a time."

So Chartreuse and I made our way up to the massive log cabin. The design of the cabin had Josh written all over it. It was almost the same design as the main building of David and Brian's commune, what I refer to as "The House of Che."

We entered through a large double doorway into a massive room. At the far side of the room sitting with five or six other people, at a large hand-hewn pine table was Josh.

As we walked closer we could see that half of the people were cultivating fresh-cut weed, and the other half were breaking up dried buds and rolling them into joints. When he saw us, Josh jumped up from the table and ran to us, hugging us both and jumping up and down. It was obvious that he was glad to see us.

I remember thinking at the time that now I knew what it must be like to be hugged by a skunk, because he was covered in Alaskan thunder fuck skunk weed. I asked him, "What all of the joints were for? Are you guys going to have a big party?"

Josh said, "No, we are going to sell these at the stampede."

I replied, "Isn't that a little risky? With the whole town filled with RCMP?"

"Are you kidding, said Josh, "They don't give a shit. Most of them will be drunk anyway, and the ones on duty are only worried about bad things like violence, robbery, and that sort of crap."

I chimed in again, "But what do you guys need money for? What happened to living off the land, and money being the root of all evil, and that stuff?"

Looking a little perturbed Josh replied, "We're still doing all of that. And money is evil. But there are some things that you just can't trade for, like pumps, and cement, and gas, you know what I mean?"

Josh gave us the 10 cent tour of the commune. As Josh was going back into Calgary with two of the commune kids, to distribute and sell the 15 bags of 25 joints each, Chartreuse and I gave them all a ride, especially seeing that Josh had promised to introduce us to Holy Alex.

When we got back into town it was very crowded, a lot more people would come into town for the night's festivities.

We headed to the park so that Josh and the kids could split up and distribute the bags of joints to the other 10 or so followers of Holy Alex that were at the park to make money for the commune during the stampede.

We parked a block or so from the Park and walked in. The two kids had five bags each, and Josh kept five bags in his large leather pouch that he always had with him.

We walked about halfway around the park and then Josh yelled," There he is."

He pointed at an old man; Josh called out to him, "Alex." Josh continued as the old man turned toward us, "These are my friends Bob, and Chartreuse, and this is Bob's dog Lazarus."

As the old man turned around to greet us I recognized his ancient weathered features from the numerous Holy Alex cards that his followers were handing out, and the one that Josh had shown me; that had saved his whole family on Salt Spring Island.

I reached out to shake his hand saying, "It's an honor to meet you sir. I have heard so much about you."

The old man's hand was frail, and yet when he gripped my hand, I thought, "Wow. What a grip." And then suddenly a rush ran through my body, kind of like a shiver, combined with a mild electric shock, and at the same moment a multicolored aura seemed to form not only around the old man, but different auras formed around everyone that I looked at.

After shaking hands, Alex hugged me and everything went back to normal. He turned to Chartreuse and hugged her with this back to me, and with her face looking right at me.

She had the strangest expression when he hugged her; she almost seemed to be in a state of Nirvana.

Then when he released her, she had a very startled expression. And then he bent down and said, "So you're Lazarus?" He gently petted Lazarus on the head and Lazarus began to pant and smiled like he had just retrieved 100 balls.

Suddenly this old man jumped up like he was a 16-year-old.

He rapidly turned to Josh and said, "You see those two guys in suits coming at us from across the street?"

And Josh replied, "Yeah?" Alex continued, "They're cops. They're after me.

Bob! You guys walk away in one direction behind me, and Josh you walk the other way behind me, and don't look back, and I will distract them."

We all did as he said, except I looked back. And to this day I still cannot believe what I saw. And you probably won't believe it either.

What I saw was an example of shape shifting. That's the only way that I can describe what I saw.

This old man who was turned towards me, and away from the two oncoming police officers, who were closing in on him, changed his face.

His face actually morphed into another face. A face I might add, that was at least 25 years younger and completely different.

I could not believe my eyes, as we walked away rapidly and the two men ran up and grabbed Alex.

They turned him around, and looking at him one of them said," Where did the old man go?"

The other cop asked, "What's going on here? Who are you? What happened to the old man who was just standing here? He's wanted for questioning."

By this time we were 40 or so feet away. And I heard Alex reply in a totally different voice, "I don't know what you're talking about officer? What have I done?"

The one cop said to the other, "I don't know what's going on here Jerry? But this is not our guy. He's just a kid for Christ's sake, and he's even wearing shoes. I don't know how these hippies pulled this off? That old bastard was right here; Shit!"

The other cop said, "We ought to take this kid in for

questioning." And the first cop replied, "On what charge? Standing in the park? Let him go. Let's get out of here before we make bigger fools of ourselves."

And with that the two cops walked away shaking their heads. And we continued back to the truck, and ran into Josh a block away from the stampede rodeo grounds.

It was an hour or so before we were supposed to meet Bryce and Layla so we went into the stampede rodeo for a while. However we didn't stay long.

I know you've heard the expression from the movie "Caddy Shack." "I like to go to bullfights on acid." It's a very funny line, but in real life, that's a crock of shit.

Anyone who could go to a bullfight, a rodeo, a prizefight, or any bloody violent event stoned on even really good weed, much less acid, and enjoy it, would have to be a sadist, a psychopath, and/or severely warped.

Chartreuse and I were just hammered on Alaskan thunder fuck weed, and we could only stand a few minutes of the calf roping competition, having spent the majority of our time trying to find our way out of the arena, and back to the truck.

We got back to the truck, but both of us were too wasted to drive.

So we took Lazarus for a walk in the park, and then came back to the truck after having some chamomile tea and food in the park.

Bryce and Layla saw the truck and stopped by. Chartreuse and I had had a good nap by then, and asked if they wanted to go back to the commune with Josh and us.

They said no, that they were going to stay in town, and leave for Montréal early the next day. We wished them luck, and everybody hugged and kissed and shook hands, and they went on their way.

I fired up the truck and drove around until we saw Josh in an alley with some guy. We stopped and I honked the horn, and Josh ran over to the truck saying "I just got rid of the last of the bags of joints. Let's head home."

I said "I need to get some gas. Do we need any supplies?" Josh replied, "No; Well? Maybe some ice cream or candy, I need some sweets."

So we got gas and food, and sweets, and headed back to the commune. It was after dark when we got there.

The place was all lit up with candles and torches, and there was a lot of activity. I parked the truck and we started up through the tents toward the long house. Along the Way, Lazarus was introduced to some of the commune dogs, but they were all cool, and all the dogs could come and go as they pleased in the camp, so I took Lazarus off of his leash.

As the three of us and Lazarus walked into the long house I saw another dog lift his leg, and pee on the leg of a chair in the main room. Someone yelled, "You know the rules. Start cleaning." And a girl came over with a bucket, sponge, and Mop, and started cleaning up the urine. I remember thinking, "That's fair."

I noticed in the huge kitchen, both men and women cooking. Huge wrought iron pots boiled away on five old wood-burning stoves. While people frantically cut vegetables, bread, cheese, etc. on a newly hewn wood block carving table, about 10 feet in length.

I asked if I could do anything to help, as did Chartreuse, and one of the guys said, "I think we are okay. But we could use some entertainment, do you guys sing, or play an instrument?"

I told him that I played guitar, and sang, and Chartreuse said she could sing a little.

The guy replied, "Great, go out front, and yell for Jimmy, Molly, Mike, and Jeff, to come up here and bring their instruments; and then go get your guitar."

I did as he said, and also threw the stick for Lazarus on the way to my truck and back, after picking up my guitar.

Lazarus and I arrived at the long house to see the wildest group of people that could ever be loosely referred to as a band standing by the kitchen in the main room.

Jimmy was a skinny little hippie kid with a 12 string guitar. Molly was a pretty zaftig blue-eyed blonde with wild crazy curly hair, she was a singer, Mike was a black haired bearded thirty something guy with a bass fiddle, and Jeff was a short fat guy with long straight hair and a goatee who played a flute.

I thought to myself, "This is going to be interesting." We all started tuning our instruments. After about 10 or 15 min. we all finally seemed to be in sort of the same key.

I started playing and singing a Cat Stevens song and everybody chimed in, singing and playing along with me. I knew a lot of songs by many different artists, so I kept playing and singing and the rest seemed to tag along better and better with each song.

After each song the group in the kitchen would cheer and applaud loudly; and then I noticed that more and more people were coming into the long house and applauding each song as well, until the huge building was almost full. Even though the majority of people were in the main building, we were still playing to the people that were cooking.

By this time I was sitting down at a table facing the kitchen. We had just finished a rendition of Neil Young's "Old Man," which I could always cover well, when suddenly two wrinkled hands rested upon my shoulders, and a soft, ancient voice almost whispered, "Very nice Bob,

I just closed my eyes and it was almost like Neil Young was here. I've seen him perform live.

It was Holy Alex. I knew it was him the moment that his hands rested on my shoulders; because before he even spoke, that same electric sensation that I had gotten when I shook his hand in the park earlier, ran through my body.

I turned to see the same ancient face from before now restored. I said, "Thank you. You are very kind."

He looked at the group in the kitchen and asked, "How is the food coming kid?" The guy in the kitchen replied, "All that we have to do now is put it on the tables."

And with that, Holy Alex, said "Well let's get to it. I'm hungry, how about everybody else?"

And the whole building shook as everybody screamed, "Yeah," in unison. Alex and all of us began grabbing food and stocking tables.

And when the food was all laid out and dished out, there we were Chartreuse, me, Josh, and even Lazarus at Holy Alex's table.

I was to learn later on, that this was quite an honor, and virtually unheard of for newcomers. But for some reason Holy Alex himself had taken a shine to us.

He was an amazing man, and over the next week and a half, or so, I learned a lot from him. Everything from simple parlor tricks, to some of the most amazing things that I've ever seen.

Of course, as Alex put it, simple tricks are easy. But amazing things take years and sometimes decades to learn.

For instance Alex told me that it took him 12 years in India, and Tibet studying with various monks and gurus to learn how to do things like change his face, body, and even clothing, at will. They also taught him how to slow his heart rate down to the point that his heart appeared to have stopped, and then bring the rate back up to normal at will.

There was another amazing feat which he demonstrated for me, while we were there. Supposedly in the 20 or so years that he purported to have lived in the Far East, he had learned the art of telekinesis as well, which he demonstrated for me one day in the woods, by moving an 8 foot piece of log with his mind.

He also had an amazing ability to communicate with animals, seemingly on their level. Which I learned is how Josh was able to call the Osprey Eagle down from the sky and have it land on his arm as he kissed it on the forehead in front of me, when he was stoned on acid at the chain lakes months earlier.

The people at the commune said that just two weeks earlier, when Alex first arrived for this visit, a giant grizzly bear like the one that tore up Brian and David's commune, and killed and wounded so many of their animals, before they could kill it, had wandered into this commune doing a lot of damage. That is, until Alex grabbed a honey pot from the kitchen, and calmly walked out to the bear dressed in nothing but his robe.

It was just after dawn. One of the guys from the commune ran out with a rifle, but Alex told him to put away the gun and get back inside. They said that Alex walked calmly towards the bear that was obviously agitated, and was just starting to tear up the chicken coop as the chickens screamed and clucked.

And all that Alex did was whistle loudly to get the Bears

attention, which he did. The giant bear left the chicken coop and ran towards Alex, letting out a loud fearsome roar. And then Alex bowed his head, while holding the honey pot in his left hand, he stuck his right arm straight out in front of him, with his hand up as if to say stop; and the giant bear who was still coming, began a cartoon like backpedal until finally managing to come to a halt, stopping so close to Alex that his muzzle was only inches away from Alex's face, that's when Alex raised his head back up.

    They said that when Alex raised his head, that he kissed the bear on the snout, and lowering his right hand, he began to pet the bear who was sitting up on his rump now. Then they said, as Alex put the honey pot up to the grizzly bears mouth with his left hand, and the giant bear began to lick the honey pot, the bear's roars and growls had turned into a combination of moans, and purrs, as the giant grizzly lapped away at the honey pot. Alex slowly put the honey pot on to the ground allowing the bear to follow the honey pot to the ground.
    Now up on all fours, the humongous bear continued to happily lick away at the honey pot.
    Alex supposedly gave the giant grizzly bear a big hug around the neck as it lapped up the honey, and then casually walked away, telling everyone to stay inside for a little while, and that everything would be fine.
    They said that after the bear finished the honey, he calmly walked into the woods and had not been seen or heard from since.

    I must admit that Holy Alex was definitely one of the most extraordinary characters that I've ever met in my life. And one of the people that I met while up there, that I will always regret not being able to spend more time with.

Chapter 15

A few more days at the Calgary commune, then a short stop at the House of Che, and then back to Michael's again

We decided to stay at the commune for a few more days so that Josh could ride back with us to Brian and David's and then back to Michael's for a rest. I soon learned that Chartreuse was what you might call a switch hitter.

We met a very pretty curly haired blonde at the commune, named Samantha. Everyone called her Sam. She and Chartreuse hit it right off.

Within a few hours of meeting Sam I could tell that there was something going on between the two of them. I don't know how to explain it, but I could tell there was quite an attraction going on there. And right about that time Billy came in saying that Holy Alex was looking for me.

So I excused myself, made my escape, and left them to their own devices, knowing that when I came back the whole thing would have sorted itself out most likely.

Billy led me through the woods on a 10 minute climb, until we were high and far away enough above the commune that the build and tents looked small. And then suddenly there was Alex sitting in the middle of a clearing cross legged in that kind of yoga position that he usually sat in.

He asked me to come over and sit down, and told Billy he could go back. I sat down next to him and asked him what I could do for him. He replied, "It's more like what I can do for you."

And I replied, "I'm all ears." He said, "Good." He rubbed his hands together like people do in the winter when they're cold. Then he turned them towards the sun and held his palms up towards the sun.

That's when he asked me to put out my right hand, and he grabbed my right hand with his right hand while putting his left hand on the back of my neck. My body became kind of numb and tingly.

He started to chuckle. And then he said, "You really have nothing to worry about unless, that is, you let your head and your heart get in the way. You know jealousy is evils' manservant, and the prime slayer of love.

I looked at him puzzled and asked, "I am sorry to ask, but what are you talking about?"

Alex smiled, and chuckled again saying, "I'm sorry. Did I misread your thoughts? Weren't you just thinking about Chartreuse and Sam? And whether or not they like each other sexually? And if they are going to have sex before you get back to camp? And if so is Chartreuse going to leave you for Sam?"

I was stunned. I stared at Alex with my eyes wide open, and my mouth agape. Billy told me on the way up, that Alex had been up there since early morning meditating.

So I immediately asked, "Did Billy tell you?" Alex replied, "No. You did. That's what you were thinking about just now."

So being me, I asked him, "Can you do that again?" He replied, "Sure." I asked him to give me a minute to compose my thoughts, and he said that would be fine.

I thought to myself, "I'm gonna come up with something really far out to see if this is bullshit or not." What I came up with was realizing that I had never mentioned my Sunbeam Tiger sports car to anyone in Canada or even Josh for that matter, so there's no way that he could have known about it.

So I began to think about driving. And cleaning my Sunbeam Tiger, and picturing that in my mind.

Then I told Alex I was ready, so he rubbed his hands together held his palms towards the sun, shook my right hand, while putting his left hand on my neck again.

This time the sensation was stronger, and I closed my eyes for a moment.

When I opened them again and looked towards him, and he appeared to be levitating with his arms folded and his legs still in the yoga position.

However I could still feel his right hand holding my right hand and his left hand still on my neck. I closed my eyes again and when I opened them this time everything was back to normal.

He pulled his hands away and said, "I don't know why? But you were remembering driving a little green sports car late at night with the top down. And then you were washing the car, and cleaning the interior the emblem on the side said Sunbeam Tiger." I was stunned.

Again I asked him, "You can read minds?"

He replied, "Not minds, thoughts. It's a little trick I picked up from a guru in Nepal. He was a very interesting fellow, "A Breath-Arian." "A what," I asked?

Alex replied, "He didn't require food or water to live."

"Jesus," was my shocked reply.

Alex continued, "Yeah. Just like Jesus."

I continued, "So not to change the subject, but since you know about Chartreuse and Sam. What should I do?"

Alex replied," Right back on topic; I like that; most of these kids would have me talking about what it is to be a Breatharian for hours. But not you Bob. You're right back on topic, and asking for guidance. Good for you. The simple answer has already been given to you. But I'll clarify it for you.

I could see in your thoughts that Chartreuse and Sam are attracted to one another. What you have to do is trust Chartreuse enough to encourage that relationship.

When you get back to camp suggest that the three of you sit together in the big hall for dinner. And then suggest that the three of you go back to your camper to get high, play music or whatever comes to mind. And after a while take your dog for a long walk.

When you come back, you and your dog get into the cab of the truck quietly, and then see what happens. Trust me. You won't be sorry."

That's when Alex jumped up and started yelling, "Look. Look; Mallards heading west." Within a second, he started quacking loudly over and over again with his hands cupped around his mouth sounding like the best duck call that I ever heard.

The huge flock of ducks began to come our way getting lower and lower as they approached us. Now he alternately waved his arms, and then cupped his hands around his mouth again making loud, and different quacking sounds.

The ducks circled overhead no more than 100 feet or so above us, close enough for both of us to be splattered at least once by duck feces. Then giving one last loud quack he flailed his arms toward the northeast and the ducks flew off in that direction.

When they were far enough away that I felt I could be heard again, I asked him, "What the hell was that?"

He replied, "That was what I've been waiting for up here since early morning. I knew those mallards were coming by us heading west today, and I needed to tell them to fly north of certain lakes on their way west to avoid the hunters in those lakes. We just saved a third or so of that flock of ducks. And that's a lot of ducks, my friend." He began to laugh, and hugged me, jumping up and down, while he hugged me, and suddenly I felt as elated as he did.

There we were, two crazy fools jumping up and down in the middle of the clearing, and I felt like I was on top of the world. We walked back to camp together, him regaling me with tales of exploits in India, Tibet, South America, etc.

That night I did exactly as Alex had instructed me, and sure enough Chartreuse Sam and I wound up back in my camper. We all got high, sang, and drank wine. And then I took Lazarus for a long walk, and when we got back, I quietly opened the door to the cab and putting Lazarus in first, I sat quietly in the passenger seat while Lazarus curled up in the driver's seat.

I must admit that it was pretty tough at first listening to the passionate moaning, alternately coming from both ladies. But thank God, Alex had gotten my mind right, and prepared me.

It was quite late and after about an hour of listening to the girls going at it, and, I must admit masturbating for a while, but falling asleep before I came.

The next thing I knew, I was being shaken awake. It was Chartreuse. She asked, "What are you doing up here?" And looking down and seeing my hand on my cock, she said, "Oh, that's what you were doing. We can help you out with that. Come on back and join us. We were about to go looking for you. We were worried." I replied, "I thought that you guys might want to be alone." Chartreuse said, "No. We want you with us. So I said, "Cool."

I raced back with her and climbed in to the camper so fast that I forgot to put my cock back in to my pants before I climbed in. Chartreuse said, "Wow. You've still got your cock out. You must be horny."

said, "Whoops". And I started stuffing my manhood back into my fly.

Chartreuse said, "Oh my God, you poor thing. You were up in the cab listening to us and jerking off." Sam said sadly "We must have been torturing the poor guy, without even knowing it." Now I began to take my clothes off, all of them. Replying, "Well, at least I fell asleep before I ever came."

Both Chartreuse and Sam replied in unison; "Good." And Chartreuse said, "Now get under the covers."

Which I did, and both ladies proceeded to have their way with me.

Even now, some 37 years later, I still occasionally re-live that night in my dreams.

With me watching Sam's flowing curly blond hair flying around in the pale candlelight as she bounced up and down on top of me. And I can still recall the smell of patchouli oil and Indian incense in the air, and taking turns making love to one girl while fingering the other; with both girls going down on me together, and me going down on them over and over.

I know that I came at least six times, and when I told them that the next morning, they both asked, "Only six times." I guess that says it all.

By the time we got up it was late, so late that Lazarus crawled through the crawlspace from the cab into the camper crying to go out. He had to go so bad that when I opened the camper shell door, and put down the tailgate, he started peeing while he was jumping out of the camper.

Then we all hugged and kissed. And I told the ladies that that was one of the greatest nights of my life, and that I loved them both. They both smiled and cried a little and we kissed and hugged again, and then we got dressed.

We were all hungry so we headed to the kitchen to get some food, and I rounded up Lazarus on the way.

We ran into Josh in the longhouse, in the great hall. He sat down with us while we ate our breakfast.

And of course the first thing out of his mouth was, "It's time to go. I've done all I can do here for now."

A little irritated I said, "You know Josh, life as we know it really does not revolve around you."

Josh being Josh replied, "In this case Bob it really does. There are a lot of people in a lot of different places that depend on me. But you're right. If you want to stay here, that's fine. I can find another ride back to Brian and David's and then Michael's. But I've got to go. I have shit to do.

Oh, by the way. Some guy rolled in this morning, and he likes your truck. And he asked me if you'd like to trade it?"

I asked, "For what?" "He's got a 71 Land Cruiser. The sucker looks almost new." Josh replied. And I jumped up yelling, "What? Where the hell is he?"

"You should've seen the Land Cruiser on the way up here. It's a tan four-door. And he should be close by.

"Wait; there he is." Josh yelled to a guy across the room, "Hey Pete. This is my friend Bob that owns the Willys." With that, the dark-haired bearded guy with a camouflage jacket and a John Deere baseball cap ran over, introductions were made, and we walked outside to discuss the possible transaction.

When I saw the Toyota Land Cruiser I couldn't believe my eyes. It was hard to keep a poker face and hide the excitement. I thought for sure he was going to notice my heart about to pound out of my chest.

He inspected my truck and said he really liked it, and of course asked if I had done all the work myself. I fought off the urge to vomit after hearing the same thing that I had heard from everyone that I had encountered on the trip so far.

At this point it looked like he was willing to do an even swap. All that was left was for each of us to drive the other ones' vehicle. And then we would drive back to Vancouver and go across into Washington, to do a transfer of titles.

I drove his Land Cruiser first and of course it drove beautifully.

When he took my Jeep out onto the highway it wouldn't go into overdrive. The overdrive solenoid was gone again. When I explained that it was the solenoid and I could get it fixed for him in Calgary, he asked the dreaded question, "Has this ever happened before?"

I couldn't lie to him. "Yes," I said. "It's a 1953 vehicle, and, even though everything on this truck is new. Engine, transmission, rear end, electrical system, I must admit that I did replace the overdrive solenoid before I left LA, and then again in San Luis Obispo and now it looks like it's out again. However, it's not a real expensive item." And that was that.

He decided to pass on the trade. And I must admit that a little while later, had I made that trade, I might have died in the wilderness.

We invited Sam to come back with us, but she wanted to stay at the commune for a little while longer. So I got the solenoid repaired in Calgary (after all of that, it was nothing but a loose wire that took a few minutes to fix.)

So after one more night of passionate love making with Sam, and Chartreuse, I rounded up Josh, and the three of us and Lazarus were headed back to Clinton BC, and the House of Che.

When we got to Brian and David's we didn't stay very long.

There was kind of a strange vibe about the place. Everyone seemed restless and nervous; even all the dogs were on edge. I asked David what was going on, and he said that he didn't know for sure, but some weird shit had been happening early in the morning before daylight, for the last couple of days, and that they had lost a couple of dogs. But he knew it wasn't animals, because the dogs just disappeared; with no blood, no signs, no nothing, just gone.

That was enough for me. As tired as we all were, I told Josh that if he wanted to stay, he could. But that Chartreuse and Lazarus and I were either going to go into Clinton and stay the night, or if possible drive all the way to Michael's.

Josh tried to get us to stay, saying that I was being silly, etc., but I held to my guns, made my apologies to David and Brian, and finally Josh begrudgingly gave in, and left with us.

We gassed up in Clinton around 5:00 pm and decided to push on to Michael's in Vancouver. It started to get dark between 8:00 and 9:00 pm so we pulled off the highway into a roadside turn out or rest stop if you will, and slept there for the night, leaving for Michael's place the next morning. We got into Michael's about 10:00 am.

Nobody answered at the gate, however luckily Josh had a key that would open it automatically. (And so we were in. That worked out well for us later on, as well.) When we pulled up to the Mansion there were a lot of cars, but no customary noise.

I looked at Josh and Chartreuse, and said, "Something isn't right. It's too quiet." They agreed.

But we decided to investigate anyway. When we walked in, there were people lying everywhere.

At first we didn't know if they were dead or alive. Was this a massive OD? Or the aftermath of an all-night party?

All of a sudden a naked girl sprawled in front us on one of the tapestry couch's let out a loud snort and rolled over. This disturbed five or six other people causing them to move as well. And the three of us breathed a unified sigh of relief.

And with that Chartreuse and I settled in the cloud bedroom which was empty, (after I walked Lazarus of course.) Josh went out to the pool house, I found out later.

When I came back into bed with Chartreuse after walking Lazarus, I remember thinking, "Wow. She sure feels good. So soft, and warm, such a perfect fit."

When I think about it these days, I know for sure now. That she was one of at least ten or twelve ladies that got away during that period of my life. Because I was young and arrogant, and no matter how good the girl that I was with was, she could never beat the next girl to come along.

Ah, the perils of a misspent youth, but ah the fun. I only wish that I could turn the clock back and do it all again. I of course would do it all again in a heartbeat.

The only thing different that I might hope for, would be that at some point I would have had the common sense to settle down with one of them.

Chapter 16

Back to Michael's, for lots of R and R, and Sex, Drugs and Rock 'n Roll the Michael way. Full throttle and balls to the wall!

So we were back at Michael's. Chartreuse and I had taken refuge in and were sleeping in the cloud room as it was called, because of the large sky filled with clouds mural that was painted on the ceiling, while Josh had gone to sleep in the pool house. The entire place was filled with naked and half naked people still sound asleep and passed out, obviously from the previous night's debauchery.

As I slept soundly having a wonderful dream about sex with multiple beautiful women, I felt Chartreuse's warm body leave my side as she got out of bed. This did not faze me however, as in my dream I was having sex with three beautiful women. A few moments later

I felt Chartreuse come back into bed and go under the covers and start giving me head. I remember thinking in my REM sleep state, how thoughtful and considerate of her to do this for me while I was with three other women. Also the oral sex was amazingly good and within a few minutes I was coming. As I moaned with pleasure I heard a large group of people laughing, and then to my right at the bathroom door, I heard Chartreuse scream out, "What the fuck is going on here."

And then the three women in my dream were gone and I was rising up in bed with my eyes wide open.

The cloud room was filled with people, with Michael in the forefront, standing at the foot of the bed naked with nothing on but an opened robe. I looked to my left and saw Chartreuse staring at me in bed with an angry look on her face. Just then the covers flew off and a very pretty young girl lifted off of my crotch wiping her mouth. The crowd in the room spurred on by Michael began to laugh uproariously again.

I looked pleadingly at Chartreuse saying, "But honey, I thought it was you."

Before Chartreuse could reply Michael blurted out, "Jesus Bob. how domestic of you. Don't tell me that you kids went and got married in Calgary, finally ending all of my hopes for the both of you."

Chartreuse didn't say a word. She just adjusted her towel marching back into the bathroom, and mumbled something to the effect of, "Michael, you are such an asshole."

Michael pointed to the pretty young girl and said, "Bob. I would like you to meet Glenda." The pretty young girl put out her hand and I shook it, as she began to grin. Michael continued, "She's quite good isn't she? I hope that I didn't get you into too much trouble? But you have to admit that if you look at it objectively; the whole thing was quite funny, wasn't it. And besides I've never known Chartreuse to ever hold a grudge. That's one of the reasons I like her, and you, I might add. So, it's 3:30 let's all have lunch."

Michael and all the people clambered out of the room, and I went into the bathroom to talk to Chartreuse. I went to open the bathroom door and it was locked. I knocked on the door and asked Chartreuse if she was okay. She sounded upset and replied, "I'm fine. Just leave me alone.

"You know I thought it was you, right?" I asked, she replied, "I'm not blaming you.

It's just that I was really enjoying us just being together. And now we're back at Michael's, and you know that that's all going to change."

I asked, "Why?" She replied, "Because here at Michael's, there will always be a prettier girl, a sexier girl; who gives better head, etc. and I can't compete with all of that."

I replied, "Why do you think any of that stuff matters to me?"

She shouted back through the door angrily, "Because you're a man, you asshole." I remember thinking at the time, "Well. She's got me there."

Realizing that there was no way to console her, I told her that I was going down to have breakfast with the others, and that I would see her down there. She replied, "Whatever."

I figured at this point that the best thing that I could do would be to show her a lot of affection in front of the others.

But I must admit that when I went downstairs, while I was talking to Josh I had a hard time taking my eyes off of Glenda who was really beautiful and had just given me some of the best oral sex that I had ever had. About midway through our conversation Josh asked me, "Where the hell are you man? You're sure not listening too me."

Turning around Josh saw Glenda just as she smiled at me, and I smiled back.

Josh said, "So she is as good as they say she is. And now the little head is thinking for the big head, huh. Bob! If you do this, and we both know you're going to do this. You're going to break her heart; and I mean Chartreuse, not Glenda."

Now, suddenly the angel on my right shoulder, devil on my left shoulder moment came. The little angel on my right shoulder was screaming, "Chartreuse is a great girl. And she loves you. You don't want to hurt her." And the little devil on my left shoulder was screaming, "But just look at her. What a fox.
She's hotter than shit, and Michael hasn't laid claim to her yet. And she just gave you the best head that you've ever gotten, and she's smiling back at you. So even if Michael put her up to sucking your cock. She obviously enjoyed it, so what are you waiting for? Forget Chartreuse, you know that you're not going to settle down with her. Admit it. Chartreuse knows what's up; she just explained that to you through the bathroom door. So get in there and get some of this hot new girl who likes you, you asshole."

I must admit that the two voices in my head, combined with Josh chattering away at me forced me into a kind of mental shutdown.

I just turned and looked at the wall until Josh got fed up and got up from the table and walked away.

I sat there for a while just focusing on the same tapestry hanging on the wall which had a picture of some 16th or 17th century children that were playing with dogs in a meadow. I was thinking to myself, "I wish that I were in that meadow with those children right now, running and playing with the dogs. No worries, no cares.

And then the little devil on my left shoulder screamed at me. "Hey, dumb ass, wake up. You have two beautiful horny women after you, and you want to run away and play with imaginary children and dogs in an imaginary field somewhere? What are you, an Idiot, why don't you get with the program?"

I looked back over at Glenda. And that's when Chartreuse sat down in front of me blocking my view.

She leaned across the table and kissed me on the lips softly and said, "I'm sorry baby. That was not your fault. Michael can be such a dickhead sometimes. I shouldn't have taken it out on you, haven't you eaten yet?"

I replied, "No, I was talking to Josh. Let's get some food." As we walked into the kitchen I noticed Glenda smiling at me, and I smiled back at her as Chartreuse and I walked past her.

We finished breakfast, and walked into the huge living room were a lot of people had gathered.

Michael was doing one of his rants, which he did from time to time. Everyone seemed to enjoy them, because even though they were always a little off kilter, they were usually very funny, and sometimes quite insightful.

In this one Michael was ranting on and on about how unfair it was that women can seem to climax over and over again and still do things like stay awake, climax again immediately, and (most importantly to him anyway) they have the ability to go to the bathroom immediately after climax. A man will usually fall asleep almost immediately upon climaxing without the use of certain drugs. And a man has to wait 30 minutes to an hour on average before he can climax again. And he has to wait 5 to 15 minutes after climax before he can urinate. And seeing that within 5 to 15 minutes of climaxing he has usually fallen asleep, that means that he either has to wake up one to three hours later and go and piss, or if he's really loaded, or passed out, he has to piss the bed. All of these things according to Michael gave women an unfair advantage.

Of course it was a lot funnier with Michael telling it. So funny that the 60 or so people in the room, both men and women were laughing as much as I've ever seen with any stand-up comedian in a comedy club. And then, of course, the room broke into applause.

Michael, upon hearing the applause, bowed and turning his back to the audience, bent over and threw his robe up over his back, mooning the crowd and exposing his genitals, which seemed to hang from his buttocks like some sort of strange misshapen

Christmas ornaments, and the crowd howled with laughter again.

Michael turned back to the crowd asking, "So what do you want to do now kids?"

And people started shouting out suggestions, "Let's go to the beach." Michael replied, "Too cold." Someone yelled out, "Let's all get high."

Michael replied scornfully, "Of course we're going to get high. That's not a suggestion, next." Someone yelled out, "Let's go out and play with the animals." Michael replied, "That's more like it. But don't try and ride the zebra, and don't fuck with the ostrich, or the kangaroo or someone's going to get hurt like last time.

And people, please, absolutely no psychedelics or uppers, if you want to do those drugs, then stay in the house and listen to music or lay in the sun by the pool. If you are going to play with the animals, just weed, and light downers, okay?"

And with that the large group broke out bags of marijuana, and popped pills, and began moving out through the back of the house in a large formation behind Michael who was always in the lead.

As the large group of hippies in various states of undress, smoking marijuana, drinking champagne, popping pills etc. talked amongst themselves while following Michael out of the back of the house; Chartreuse and I stayed where we were in the living room watching the merry band leave.

Chartreuse looked at me with this sort of disgusted expression saying, "That Michael. He always has to run things. He's like a ringmaster in the circus, or something."

I don't know why I said it, but I replied, "Well. It is his circus. Maybe that's why they call it Michael's Flying Circus." Chartreuse, now a little angry, asked, "Are you taking his side. Oh my God. You're starting to look up to that asshole, aren't you?"

I replied, "Chartreuse. The man is a multimillionaire, who can have, or do just about anything he wants. And yeah, I'll give you the fact that from time to time he can be an asshole. But considering his position, he's usually pretty fair, he can be very funny, he's quite smart, and I hate to break it to you, but all in all over the last few months that I've gotten to know the guy, I have grown to like him a lot."

Chartreuse's face began to redden. Her voice began to rise

and she replied angrily, "So I guess it doesn't bother you that he had an intimate relationship with me for a year and a half and then when the first new super-hot girl came along, he dumped me and then handed me off to you as a present."

I replied, "Well I guess it doesn't bother me as much as it bothers you."

Chartreuse was now staring daggers at me. As I continued, "And besides, that's not the way I remember it. As I remember it, Michael didn't hand you off to me as a present at all. He started fucking a new girl, and you and I hit it off after you and I and Michael and the new girl had a four-way together. Remember?

However, none of that has anything to do with the way that I feel about you, or Michael, or that new girl of Michael's who has already left here, and moved on now."

Chartreuse began to calm down some. Putting down the table lamp that she was about to hit me with she said, "Wow. You're right Bob. I was jealous of Michael and angry at him for dumping me. And I was jealous and afraid of losing you to that new girl, Glenda. I saw the look on your face as she made you come this morning, and I've never been able to put that expression on your face when I have blown you. And she has me worried." Chartreuse looked sadly down at the floor.

I jumped over and sat right next to her on the couch. I put my right arm around her, and with my left hand I lifted her face up to mine, a tear trickled from her left eye. I kissed her, and we hugged, and I said, "Look baby, there's something you need to understand,

Glenda, as pretty as she is, as good as she gives head, isn't the threat here. She will never ever change how I feel about you.

The real threat here, if there is one, is our age, and our lifestyle; you see as much as I care about you, I'm not ready to settle down. To be honest with you I don't know if I'll ever settle down. (How prophetic that statement was.) I can only guarantee you one thing honestly. And that is that if I do have sex with Glenda, I won't leave you for her. I'm not Michael.

You see baby when you get down to it, the companionship, the conversation, and the fact that you feel awesome just lying next to me in bed, trumps anything that she can do to me sexually.

So I may sleep with her, but I won't stay with her. And if it makes you feel more comfortable the three of us can do a three-way. And that way when the sex is all done, and we all fall asleep together, me cuddled up to you, with my arms around you, and her cuddled up to me on the other side, then maybe you'll finally understand what I'm talking about."

Chartreuse looked into my eyes and said, "Okay, Bob, whatever you say. Just take me right here, right now." I said, "Right here, in the living room? We've never done it out in the open like that before. What if they all come back in?"

She replied, "Who cares, let 'em watch. I hope that it's Glenda, so I can show her a thing or two." We both laughed, and started shedding our clothes. I don't know if it was the dangerous quality of doing it in that huge open living room, where anyone could walk in at any time, or what. But that was some of the best sex we ever had. And we started doing it more often at Michael's to his happy amazement, and encouragement.

One aspect of our semi-public sexual antics was Michael's affinity for video-taping people who were making love without their knowledge or consent; it was something that he lived for, kind of an addiction. However he was not content with just videoing people's sexual encounters without their knowledge, he also loved to play them on the big-screen TV in front of a packed room of people with no warning.

The next day, for instance, Chartreuse and I were in the packed living room with 50 or 60 people, some eating, some getting high, some watching the big-screen, and playing board games, etc.

Chartreuse and I were sitting on the couch talking, and then she pointed at the big-screen, shouting, "Look at that". I turned to look at the screen to see what appeared to be an out of focus ass hole, and a bouncing pair of testicles.

I laughed and commented, "Wow, that son of a bitch is really getting after it, and those are some big hairy balls, and he's really giving it to that girl, I wish we could see her face, listen to her moan."

Right then the camera panned back and moved to the side.

The entire room broke into uproarious laughter, some people laughing so hard that they fell off of their seats and onto the floor.

You see, as the camera moved to the side and panned in on the couple's faces, it was me and Chartreuse from a few months back.

Upon seeing this my face was as red as a McIntosh apple. But after a few moments of embarrassment, Chartreuse and I began to laugh as hard as everyone else. After all it was very funny, even though it's a little harder to laugh with your foot in your mouth.

A few days later we had our three-way with Glenda and it was amazing, and it ended just the way I predicted it would.

However the one aspect that I could not predict was that Glenda continued to share our bed for another week and a half until she left Michael's with a group of kids heading down to Oregon, where she was from. You see, the one thing that I never thought of in my prediction was that Glenda was as good at giving a woman head as she was a man. And I must admit that I never could put a smile on Chartreuse's face as good as Glenda, or later on Amber could.

If I were to meet another Glenda or Chartreuse, or Amber, or Kathleen, etc., today I would settle down in a heartbeat. Ah. Those woulda, coulda, shoulda moments in time? I think that we've all had our share of those in our past.

After all, I'm sure that that is the reason that God gave us all a memory, because if you are one of those people that does not believe that God has a sense of humor, then you must not watch the news, know anything about history, or have never read any religious manuscripts.

Chapter 17

Back to the House of Che, and a life-Changing Meeting with a Brother of the shields

After almost a month at Michael's, Josh was getting cabin fever. And I must admit that as much fun as it was at Michael's I was ready for a change as well; maybe partially because as much as I liked her, Chartreuse was getting a little clingy. So Josh and I decided to head back to Clinton and the House of Che, to look in on Brian and David and their people.

Of course Chartreuse wanted to go with me, but I pointed out that it was too dangerous and the weather was getting cold, and that she would be better off and safer staying at Michael's. I also pointed out that we wouldn't be gone for that long. So she finally acquiesced. And Josh, and Lazarus and I were on our way back up to Clinton.

We stopped in Clinton to gas up and buy supplies. We decided to buy 10 half gallons of assorted ice cream and ice it in coolers as a present for the gang at the House of Che, seeing that ice cream was such a rare treat for them. So there we were heading up the logging roads out of Clinton toward the commune. I was driving, and smoking a joint, Lazarus was up in the opening between the camper and the truck cab, and Josh was working on his second half-gallon of ice cream.

The radio was blasting Jimmy Hendrix' "Foxy Lady." That radio station was doing a Hendrix marathon. I asked Josh, "You're such a little guy. Where the hell are you putting all of that ice cream?"

Josh replied, "You don't really believe that we are gonna get to eat any of those ten half-gallons iced in the camper do you? Those folks probably haven't had any sweets in at least a month. They're gonna be like a pack of wolverines in a butcher shop, when it comes to that ice cream." I laughed and said, "Maybe you're right. But that still doesn't answer the question of where you put all of that ice cream. What've you got, a hollow leg or something."

With no obstacles like fallen trees or washouts on the logging roads we made good time and got to the commune around 2:30 PM. that afternoon.

We got the normal greeting from a pack of 100 or so assorted dogs barking loudly, and a new guy that we hadn't seen before coming toward the truck with a rifle. I remember thinking, "Oh great. Shot by some newbie that doesn't know us. Wonderful."

But before either Josh or I could say anything, David yelled loudly over the barking dogs at the guy. "Put down that gun. You dumb son of a bitch. That's Bob and Josh. What an idiot."

Then he yelled even louder, "Dogs..." And the entire massive pack of dogs went silent in an instant.

It became so quiet that you could actually hear the wind in the trees. Until the newbie spoke up saying to David, "I'm sorry I didn't know." David said, "Don't apologize to me; apologize to them." Which he did, and we shook his hand and said that it was fine.

David came up with a big grin on his face, grabbed us both gave us a big hug, and said, "Good to see you guys. We've missed you. Can you tell we've been busy while you were gone? We've put up two more corrals, four new outbuildings, and a big new stone barbecue.

And on that note, your timing is impeccable, because in a couple of hours were firing up the barbecue, for barbecue venison, and chicken, along with baked potatoes, corn on the cob, and we traded the neighbors for four elderberry pies and a 5-gallon jug of elderberry wine. And we have all of the Alaskan Thunder Fuck that you can smoke.

So tonight in your honor, we are going to party hardy. Yee haa!"

I replied, "And we brought you guys 10 half-gallons of assorted ice cream as a present."

David replied, "Cool, man, cool." David screamed out toward the camp, "Hey everybody, we've got ice cream for the party." And everyone within ear shot let out a big cheer in unison. David continued, "And we can put it in our new underground ice house / cold storage room." I replied, "Cool, man, cool."

We grabbed the coolers and carried them into the cold storage room. It had a 6-inch thick door with huge iron hinges that took two guys to open; and hand hewn log stairs that went down into a 15'x15' excavation, with rock and mortar walls and gently sloped tin roofing with tar paper underneath, and 12" thick sod for a roof over the tin and tar paper.

I was quite impressed with the construction and the fact that it was the middle of a warm sunny afternoon, and you could still see your breath when you were down in it.

I asked where they were getting all of the materials from. David said, "We still get a lot of stuff from the dump. But we are making surprisingly good money from the horses, and one of our new guys is great with leather, and he's been selling stuff in Clinton and chipping in most of that. But we are doing really well selling and trading weed for stuff."

I replied, "Isn't that a little risky?"

David replied, "Not the way we do it. We're growing acres of the stuff along streams and around the remote chain lakes. We plant and harvest on horseback. We lose about 15% to critters, mostly deer. But we still average between 30 and 60 pounds a summer. So no more cold hungry winters my brother.

We sell it five – 15 pounds at a time to a friend who pays us a good price for it. Then he goes and sells it in cities to the east of us, and when he comes back for more he gives us a percentage of what he sold on top of what he has paid us already when he pays for the next batch. So we're doing good brother."

My next question was, "What if he gets caught. Won't you guys be in trouble?"

David laughed, "You guys right out of the states are so paranoid. Bob, the guy has already been caught twice. This isn't America; both times that he got caught he just paid a fine. And he would never rat us out. He's our brother, and more importantly he's not gonna kill the golden goose." I replied, "Cool. You've obviously have got it covered."

I helped fire up the barbecue, and that night we had a hell of a party, with lights and electricity no less. The boys had come up with the money for a generator, string lights, and even lights in the main buildings.

I was truly impressed. The food was great, the wine was passable, the weed was awesome, and the entire small community ate, laughed, danced, got loaded, and generally had a grand old time into the wee hours of the night.

Brian pulled me aside during the festivities in order to point out the three or four new girls that were single to me. They were all decent looking and one was really cute.

I don't know what it was, whether it was Chartreuse in the back of my mind, or just that all of the sex at Michael's over the last month or so, had worn me out, but I decided to call it a night early, and walk Lazarus and then just go back to the camper and read. I had been reading Hyemeyohsts Storm's book, "Seven Arrows," a book about the trials of the Great Plains tribes, and North American Indian religion. And the Brothers of the Shield, which were the Native American Indians version of the priesthood; it is a fascinating book, and I finished it about 2:00 am.

Josh woke me up about 10:00 am the next morning. They were having breakfast in the main house.

David and Brian wanted to show us the rest of the things they had built, and all of the new things that they had purchased, traded for, and found discarded at the Clinton junkyard/dump.

They showed us the belt driven portable lumber mill that they had purchased and hooked up to the rear wheel of a VW Bug to drive it. With it they claimed that they could now mill any size of lumber from beams to fencing material.

David's old lady was really proud of a large hand carved Victorian era four-poster bed that David had found at the Clinton dump.

They also found an old working Victrola hand cranked from 1904 and four boxes of old wax cylinders that still played fine.

One of the cylinders that I got a kick out of was Rudy Vallee's old hit from the late twenties, "Your Time is My Time." Mostly because both David and Brian hated it;

Once I found out that fact, I would wait until they were in the middle of some job that they couldn't stop right away for safety reasons, (like setting a beam, or lifting a newly framed wall) and then I would crank up the Victrola, put on that song, aim the megaphone in their direction and wait until I saw them come running towards the house.

And then I would snatch the cylinder off the player and run and hide, so that they couldn't break it.

I did it over and over again, until David threatened to smash the Victrola. I knew how much his old lady loved that thing, so I finally stopped doing it.

But I kept the cylinder. I hid it in my camper and brought it back to LA with me. Every once in a while to this day, I will think about that twangy voice singing "Your time is my time, my time is your time." and just start laughing out loud.

The walls of the commune buildings were adorned with numerous oil paintings picked from the dump with nicely carved wood frames. And they took us out to the tool shed and showed us an assortment of nice tools they also had picked from the dump.

That was the final straw for me, because I did need some tools. And I announced to the guys that I was going to head down to the Clinton dump right away.

Josh wanted to go on one of his week or so long walkabouts anyway. So that morning Lazarus and I headed towards Clinton, and the dump.

We arrived at the Clinton dump a little after 1PM. I was surprised that on a weekday there was no one there. It was obvious that people had been dumping there for a while.

The dump was large for a small town. I would guess about 40 yards in diameter or more.

Lazarus ran ahead of me in the dump, and would come back to me when I would find something that looked interesting, or an area that looked worth digging in.

Right off I picked up an old framed photo of a horse and rider dated 1932.

And when I set it aside to keep, I noticed what appeared to be a toolbox underneath some scrap that lay under the picture. It took me about 15 minutes to resurrect the toolbox, but it was a real score, filled with all kinds of great tools, a lot of which I needed. I set it with the picture, and then Lazarus ran up to me seeming kind of agitated.

I asked him what the matter was, and he just looked at me anxiously and kind of whimpered.

Suddenly off in the distance I heard a high-pitched sound. "Wheeeeuhhh Wheeeet. Wheeeeeuhhh Wheeeeet." Way on the other side of the dump

I could see what appeared at a distance to be an elderly gray-haired Indian woman in buck skins with fringe, waving to me and yelling out this weird high-pitched cry.

I waved back and Lazarus and I started making our way across the dump to meet the strange individual.

As we got closer I could see that it was a gray-long haired Indian man that greeted me.

Lazarus got to him before I did and the old man leaned down and petted Lazarus on the head. Lazarus seemed to mellow out right away as soon as the old man touched him, and as soon as the old man stopped petting him, Lazarus sat and stared focusing on the old man and forgetting about me; the only other time that Lazarus had done that before was with Holy Alex.

When I saw this reaction I remember thinking to myself, this is gonna be a trip.

As I got within 10 feet of the old man I could see his dark wrinkled sun beaten chiseled face, his ax-like nose, his gray eyes which seemed to look right through you, his long spindly wrinkled spider like fingers that reached out towards me as he extended his hand in friendship, a cracked crooked smile on his face accentuated by numerous wrinkled lines that cascaded from the corners of his mouth onto his jaw and up under his cheeks almost like the lines in the feathers of a peacock's tail.

As I put my hand into his hand to shake it, I decided to give him a firm handshake; however his grip was much stronger than mine. But as soon as I released my grip he released his. "Indian one, paleface zero", I thought.

In a very low soft gritty, almost whisper of a voice he said, "How are you doing today, my son? A beautiful day to go a junkin' isn't it. You white people sure throwaway a lot of good stuff."

I replied, "Apparently so. My name is Bob, nice to meet you."

He replied, "My name is Little Bear, but you can call me Father."

As I replied, "Very nice to meet you, Father." I thought, "No way. I finish "Seven Arrows" last night, and today I meet a Brother of the Shields. This can't be happening." I had to ask, "Father, are you by any chance a Brother of the Shields?"

He looked very surprised and replied, "Yes, I am my son. I'm one of the last of a dying breed. But tell me, how do you know of the shields?"

Looking into his eyes I replied, "I just finished a book last night, which tells the story of the Brothers of the Shield, called "Seven Arrows." I can show you this book if you like?"

Yes. I would like that. He replied. But first let us see what we can find. And then we will look at your book."

As we scavenged the dump together, talking, and sharing our finds,

I asked him what he was searching for in the dump.

He replied that he was looking for tools and car parts primarily, but, from time to time, that he would find Indian artifacts from various tribes that sadly had been discarded by his own people.

He told me that every time that he found a discarded piece it troubled him greatly.

After wandering the dump and finding some amazing things, he had a large burlap bag filled with things, and I had a good-sized pile of stuff myself, including a big heavy bell that still put out quite a loud ring. It would be perfect for the commune.

I asked him where his car was. He replied that it was at home, in a very special and sacred place.

I asked, "Well, how did you get here?" He replied that he had walked.

I asked how far it was to his home.

He pointed to the north and said, "It is a little ways that way, my son.

I asked him if he would like a ride back home. He replied, "The walking is good for me. But that would be very nice."

We loaded up our new found treasure, and he directed me back to his home.

On the highway on the way back, a car about 50 feet ahead of us on the highway hit a cat, flinging it to the side of the road.

The old Indian man grabbed my sleeve, and shouted, "Pull over. Pull over. Just past that cat," And I did.

The old Indian gentleman jumped out of the passenger side of the truck, and I jumped out of the truck following him.

We both ran up to the cat, which appeared to be in very bad shape. His breathing was extremely labored, and he obviously had very bad internal injuries. Blood was coming from his mouth and nose. His eyes looked very frightened.

The old Indian began to chant while lightly running his fingers over the cat's body. As I watched the cat's eyes, the fear seemed to leave them, and was replaced by a look of calm.

I can't remember exactly how the chant went but it was something like, "Hey Ya Ya Ya Ya Yah. Hey Ya. Hey Ya. Hey Ya Ya Ya Ya Yah."

He put his head down and slowly lifted the cat's head, putting his forehead to its forehead. Chanting all the while, and finally picking the cat up, and cradling it in his arms as he continued to press his forehead to the cats fore head, chanting while he danced around with the cat cradled in his arms until it finally passed away. At that point he stopped his chant, and looking down at the cat, he took his right hand and closed its eyes and cradled it in his left arm.

And then to my amazement he walked over to the camper, lifted up the camper door and chucked the cat's lifeless body into my camper like a bag of potatoes. This scared the hell out of Lazarus.

I don't think that he'd ever seen a dead cat, or a live cat for that matter, ever come flying at him like that before.

It scared him so bad that he jumped up into the cab from the camper, and would not go back in there until we arrived at our destination and removed the dead cat. When the old Indian man did this I was so shocked, and I asked loudly, "What the hell was that?"

The old man laughed a little and replied, "Oh. I'm sorry, my son, that must've been very confusing for you.

You see I helped the cat cross over to the other side, and I took away his pain and suffering on this side. So that when I sang him across to the other side he would not live in pain forever on the other side.

But now his spirit has crossed the great river, and he is happy and dancing and playing on the other side.

So now we will take his body home, and use it ,so it does not go to waste, and so that he will be remembered on this side, I will make a great cat stew from his flesh for dinner tonight, and so we will remember him tonight.

And then I will make a nice pair of moccasins from his hide, so that when it is cold, I will look down at my moccasins, and I will say my feet are warm because of the little brown cat that died along the highway, which now plays, dances, and chases fields full of mice on the other side.

"And on very cold days I will sing his praises, and he will always be able to stop his playing and dancing on the other side of the great river of life and death, and look across to this side and know that he is still loved, and honored, and remembered."

As the daylight was fading we wound our way down the long lightly traveled dirt path to his home.

A real Indian teepee made from animal skins, with weathered painted images adorning it. It had a stream on one side, and a small pile of antlers on another side, and a pile of garbage on even another side.

This would be my home for the next three or 4 weeks. This would be my spiritual reawakening. This would be where I would learn what it meant to be a Brother of the Shields, and more importantly what it meant to truly be in touch with the planet, with nature, and if you will, to be in touch with God.

Those three or 4 weeks changed the way that I have looked at life, religion, and every important challenge that this world faces on a day-to-day basis ever since. It changed who I am as a human being. How I look at other human beings. How I look at all other species. In short, it changed my perception of everything—forever.

Chapter 18

Learning from Father about the Circle of Life and the Ways of the Shield

As darkness set in I decided to throw the stick for Lazarus while father skinned and cleaned the cat. He salted and stretched the cats hide, and cleaned the meat, putting some of it in a pot inside the teepee and walking the other parts out to a flat rock about 150 feet from the camp. I tagged along that's how I know, and when we returned I asked him why he had taken the remnants of the cat out to the rock.

He replied that he would've given the remnants to my dog, but that he had assumed that I would not want my dog to have a taste for cat blood. So he took the remnants to the gifting rock.

I thanked him for not giving the cat scraps to Lazarus, telling him what had happened at Black Tree Commune, and then I asked him what the gifting rock was, and he replied that that was where he would place gifts for the meat eating animals.

I was to learn more about this practice later in our conversations. He told me that he was going to gather fix in's for the stew, and asked me if I could gather some more firewood.

I said I would. And roughly an hour or so later he was back with his leather carry sling loaded with various vegetables and plants.

As it was now getting dark we went into the teepee and sat around the fire. I brought in my kerosene lantern, and some wheat flour, yeast, and a bowl, and a jug of water to make bread to bake on his center fire flat rock, which was used for baking.

When I turned the kerosene lantern up father declared, "It puzzles me why the white man has to turn night into day, and day into night." I replied, "Is it bothering you, Father? I can turn it down, or off if you wish." Father replied, "No. That's fine, my son."

"I should be used to it by now, because when I stay overnight in town from time to time, even my people have taken to the white man's ways, and live in their boxes with little sticks that come out of the walls that turn night into day with one touch. It is a wonderment, but still very annoying.

The first time I witnessed it, I ran out of my nephew's box thinking that it was lightning. I asked myself, "Do these white men think that they are the Great Spirit? But now I have grown used to it, and simply consider it another annoyance created by the white man to keep my people far away from the medicine wheel of life."

While he had been talking I noticed what looked like a small pile of Death Angel mushrooms interspersed with all of his other stew fix in's. Everything else from what I had learned from Josh looked okay. Cattail root, thistle, Nettle, fried chicken mushrooms, wild potatoes, and onions, etc.

But even I knew that Death Angels were deadly poison. Startled, I asked, "Father? Aren't those Death Angel mushrooms? You're not putting them in the stew are you? You know they're deadly poisonous."

"Do you mean the happiness catcher mushrooms?" He asked holding up one of the death Angels.

Startled I said, "No offense, Father, but that is a Death Angel, not a happiness catcher. And if you are putting those in the stew, I'm going to have to pass on the stew."

Father began to laugh, saying, "My son, what you do not understand is that many things that kill the white man do not harm the Indian at all. And only harm the Indians that have become white men.

It is only when one chooses not to live in harmony with nature, and understand nature, and chooses to ignore and destroy nature, that nature is forced to fight back. After all it is only self-defense on a grand scale. The problem is that the white man chooses to destroy everything in his path that does not want to become white.

The reason the white man refers to the happiness catcher mushrooms as Death Angel mushrooms is because when white men first saw them they did not talk with the mushrooms they did not take time to admire their beauty.

They simply walked up and tore them out of the ground and cooked and ate them. And the first few times that they did this they tasted good.

So for a short time this process continued until the happiness catchers who had always been talked to, and admired, and caressed by the Indian, got tired of being abused, ignored, and slaughtered.

And now if a white man picks a happiness catcher and eats it he or she will get very sick, or die.

But I know the way to pick a happiness catcher, I tell it how beautiful it is, caress it, and if necessary sing it to the other side, reminding it of how it will be remembered on this side."

I looked at him befuddled and said, "That's great for you, Father, but in case you forgot, I am a white man."

Father began to laugh again. He said laughingly, "You still do not understand, my son. The poison enters the plant after it is taken, because of the way it is taken. And not because of who eats it afterwards. It's the same with tobacco.

The Indian reveres the tobacco, and lets it grow wild as it should, and sings its praises, and harvests it gently while showing reverence for it as a species, and not a crop, to be slaughtered.

So, the wild tobacco is not poisonous to Indians, only to Indians who live like whites, and smoke the white man's tobacco, and drink the white man's stinging water until they are drunk, and become fools.

That is because the Great Mother and the Great Father believe as I do that fools should die, because as long as they live, they cause harm to the animals, the land, and all of the non-foolish people." He continued, "I smoke tobacco, and have occasionally for most of my life.

However I can walk from here to Kamloops without stopping. I have run many times to Clinton from here without stopping or ever breathing hard.

I suggest that you take a small sip of the broth first, if anything is going to happen you will get sick within a few minutes, and you will not die. Then when you see that you don't get sick you can eat as much as you like without worrying."

He finished cooking the stew and I made the bread, and fed Lazarus his dinner.

Father handed me a wooden spoon with a very small amount of the broth, I halfheartedly swallowed it. Beads of sweat formed on my brow as I waited. 5 min., 10 min., 25 min., and nothing changed. I was fine. He handed me a bowl of the stew and slowly and reluctantly I ate it with a massive amount of bread.

I had to admit that he was right. I got a little bit of gas but other than that I was fine. I recall thinking to myself; wait till I tell Josh this one.

He asked me about where I was from, and I regaled him with stories of Los Angeles, and living by the beach in the Marina, and of being a singer, and making furniture, and how my parents had died only three months apart, and how I had attempted suicide, and Lazarus had saved me, and how the only reason that I was sitting in front of him was because my friend Klaus had told me that I needed to get out of Los Angeles to clear my head.

And that so far my friend had been right when he had said that this trip was going to be a magical trip. And that he, "Father," was just more living proof of how magical the trip had become.

He said that we should smoke on it, and pulled an ivory and silver peace pipe from out of a white ermine pouch.

Now I knew that we may have a problem. Because I knew that refusing to share a peace pipe with an Indian was a big no-no.

I asked, "Father". I understand that it is discourteous to not share a pipe. However I have a problem. I am allergic to tobacco.

He replied, "Don't worry, my son. This tobacco is blessed, so even though you're a white man it shouldn't harm you."

I replied, "No, Father. You don't understand. When I was a three-year-old child I ate a pack of cigarettes, white man cigarettes, and became deathly ill; and I have been allergic to tobacco ever since. Would it be all right if I smoked from my own pipe? And smoked some of my marijuana instead? We would still be smoking together wouldn't we?"

Father laughed saying, "You whites are such a puzzlement too me. Why you like that crazy weed I will never understand.

My nephew gave me some last year. He said that it was very good, and that it would get me very high. And even though it smelled like a skunk, I took his word for it.

You see, to me getting very high means that I will be taken closer to the other side without crossing over, allowing me to be for a short while with the Great Father and the Great Mother, and the spirits of my ancestors!

After I walked home, and made a fire, the first thing that I did was to fill my pipe with the skunky weed. And I must admit that even though the smoke smelled like a skunk it didn't taste that bad.

I smoked another pipe full, because no heavenly ascension had occurred at that point.

After another pipe full I still remained seated on the hide of my giveaway animal inside my teepee.

So I figured that I should at least try one more pipe full to see if at least the Great Father and Mother would show themselves to me.

Halfway through the last pipe full I began to feel very happy, and decided that I felt like singing, and that singing might help my ascension up to the shore of the great river. So I stood up and began to dance and sing around the fire, dancing, singing, smoking, laughing, and chanting to the heavens. I did this until my pipe was empty.

I sat down, and I realized that I was very hungry, and I had just eaten at my nephew's house, so I wondered, why I am hungry?

I was hungry, but there was nothing to eat. And it was after dark, but I was very hungry. So I made a torch, and I grabbed my bow and arrows, and threw the flap back on the teepee, and went out to find something to eat. However when I went out into the darkness and held up the torch, my entire campsite appeared to be surrounded by all kinds of horrible monsters. I ran back inside, and sat trembling with bow in hand for the rest of the night, chanting for all the great spirits to protect me.

When morning came I peeked outside and the monsters were gone. And since then I have determined to leave the crazy weed to the white men. But if you prefer to dance with the monsters then please get your pipe and smoke your crazy weed. And we can smoke together before we sleep. However if you don't mind, can you and your dog sleep in your truck tonight so that the monsters surround your truck and not my home."

I told him that that would be fine.

We smoked for a little while, and he told me that I was welcome to stay with him as long as I liked. And he was happy that I wanted to learn about the Shields.

When I got my pipe and weed I had grabbed my copy of Seven Arrows, he leafed through it and commented, "I like the pictures very much, and the symbols, the shields, the sacred circle and the picture of the peoples of the various tribes are interesting, even though they appear to be from long ago. My problem is I've never fully learned the white man's scratchings. I only have learned what I need to know to survive. I have learned to speak the white man's language better than I can read or write it."

I replied, "Then while I stay with you, I will teach you more of reading and writing the white man's language, and you can teach me more of your religion, and your people, and how to live more in harmony with nature, and the less like an ignorant white man."

Father laughed loudly, and said laughingly, "My father taught me that the bravest man is not the man who talks about himself and of his bravery. The bravest man is the man who can laugh at himself and quietly do brave deeds."

And on that note he laid down to go to sleep, bidding me, "Goodnight my son", and I walked the dog, and Laz and I went to sleep in the camper.

Before I went to sleep I was thinking "WOW! Now I am going to get to learn about the Shields, and right from the horse's mouth, as they say. And I can get even closer to nature, (I'll bet even Josh will be envious.) I'll bet Father can teach me even more about living off the land than Josh has."

This really has been a great trip. Michael's permanent party, the House of Che, and the other communes, even fighting forest fires was exciting, and all of the great girls."

Suddenly, I began to gasp for air. Laz had cut one of his worst farts ever. "Goddamn it Lazarus, You son of a bitch." I screamed, coughing. "I'm gonna quit adding dog food to your lay mash. This is bullshit."

We both scrambled out of the camper and let it air out. Laz took a crap and I peed. Then we climbed back in and I lit a bunch of incense. We both dozed off dreaming of what exciting adventures lay in store for us the next day.

The next morning I awoke to loud barking. Lazarus was going crazy. There was something outside of the camper.

I couldn't see anything when I looked out of either of the side windows, however when I looked out of the camper shell door window by lifting up the curtain which covered it.

I was startled to see a large bulbous nose which appeared to be leaning down and up against the window. The large nose snorted, cascading a vast amount of steam and snot, which virtually covered most of the window. This obscured the window to the point where I could barely see anything out of it.

My dog was still going crazy, and giving off that strange warning growl that he did when there was danger.

As I pulled my rifle out and racked a round into the chamber, I remember thinking, "First of all this is something big; it is most likely a moose, but it might be a bear. In any case whatever it is I better be ready, but for now I'll see if I can wait it out.

I hope Father is safe, if it's a mother moose with a calf we're all screwed. I looked down at the still dented tailgate from my last encounter with a mother moose with calf.

As I gazed upon the dented tailgate, rifle in hand, the entire truck lurched forward slamming me against the back of the truck bed and camper shell.

Oh shit. I thought. It is a moose. Even a grizzly couldn't move a four-wheel-drive truck in gear with the emergency brake on like that.

The truck lurched again even harder this time. Lazarus had stopped barking and jumping around and growling. He now cowered next to me shivering and whimpering and looking up at me as if to say, "What are we going to do now, dad?"

As the truck shuddered again I took one hand off of my rifle and petted him and smiling down at him I reassured him by saying, "I won't let it get us kid. Don't worry; if it comes through that door no matter what it is, it's dead." The truck shuddered violently again.

I heard father outside mumbling something. But I couldn't make out quite what it was that he was saying.

I yelled from inside of the camper, "Father. I can take care of myself I have a gun. Please run, and save yourself."

Father replied, "Fear not, my son. There is nothing to worry about. This will all be over in a few moments. But please do not use the gun; that is unnecessary."

Next he screamed out three high-pitched screams; "He, He, He." Then I heard the clump, clump, clumping of large round hooves sauntering away from the camper.

I cracked open the camper shell door and looked off to the right through the side window, and sure enough there was a large bull moose casually sauntering away. I slowly opened the camper shell door, all of the way.

And there was Father, standing there with a large grin on his face; in his buckskins, he was holding his ceremonial spear.

I asked, "Father, what was that all about?"

Father replied, "He was hungry and smelled food inside of your truck box." I asked, "How do you know that?" Father laughingly replied, "Because I asked him what he was doing here. And he said that he was hungry and he could smell a strong odor of food inside of your truck box."

I replied, "The only food I have in here is human food, and the lay mash that I feed Lazarus."

Father said, "Well that explains it. Lay mash is fine dining for a moose."

I climbed out of the camper, and putting the tailgate down, motioned to Lazarus to come out as well, I knew that he had to go to the bathroom, as did I. Lazarus came to the tailgate and ran and looked on either side, he whimpered a little bit and finally jumped down, and then ran over to a rear tire and lifted his leg. Standing a few feet from him I turned away from Father and took a pee myself.

As I peed I said to Father, "Father I have so many questions for you. How do you talk to the animals? How did you get a bull moose that wanted my food to just leave like that? Can you communicate with all animals?"

Father replied, "We have a big day today, and I have much to show you. But, I will answer your questions over the morning fire my son." I said, "I have food, bacon and eggs, and flour and syrup for pancakes. And we can have our choice of coffee, or tea."

Father replied "I normally do not take food in the morning. But as it will be a long day with a lot of walking maybe a little food would be good.

This white man's drink, coffee, I had once, and it made me very, very nervous, as the whites like to say, 'jittery.' The drink that they call tea made me nervous as well, just not so much bad."

I answered, "Father. I have a tea that I guarantee you, will not make you nervous, and will actually make you feel very good, even calm you. I drink it when I fast, or go without food. It is called Red Zinger. I will make enough for both of us so that you can try it."

Looking perplexed Father said to me, "I know that I am not very well versed in your white man's language, but a drink called "Red Zinger" does not sound to me like a drink that would have a calming influence?"

So Father made the fire and I made the food and the tea. We sat around the fire, eating and drinking as he explained to me how he had so easily dealt with the large Bull Moose.

He told me that it had taken 15 years of training from his Father, and another 25 years of practice to learn how to communicate with the animals.

The way that he explained it, it was a form of telepathy combined with verbal chants, and various sounds that the animals understood like the high-pitched squeals that he had used on the moose.

I immediately asked him what he had said to the moose.

He replied that he had simply come out and asked the moose, "What are you doing at my home, Brother Moose?" And the moose told him that he was very hungry and smelled food inside of the large box and was simply trying to get into it to satisfy his hunger. Continuing he said, "I told him that it was unnecessary, and motioned with my spear to a field of sweet honey grass peppered with even sweeter bluebonnet blossoms.

I reasoned with him, "Why hurt your self trying to break into a box to get food that is not as good or as fresh as the honey grass and bluebonnet blossoms that are there for the taking, only a few minutes' walk that way. He thanked me for the help, and asked if there was anything that he could do for me. And I replied, yes, you can. There is a frightened white man in the box with a fire stick. So please be on your way, for everyone's sake. Then I loudly chanted "He, He, He." Which he knew too mean, and be quick about it."

I looked at Father over my eggs and bacon, took a drink from my mug of Red Zinger tea, and said, "Father. Do you mean to say that you had a complicated conversation like that with a Bull Moose?" He replied, "Yes, my son."

I was here to learn from this man, so I wasn't going to start off the first day by doubting him. I asked, "Can you communicate like that with all creatures both great and small?"

Father replied, "Yes. But not to the same degree, the smaller animals are usually easier. And larger animals and in particular predators are usually a little more difficult, especially if they are hungry.

For instance, my son, if I run into an angry grizzly bear, or a very hungry mountain lion, or any badly injured dangerous creature, I will show respect and reason with him or her. Reminding them of things they already know, like the fact that human beings are the deadliest creature on Mother Earth, and that even if he or she manages to rub me out, he or she will also be rubbed out in the process by my arrow, my knife, or my spear.

And, being that I have been rubbed out, I will have sung my death song so that I can cross the great river to the other side; but being that we both are rubbed out I will not be there to sing he or she across the Great River of life and death.

So that means that he or she will be destined to walk the wind on this side of the Great River forever, and never find peace. So why not go our separate ways, and continue our journeys through life with respect for each other. So far this conversation has almost failed me only once my son."

"When was that Father," I asked?

Father replied, "Over 20 winters back I had killed a deer, and after apologizing to the deer and singing him to the other side, I cleaned him, skinned him and cut him into portions which I loaded onto my snow sled to take back to my teepee.

It was very cold, and the journey was very difficult pulling a sled through the snow in my rapped moccasins and snowshoes. That is when I sensed danger, and pulled my bow from my shoulder.

There in front of me on a large rock was a very large mountain cat. To this day it is the largest cat that I have ever seen. It let out a great screaming roar.

Drawing the arrow taut against the bowstring, I looked into the large cat's angry eyes, and spoke to him. 'Why are you so angry friend cat?' I said. The cat drew a deep breath and looking back into my eyes with a piercing stare he replied, 'Because I am very cold, and have been in search of food for many days, and finding none I cannot go back to my cave with a full belly, and be warm, and sleep, which is what I must do. I smell that you have food which is what I need. And if I must kill you to have this food, then so be it.'

I knew at this point that my normal reasoning would not work with this creature, so I tried a new strategy.

"Friend cat,' I said, 'I understand your pain, however I cannot let you kill me, and if you try, I will be forced to kill you with my arrow.

But if you will hear me out, I believe I have a solution that will work for the both of us.

On my sled I have a freshly killed deer, as you know. I will share my deer with you pulling half of its body off of the sled into the snow for you to consume and take back to your cave for later. This I will do for you.'

The large cat growled again and said to me, 'But I am very, very hungry, and I want all of the deer. And why should I settle for half of a deer, when I can have the whole deer and maybe you as well.'

I replied, 'Friend cat. This scenario that you propose works both ways. I am very good with my bow, and I guarantee you that I will at least wound you, if not kill you, with my first arrow before you get even halfway to me.

And I will rub you out with another arrow and my spear before you can ever touch me. This I do not want to do, but it is your decision? Half of a fresh killed deer, along with the rest, warmth, and full stomach that you deserve, or I can take you home along with the deer, and consume your flesh, and adorn my Lodge with your hide. Personally I hope that you will reconsider my offer, because I do not really want to kill you, because killing you, cleaning your carcass, and adding the weight of your carcass to my sled I would find very tiresome right now.'

And then drawing back my bow and arrow again, and aiming it at the giant cat's heart, I looked into his eyes and said, 'What is your choice friend cat?'

The great cat reared up on his hind legs, and pawing the air with his right paw, and looking me directly in the eyes he replied, 'Better half of a deer in this world then nothing in the next.' And with a blink of his left eye he thanked me.

I pulled half of the deer carcass off of my sled and started pulling the sled toward my camp, always looking back over my shoulder just in case.

Before I got completely out of sight I saw the great cat take away the entire half deer carcass to hide in his den.

And just as I pulled out of sight I could see him happily gnawing on the last piece of the carcass left behind in the trail."

I asked, "You must've really been happy, Father. I mean that you didn't have to kill the great cat or be hurt or killed yourself.

Father replied "I was my son, but I was even happier about something else."

I asked, "And what was that, Father?"

He replied, "It was very cold, and I was very tired. And now I was pulling only half of the load. So I made it back to my Lodge in a little more than half of the time. And that made me very happy indeed my son."

Chapter 19

Father and I share stories of our ancestry, and he continues to teach me the Way of the Shield

Father and I continued to talk until early afternoon.

I asked him about his ancestors, and he told me that he only knew of his ancestry as far back as the Buffalo times.

When it is said that the Buffalo covered the plains like a dark ocean As far as the eye could see. In those days the two great tribes of the northern plains were the Sioux and the Cheyenne.

They worshiped Wa- Ta-Tonka their word for the Buffalo. And thanked the great Mother and Father for the abundant gift that was showered upon them. These days were known as the happy times. And with the exception of occasional skirmishes with tribes like the Crow and the Pawnee, two of their enemies, the Sioux and Cheyenne lived in harmony and peace; even inter-marrying tribe to tribe from time to time.

The father of his father's father, a Lakota Sioux brave married a beautiful Cheyenne girl during these happy times, a practice which continued right up to the terrible times after the Little Bighorn in which his father's father fought very bravely.

But when the whites began to rub out the Sioux and Cheyenne with fire sticks, long knives, and disease; his father's father took his family north, with the great Chief Sitting Bull into the land of the red soldiers after hearing of the kindness of the great white mother across the great water.

And his father's father and family decided to stay and live in this northern land, because these whites were not butchers, thieves, and liars like the southern whites; which are what they called Americans, at least for the most part, that is.

He and others had warned Sitting Bull that if he took his people south again, they would end up like many of the Cherokees, and other tribes. Rubbed out by the southern whites, and even killing one another.

And that is exactly what happened. Sadly the great prophet Sitting Bull could not see his own fate and that of his people.

His father's father had learned the ways of the Shield before coming north and taught his father.

However his father's brother, his uncle, went the other way and spent his time making friends with the whites. And this was not necessarily a bad thing, because he could always help settle disputes with the northern whites.

He himself had never married, choosing rather to marry himself to the land. I asked him why?

And he replied that once he found that he didn't need to marry a woman to sleep with her the whole idea of marriage for him became nothing more than a nuisance.

He interrupted his train of thought by saying, "I must admit to you my son that the ways of the white man have always puzzled me greatly. They always seem to be in a hurry to go nowhere. And they seem to be obsessed with boxes. They live in boxes. They ride around in boxes.

They urinate and defecate in a box that has a small stream in it that whisks their urine and feces away with the flip of a lever. And they keep this box in the same place that they bathe.

They drive around in boxes.

Beautiful boxes that should be worshiped for their beauty instead of used like a tortured beast of burden. They receive their messages in little boxes. And talk to each other over great distances through wires connected to boxes with little horns attached.

They even have vision boxes which they call television which would be a wondrous thing if one could witness the Great Spirit Quest visions of the Great Chiefs of the past, however on these boxes all that you can witness are horrible things, violent things, and crazy white man things.

Like people trying to trade silly things, such as food, and soap, and bigger vision boxes. And apparently now they're selling and trading women on the things also.

Even though my brother says that they are only selling the clothes and not the women. I asked him what are the women going to do without clothes, it gets cold up here. I'm sorry my son but the ways of the white man greatly perplex me."

I asked, "Father, you speak very good English. Where did you learn?"

He replied, "My father wanted my brother, myself, and my sister to go to the white man's school. My brother and sister attended the white man's school in the daytime and played after school with the white children.

However I attended the white man's school in the daytime and learned the ways of the shield from my father afterwards and on weekends.

On our land we had three white man's boxes or houses as they call them. And three lodges. My brother and sister lived in the boxes most of the time, and just like the whites they cut their hair.

My father and I lived in the lodges along with my mother most of the time. She would only put up her hair and dress like the whites when she went to town, or stayed in the boxes with my brother and sister.

We owned a truck and three horses. My mother was the only person who could drive the truck until my brother turned 16.

My father and I never learned to drive. We went everywhere on horseback, or we walked.

My brother married a white woman, and my sister married a white man.

And when my father died I helped him across the Great River, and I told my mother, brother, and sister that I was going to continue my learning of the Shields away from the whites; which is what I did.

I would come in and visit them every few months to let them know that I was well. One day I was walking across the field to see them, and my sister came running to me screaming, 'We couldn't find you anywhere. Mother is very sick.' She said, 'The doctor says that she is dying.'

'What doctor?' I asked her. 'Dr. Adams,' she said.

I angrily shouted, 'A white doctor? Of course he says that she's dying. They all want to rub us out anyway.'

I ran into the room in the house box where they had her.

She looked very white and frail. I leaned down and felt her head it was very hot. She opened her eyes and saw me, and she told me that she was so glad to see me.

She also told me that she knew she was dying, and that she wanted to be buried with my father in the old way.

And she told me not to let my brother and sister bury her in the ground like trash, in the white man's way.

So I fashioned carry polls to the back of my horse and stayed with her until she passed, and then I sang her to the other side while my brother and sister both cried.

Once I was secure in the knowledge that she was with my father on the other side of the great River. I bundled up her body, and dragged it behind my horse and built a burial stand on the hill next to what was left of my father's burial stand from many years before.

As I closed my eyes and danced in a circle around the old and new stand, I sang the praises of my mother and father.

And I could see them embracing and dancing together on the other side of the Great River and my heart soared, for I knew that nothing could harm them anymore.

They were together forever, and their new life was a good life. Yes. I cried, I laughed, I sang, and I danced all night, until I could dance no more. And I could stand no more. And as I collapsed on to the ground and the sun began to rise.

I thought to myself, my parents are back in the happy times. That is when I opened my eyes and rejoiced as I looked into the beautiful dawn.

And then I lay my head down upon the grass to rest and sleep, smiling as I closed my eyes to sleep.

The vision of my parents waving to me from the other side was my last vision before I fell asleep."

He paused for a moment, and then said, "But what about you my son? Who were your ancestors?"

I replied, "Of course I will tell you Father. But before I do, I must tell you how sorry I am for the loss of your Mother and Father; And how beautiful your story was." I wiped the tears from my cheeks.

And he replied, "Thank you my son." After regaining my composure I began to tell him the story of my family.

"My father was pure German. His father and mother were pure German and moved in 1914 from Mannheim, Germany to Mannheim, Pennsylvania."

Father replied, "Ah, the warrior tribe from across the great sea. I have heard of these people. Like most of the, whites they were never content with their own land. Always wanting to conquer other tribes, and take their lands, and dominate their people."

I continued, "And my mother's side of the family was quite a mix. When they arrived in America they were a Scotch and Irish mix."

Father interjected, "Yes. I know of these people; the fire haired people with the great tempers; from the islands in the great sea known as "The Angry Land."

I asked, "The islands known as the angry land?" And then it hit me Ire-land. What's another word in English for anger? It's ire. And I've met very few men or women from Ireland who didn't have quite a temper when provoked.

Father chimed in again, "My brother married one of these fire haired women from the angry land. And one night he drank too much of the stinging water, and she hit him over the head with an iron skillet and almost killed him. Or at least that's what my sister told me.

I know that when I go to my brother's house she is always angry at me, yelling at me, making me bathe so that I smell like flowers, and taking saddle soap to my leathers, so that when I go back into the woods the animals don't know my scent, unless I run all the way back from his house to my Lodge, and sweat my scent back.

I swear that one day that fire haired woman is going to get me killed with her perfumed soaps. Anyway, go ahead with your story my son."

I continued, "Well that's when things start to mix up a little when the McGuffin's, (My mother's side of the family) came to Texas, and a lot of things happened. I apparently had a great, great, great uncle that was at the Alamo where the Texans fought the Mexicans for independence.

I have also been told that I also have some Comanche blood as one of my great, great, great; aunts was captured by and became a bride of Quanah Parker, the great Comanche Chief. And I may have some Navajo blood as well, because a relative on that side of the family was apparently orphaned by the Yaquis', and adopted by a Navajo family who had done well as sheep ranchers."

Father said, "Yes, the Cliff Dwellers who were almost rubbed out completely by the blue coats, led by the butcher Kit Carson.

Like the Cherokee and many other tribes, many died on the trail of tears. At least the whites finally let the cliff dwellers stay on their land, because the whites had no use for it.

And eventually they prospered. If you have Navajo blood you should be smart and artistic. Also you must be very brave, and a fierce warrior, because the Comanche were very brave and fierce warriors.

The Yaquis, who slaughtered your ancestors, were not only brave, and fierce, but they were crazy as well. Both the Comanche, and the Yaquis', and the Apache, were feared by the whites; because they could be crazier, more savage, and usually even crueler than the whites.

As a boy my father would frighten me, my brother, and my sister with stories of these savage people. And both your Mother and Father crossed over to the other side recently, my son?"

I replied, "Yes as I said, they both passed away earlier this year Father."

Father replied, "That is very sad my son, but enough of all this talk of sadness. It is getting late. We must go catch dinner before dark."

I excitedly said, "We're going fishing? Great, I'll get my rod and reel."

"No my son", we will need no string and stick. We will catch our fish the Indian way."

"And how is that father?" I asked.

"We will use the spear, my son; of course." Father replied.

I answered "Okay. I have a spear, too." Father said, "Well, get it my son. And let's be on our way."

Soon, there we were, walking along the banks of a small stream, with Lazarus running ahead of us; and he was as happy as a clam.

I saw a fish in the narrow mountain stream, which at that time of year was about 35°F;

I took my forked spear and started stabbing at the water splashing it all over me.

But it was like the fish could anticipate my every move. After 40 or so attempts to spear the fish my arms were throbbing and I was soaked with ice water and beginning to shiver. Father was having a grand old time watching me make a fool of myself.

He laughingly said to me, "You'll never catch any fish that way my son. Do you want to see me catch that fish the Indian way?"

I replied almost pleading with him, "Please show me, Father. And please catch a lot of fish; because if I don't eat well tonight, after this day I'm probably going to get pneumonia."

"All right my son, watch closely." He began to walk along the edge of the creek moving his spear like a wand in a serpentine motion almost directly over the fish as it weaved in the water.

As he did this he sang and chanted, suddenly sweeping the point of the spear rapidly from one side of the bank to the other. Almost like an orchestra conductor uses his baton to conduct a symphony. When he would do this his pitch would change and get higher as the spear head moved towards the bank.

He continued this process walking about 30 feet up the creek following the fish. This took only a few minutes, and then unexpectedly the fish to my amazement followed the spearhead and jumped out of the water and onto the bank.

The fish was flopping wildly on the ground. Father put down his spear and picking up the fish he did the same thing with the fish that he had done earlier with the cat, singing the creature into the afterlife.

I followed him for two or three miles upstream while he did this, making fish jump onto the bank, singing them to the other side, and then stringing them onto two gill lines till he had charmed 12 fish onto his gill lines. Also he had placed six smaller fish back into the stream saying, "It's too soon for you little brother, or little sister. Have a happy summer, and eat well. I will see you again next year, or the summer after."

He handed one line with six fish on it to me, and said, "We will eat well for a while, my son. And all the fish are happier on the other side. They are in a giant lake with much room to swim; and many fly's and smaller fish to eat. They are all much happier now, and send us many thanks."

As we walked back to camp I began to warm up some from the exercise and the sun.

I threw the stick for Laz, and I realized that he was happy, and I was happy, and Father was happy. And once again on this trip all seemed to be right with the world.

I wondered what great stories and insights Father would have for me at dinner.

Whatever they were, I was now the student and he was clearly the teacher.

And this time, unlike in college; this student was eager to listen, eager to learn, and eager to appreciate; because unlike college; I wasn't being taught abstract mechanical theory, or the like.

I was being taught how to communicate with nature, in the wild, directly, and Father definitely had my FULL attention.

My sketch of Lazarus in the Camper

Chapter 20

A brief break from life with Father, a quick trip too horny town, and then on to satisfaction city with Lucy Lou, and then back to my spiritual journey.

We got back to Fathers lodge a little before dark. We fried half of the fish, and salt dried the other half.

Father and I exchanged stories over dinner. And then he told me that he was going on a spiritual walkabout, but that I was welcome to stay at his camp as long as I wanted.

I asked him how long he would be gone for. And he replied, "I'm not sure, my son. I seek wisdom from the Great Father and Mother, and when I gain this wisdom, and only then, I shall return. So you may stay here if you wish until I return. Or you may go elsewhere, and return from time to time to see if I have returned, whatever your heart desires, my son."

I replied, "Well, I could go back to David and Brian's? Or, there are some fire roads that I have wanted to check out between here and Kamloops. Maybe I'll do that?"

Father looked at me lighting his pipe after the big meal of fish and veggies saying, "Good, you have a plan. It is always good for one to have a plan in life. Even if that plan is interrupted, one can always make another plan. Isn't life wonderful, my son? It's always exciting because one never knows what lies around the next corner."

In our dinner conversation I learned that Father had never tasted wine, only whiskey.

I had a half bottle of Chardonnay in the camper, so I wrapped a string around the bottle and stuck it in the cold stream that ran next to Fathers lodge. After letting it chill for 30-40 minutes or so, I pulled the chilled bottle out of the stream and walked back into Father's lodge.

I took a swig from the bottle and it was nicely chilled, so I asked Father if he would like to taste it; explaining to him that it didn't burn the mouth and throat like whiskey did. I forgot that he told me that the drink of whiskey that he had had was some 15 or so years earlier.

Father said that he would like to try it, so I handed him the bottle.

After smelling the opening at the end of the neck of the bottle, he took a very tentative small sip. He let it sit in his mouth, and then after swishing it around in his mouth, he finally swallowed it.

Looking at me with a sort of blank expression, he finally smiled and asked, "White men made that?" I replied, "Yes, Father."

He went on, "It is much better than the stinging water, slightly bitter and a little sour. But I must admit, it is drinkable my son, amazing."

I asked, "Would you like some more, Father?"

"Perhaps one more small taste, my son, all of the white man's drinks can be a cruel mistress. All that one has to do, to know this fact, is to witness what they have done to my people."

He took another small drink and handed the bottle back to me.

Over the next 20 min. or so I finished off the rest of the half bottle of Chardonnay. While Father told me how if you can do the Raven dance well enough, you can actually get a Raven in a tree to mimic you, and do the dance with you.

That's when Father stopped his story saying, "Oh my son. Now I know that this is a white man's drink."

He started to tip to one side and had to steady himself with his right hand.

"Why Father?" I asked.

"Because it comes with the spinning sickness that always accompanies the stinging waters. That is just like white men. They come up with stinging waters that don't sting. But still make you just as sick.

What a fool I am. I know the treachery of the white man, and still they fooled me again."

I asked, "I'm so sorry father. Are you all right?"

"I will be fine, my son. I will do what I did the last time I drank the stinging waters. I will sleep until the spinning stops, and then suffer through the great head pain tomorrow until it goes away."

I asked softly, "Father? Do you trust me? Do you realize that I never would've given you the wine, if I had known that it would make you sick?"

"Yes, my son. He replied, you may be mostly white, but you are not treacherous. You are a good man. And I do trust you."

I continued, "Father, I'm going to get some medicine for you. It is white man's medicine. But it will ensure that you do not suffer the great head pain tomorrow, and may help to stop the spinning sooner tonight."

"What is this white man's medicine that you speak of, my son?" Father asked.

"They are little white pills, called aspirin." I said.

"Yes. Father exclaimed. My brother takes these for his spinning sickness. Thank you, my son."

I gave him the aspirin, and he went to sleep in his Lodge, and I walked Lazarus, and then we went to sleep in the camper.

When I woke up in the morning he was gone. Off on his spiritual walkabout.

I made some breakfast for me and Lazarus and we headed into Clinton, and stocked up on supplies and topped off both gas tanks.

I decided to check out a logging road that looked interesting on a trip back from Kamloops.

With Lazarus sitting up in the passenger seat looking all excited, we headed off into the wilderness for our next adventure.

We drove and drove, until I spotted what I thought looked like a good place to camp. So we pulled over and set up camp. I spent my time gathering firewood, cooking dinner, and I was getting good radio reception, so I listened to the radio while I leafed through some magazines that I had purchased in Clinton.

One was a men's magazine, which reminded me that I hadn't gotten laid in a while.

I don't know if it was the joint of Alaskan Thunder Fuck that I smoked after dinner, or what, but suddenly I got really horny, turned off the radio, walked Lazarus, and we climbed into the camper, I jumped into my sleeping bag and proceeded to jerk off. After climaxing I dreamed of having sex with all kinds of different women, many that I had slept with, and many that were imagined.

However, Chartreuse kept coming back into my dreams many times during the night. I woke up the next morning feeling 10 times hornier than when I had gone to sleep the night before.

I smoked a joint thinking that it would calm me down.

But it had the opposite effect; and I got even hornier, if that was even possible. I turned on the radio, and cranked the volume.

I was really stoned, with an almost irrational and definitely irresistible desire to get off.

I took all my clothes off, climbed up on the tailgate, then climbed onto the roof of the camper shell and began to jerk off in front of God and everybody, even though I was on a hilltop of meadow grass in the middle of nowhere, miles from any kind of civilization.

At first I jerked off to the blaring sound of Wilson Pickett's "Mustang Sally". And massively climaxed all over the roof of my camper shell midway through the Rolling Stones song, "Satisfaction" which couldn't have been better if I had called in and requested it just before I climbed on the roof of my camper, and continued abusing myself.

I remember thinking as I climbed off the roof, wiped myself off, and collapsed on to my sleeping bag, "Screw this shit. I've got to go back into town, or up to the commune, or even back to Michael's back in Vancouver if I have to, and find a woman to fuck. This shit is crazy."

But being a guy, I turned off the radio; I put on my shorts, and I lay down for a few minutes, and fell asleep.

I woke up three hours later at around 1:30 PM, and I was starving. I was so hungry I didn't even take time to make a fire. I opened a can of chili and cooked it on the cook stove.

This was normally emergency food. As soon as I finished eating, and feeding Lazarus, I loaded up the truck and Laz and I were on our way back to the highway, and to Clinton first, and then the commune, and back to Vancouver if necessary.

I needed a woman; Like yesterday.

We made our way back to the highway, and headed back toward Clinton. We went about 10 or 12 miles, and then, there alongside the highway, with her thumb out, was a cute little dishwater blonde, in ragged bellbottoms, a tie-dyed tank top, a backpack, a beaded bag, and sunglasses.

I looked up and loudly proclaimed, "Thank you God." I pulled over just past her. I motioned Lazarus to climb back into the camper shell.

As he jumped into the back, she opened the passenger door. I asked, "Where are you headed?" She replied, "Any place that's fun, and cool." I said, "You too?"

She laughed, and climbed up into the passenger seat. I took her backpack and shoved it back into the camper with Lazarus.

As she climbed up into the truck I could see her nipples protruding out through her tie-dyed tank top. And she was very well endowed.

Lazarus jumped up into the opening between the camper shell, and the cab. At first she was startled, and then she started to pet Lazarus and say, "Aren't you a cutie."

We exchanged names, and she said that her name was Lucy Lou, and that she was from South Carolina, by way of LA, and Haight-Ashbury. I told her that I was from Marina Del Rey, in LA. She had been to the Marina, and to Malibu, and talked about how beautiful they both were; and how much she loved the beach.

She asked me where I was headed. And I told her that I had been living with an American Indian Priest, but he was out on a spiritual journey. So that I was just exploring the territory until he got back, and could teach me more; and that I also had friends that had a commune outside of Clinton. And that I had another friend who was a multi-millionaire with a mansion in Vancouver that he kept constantly stocked with freaks.

But that right now I needed some relaxation, so I was planning on getting off of the highway in Clinton and driving the logging roads up past my friend's commune to a beautiful little valley with some small chain lakes.

I explained that if she wanted, I could let her off in Clinton to continue hitchhiking, or she was welcome to come along with me to the chain lakes if she wanted.

While I was saying this to her, inside my head, I was screaming, "Please come with me. Please come with me. I'm so god damned horny. I'm so god damned horny."

On the outside however, I was as cool as a cucumber. She thought for a second, then looked over at me, and said, "You said you're a musician? And you've got some good weed? Could we stop in Clinton and get some food and wine?"

I replied, "Yes. Yes. And Yes. And don't forget the ice."

She laughed and replied, "Are we there yet?" immediately cracking me up; because that was the first time that I had ever heard that expression.

And so after stocking up in Clinton, and pulling over for numerous logging trucks along the logging roads, we finally pulled into the campsite that Josh and I had made a few months earlier at the small chain lakes just as it was getting dark.

Luckily no one else had been there in the meantime, so the pile of stacked firewood that we had left, and the stone fire pit that we had built were just as we had left them.

So I got a nice fire going really fast, and after covering ourselves with pennyroyal and sage oil for the mosquitoes, we ate some of the food that I had purchased in Clinton.

I pulled one of the bottles of wine out of the cooler, rolled a joint, and we brought out and sat in the portable chairs that I had in the truck, drinking wine, and passing the joint back and forth while I threw a stick for Lazarus.

She asked me if I could play something for her. So I pulled my guitar out of the camper, and sang her a couple of my original songs.

And then I made up a song for her. Right there on the spot. I've always been good at that. It's been 30 some years now, and I can't remember the whole song. But it went something like, "Oh Lucy Lou. I'm so glad that I found you. Didn't know what I was gonna do, until I met my Lucy Lou. Yes Lucy Lou, if you'll just let me be with you. I promise to be true, to you, my Lucy Lou."

The song went on and on, the verses showing up in my head one after the other, until the last verse, "No matter which way we go, or whatever we go through, when all is said and done, I will dream of you, just you, my Lucy Lou. Yes, I will dream of you, just you, my Lucy Lou."

By the time I finished the last verse, tears were running down her cheek, however she was smiling so I took that as a good sign.

I turned away from her momentarily to set my guitar down, and when I turned back to face her, her face was inches away from mine.

She said, "That was incredible. How did you do that? I mean it was so beautiful. And we just met. But it's like you've known me for years. Another tear ran down her cheek. And I started to explain, "You see I have this kind of gift of being able to rhyme."

She interrupted and leaning into me she said, "Oh, who cares, just kiss me."

We made out in the chairs for a few seconds and then slowly got up still kissing, and made our way into the camper shedding clothes as fast as humanly possible.

My penis was so hard that I had trouble unzipping my jeans, having to push it out of the way with my hand down my pants in order to avoid a catastrophe.

She was the typical hippie girl, again, just the kind I liked, and still do. As I remember it, we attempted to circumnavigate the copy of the Kama Sutra positions book that I had snagged from Michael's house.

I kept thanking God over and over again for the gift that he had graciously given to this poor, hapless, horny stranger. This girl was amazing, and she was just what I needed.

Normally, I think that she might have been too much for me; because, as soon as we would climax, within 10 or 15 min., just as I was starting to doze off, she would get me going again.

This went on through the night until just before dawn, when we both screamed out our last orgasm, and she flopped on my chest and fell sound asleep, with me still inside of her. As we nodded off I pulled the sleeping bag over us.

And that's the way we woke up the next morning.

The only thing that woke us up was Lazarus barking loudly at something. He was in the camper with us, barking out the back of the open camper shell.

We both rose up. Her turning and looking behind her and me raising up on my elbows, and looking around her. I had made the mistake of leaving Lazarus's bag of lay mash out against the side of the cooler, and a 15 point stag elk was having his way with it. He was a really impressive and beautiful creature.

However I don't think Lucy Lou had ever seen one before, and especially not that close, because she let out a bloodcurdling scream.

This scared the crap out of the elk. His eyes appeared to flare to almost saucer size. He reared and turned in panic, and as her scream grew louder he ran away

I shouted, "Calm down. It's just an elk. They won't hurt you.

Save your screams for a grizzly, or a mother moose with a calf, or a mountain lion, something that deserves a scream."

She immediately fired back, "How was I supposed to know that that thing wouldn't hurt us. It was big, and all those horns."

I replied, "It's just like a big deer."

Her comeback was priceless. In her Southern drawl she exclaimed, "Deer kill folks in South Carolina all the time."

I started laughing, and replied, "You've got me there, darlin', touché. Let's hope that we don't run into any killer deer either."

We spent four or five days at the chain lakes. She was just what I needed, and just at the right time.

The whole trip had been so magical in that way. I know that I've said that many times before, but you had to be there and experience it the way that I did, that is at least to know what I mean.

And as fate would have it I decided to stop at the House of Che on the way back from the chain lakes. It was on the way after all. And I wanted her to meet Brian and David, and the others at the commune.

When we arrived, as usual we were greeted by all of the dogs barking and announcing our arrival; however by now they knew my truck, and were only barking and not growling and barking, like they usually did. It was more of a loud harmonious greeting style of barking.

When I finally stopped the truck with all of the 80 to 100 dogs surrounding us Lucy Lou seemed a little too scared to get out of the truck. I told her not to be scared, and got out myself, and Lazarus came through the camper opening into the cab and followed me out into the midst of the dogs.

I tried to call him back, because I was a little bit nervous about him running into the middle of all of these dogs.

For all I knew Brian and David had added some new dogs to their huge pack of strays, and I didn't want to get into the middle of some huge dogfight, and to get torn up myself in the process of saving Lazarus.

But luckily Lazarus's instincts were better than mine, because all of the dogs were glad to see him. Everybody sniffed everybody else's privates. And all 80 to 100 tails wagged profusely, including Lazarus's tail. Licks were exchanged, and everything was cool, so I told Lucy Lou that she could get out of the truck, and she did.

She began to pet the dogs as four or five people from the commune came up to greet us.

Jimmy was the first to greet us saying, "Hey Bob. Where the hell have you been? We've all been worried about you. Brian went with a couple of the guys into Clinton looking for you. Who's your friend?"

I asked, "Why were you guys worried about me?"

Jimmy replied "Are you fucking kidding man? Almost two weeks ago, you tell us that you're going to go check out the Clinton dump. And then you fucking disappear."

I said, "Oh shit man. I'm so sorry. I had no idea. I apologize. I guess I have a lot of apologies to make to everyone. Is David here? Oh, by the way. This is Lucy Lou. She's from South Carolina."

Jimmy being Jimmy replied, "Well. Lucy Lou. How do you do," finishing it off with one of his little Jimmy giggles.

We all went into the main house. I introduced Lucy to the members of the commune that I knew, and to David, who had come up from behind me.

Covering my eyes with his hands, he asked me, doing his best Charlie Chan impression, "Guess-a-who this is, inimitable number one son."

I replied, "Seeing Charlie Chan is dead, it must be David."

David introduced both Lucy Lou and me to the newcomers and the passers through (as I called them).

Sadly one of the couples passing through was heading into Vancouver, and then onto Salt Spring Island, a place that Lucy Lou wanted to see really bad after I had told her of my Amanita

Muscaria psychedelic mushroom experiences with my buddy Klaus on Salt Spring.

They were leaving the next day. And I couldn't go, as I needed to go back and see if Father had returned, to continue my life lessons with him.

So we spent one more blissful sex filled night together and then said our tearful goodbyes the next morning, after exchanging permanent phone numbers and kissing and hugging over and over. We all had a great breakfast at the commune before Lucy Lou and the couple left.

I told David and Brian, Brian having returned the night before, about Father, and learning about the ways of the Brothers of the Shield from him right after reading "Seven Arrows", and how I met him at the Clinton dump.

Brian asked, "Is that that old long gray-haired Indian that wears buckskins and moccasins and walks everywhere? I think they call him "Little Bear."

I replied, "That's him."

Brian and David said almost in unison, "Jesus Bob. Everybody in Clinton just about claims he's crazy. They both laughed a little.

I replied angrily, "Have you two ever read the book, "Seven Arrows"? Do you know anything about American Indian religion? Have you ever read "Black Elk Speaks"? Do you know anything about the "Brothers of the Shield"?

Brian and David both went "Deer in headlights", and then looked at one another. And before they could speak I shouted, "I'll answer that one for you.

The answer is No. You don't know anything about any of it.

Do you know what that makes you, a couple of ignorant white men, out of touch with nature, out of touch with spirituality, out of touch with God, and out of touch with life as we know it!

And so you can laugh. You can call the man crazy. But please do not do it in front of me. I am learning amazing things from this man and witnessing amazing things in his presence.

You see belittling him in front of me only makes me think less of you. Not him. I love you guys like brothers, and we've gone through some serious shit together.

"But when it comes to Father or 'Little Bear' as you call him, you would do well to attempt to learn what you can from the man, instead of making fun of him. I know what I'm talking about.

However on that note, I'm going to shake both of your hands, and give you both a brotherly hug, thank you for the great hospitality, and be on my way.

You see, I need to go see if Father has returned from his spiritual walkabout, because I'm very eager to learn more from him.

Again, I'm sorry for worrying you guys. But now that you know where his camp is, and that that's where I'll be, there shouldn't be any more worrying about me; unless he hasn't returned, in which case I will come back here in the meantime. That is, if I'm still welcome after chewing your asses like that."

Brian and David broke out in laughter, and we all laughed, hugged and shook hands, and I gathered up Lazarus, and we headed back to Fathers' campsite.

As we drove down the long winding barely visible dirt path of a road, and could see his lodge; the rickety old painted skins draped upon, and partially stretched across the old weathered hand hewn lodge polls that made his teepee. I could see a faint wisp of smoke coming out of the smoke hole where the lodge polls met.

This meant that Father had returned from his recent journey of enlightenment.

As the excitement welled up in my chest, I turned to Lazarus who was also very excited, spinning in the passenger seat, and looking at me excitedly, and panting.

And I said, "Look Laz. He's back. He's back. "As I drove down the last 50 feet or so to his camp, steering with my left hand, I petted Lazarus with my right hand happily saying, "That's a good boy. That's a good boy. Yeah. We're going to have fun. We are going to learn about life; and nature, and Indians, yeah. That's a good boy!"

As I brought the truck to stop, Father emerged from his lodge. With his pipe in his right hand, he waved to me with his left hand. And as I turned off the motor of the truck,

I heard him say in that whisper of a voice of his, "Welcome back, my son. Please come inside, so we can sit by the fire, and tell each other of our journeys. And what we have learned from our journeys. I have smoked salmon, and wild potatoes and greens to share with you tonight. Please, come in my son, we have much to discuss."

And with that, we both smiled at one another, and Lazarus ran up to Father, and bowed his head to graciously receive a soft pet on the head, and we all entered Father's lodge. And as we all entered his lodge he patted me on the shoulder and said, "It is truly good to see you again, my son."

And I replied, "And it is truly good to see you again as well, Father." I remember thinking to myself as I entered his lodge, "Well Bob, you've quenched your sexual appetite for a while, it's time to put away childish things and start learning about all the important things, the really important things in life.

And so, over the next week and a half I did.

And I would learn things that changed my life and my outlook on life, and my outlook on the world, and my outlook on mankind, forever.

Chapter 21

Learning more from Father, finally seeing his Precious, a crazy swapping session, and a grateful thank you and goodbye, and then back to the House of Che

Father and I exchanged stories that night into the wee hours of the morning.

I told him more about living on the beach in Marina Del Rey, and how I had been playing music, and building furniture for a living.

I recounted this time in detail, how my parents had both died only three months apart, and how I had attempted suicide myself soon afterwards, and how Lazarus had saved me from a watery grave.

He told me of growing up as a boy in Canada; and going to the white man's school with his brother and sister. And how that at a young age he decided to follow in his father's footsteps and become a Brother of the Shield, and learn the ways of the Shield; while his brother and sister made friends with the white children, and learned the ways of the whites, like almost all of the other Indian children.

When it became so late that sleep would no longer be denied, I said good night and went to the camper and went to bed after giving Lazarus a short walk.

Early in the morning Lazarus was crying to go out, so I opened the camper shell door and he jumped out, and I went back to sleep.

I don't know how long I was asleep, but sometime later in the morning I was awakened by Father's voice coming from his lodge.

I looked at my watch and it was 10:30 AM.

I thought, "Wow. I must've really been tired." I got up and got dressed.

And that's when a wave of panic overcame me.

Where was Lazarus? I let him out of the truck at the break of dawn, and he had never been gone for more than 30 or 40 min., and this time he had been gone for hours now.

I climbed over the tailgate of the truck and down onto the ground. Walking rapidly toward Fathers lodge, I stopped just outside of the entrance which was open with the lodge flap tied back. I peeked around the edge of the entrance to see who he was talking with.

I didn't want to burst in on him whether I was panicked, or not.

As I peeked into the Lodge, a sense of relief and amazement overcame me. That is because Father was having a conversation with Lazarus.

I watched in disbelief, and then amazement as Father would speak to Lazarus who was sitting directly across from him.

Lazarus's eyes focused on Father, his body completely still; from time to time he would turn his head from side to side as if he were pondering Father's words, in a pose that mimicked the famous Victor Victrola dog from long ago. I must've watched them for half an hour or so.

Father would speak softly to Lazarus, sometimes asking questions, and sometimes seeming to answer questions from Lazarus.

While Lazarus maintained the same pose, occasionally softly whimpering, and sometimes pawing the floor of the lodge, and cocking his head from side to side.

The conversation ended with Father saying to Lazarus, "You have had an amazing life little one. It is sad that you are burdened with the scorpion tail which makes life so hard for you with others of your kind.

But you have the gift of great intelligence which will continue to help you to overcome all of your physical burdens.

Hopefully the knowledge that I have given to you this morning will help you in your journey through life as well.

And your love for Bob and his love for you will continue to protect both of you throughout your journeys. Now go wake-up Bob, before he sleeps the day away. Go little one."

And with that Lazarus jumped up and ran out of the Lodge. He ran right past me towards the truck, until I called out "Lazarus. Lazarus."

And then he ran back to me jumping into my arms, I hugged him and petted him, and yelled to Father inside the lodge, "Father.

I'm up. I'm going to make some quick breakfast, and feed Lazarus. You're welcome to join us if you wish, or we will come in and see you when we're done eating."

Father replied, "Make your breakfast, my son. I will be out in a little while."

This was almost a daily occurrence over the next week and a half.

We would talk both day and night; Father explaining to me why the mountains were there. Why the stars in the sky did not fall from the sky.

Essentially, during that next week and a half that I spent with Father, I learned the old ways, the pure ways, the ways of living in harmony with nature; the ways of not always taking from the planet, but giving back to the planet as well.

The ways of a people who could not conceive of owning the land, the land which belongs to everyone. A people who were stunned by the slaughter of the Buffalo, the revered Tatonka, who were slaughtered almost to extinction; you see they could not conceive of killing solely for killings' sake.

I learned much about life and nature from him.

And he learned much about the ways of the whites from me. Among many other things, he changed the way that I look at ALL animals.

For instance when we were out walking one day, we came upon a large coiled rattlesnake. I picked up a large rock and started to raise it over my head to kill the snake.

Father put his hand on my shoulder, saying, "Please put down the stone my son." I replied, "But Father. Shouldn't we kill, it?" And with Father's reply my lesson began,

"Why must we kill it, my son? Has it harmed us? Did it not warn us? It is a viper, and could've laid in wait in the bushes, and struck out and bitten us both. But instead, it chose to warn us. So should its reward for warning us be death?

The answer is NO, my son. This creature deserves its life like all other creatures. The only time that you should take another creatures life is if it is trying to take yours, or if you need its body for food to sustain your life.

And even in such cases its life should be taken only when no other alternative is possible and with the reverence that should come with such an act. All creatures, man or animal should always have their spirit sung to the other side with a prayer of either thanks or apology, or both. That is the way it is done. That is what the whites will never understand."

I put down the rock. And Father began to approach the snake.

"Look out, Father. He's a big one. And he looks really mad." I said.

Father replied, "She is not mad. She is pregnant. And she is frightened for her babies."

He began to talk softly to the snake, "It is all right, little sister. We wish you no harm."

As he talked softly to the snake the buzzing of its rattle slowed to a slow clicking sound. As if the snake understood what he was saying.

Father continued, "You must get off of the trail little sister. It is not safe for you here."

He motioned up the hill and continued, "Only 75 feet in that direction is a cool dark den, were you can eat rat, and rest and be safe.

Now go little sister. Go and be safe."

He motioned with both hands in the direction of the den. The rattler slowly uncoiled and slithered off up the hill and into the crack in the rocks that he had motioned towards. As the snake slithered into the den I stood there dumbfounded.

I said to Father, "You have to teach me how to do that, how to speak to animals."

Father laughingly replied, "I told you, my son, it took me many, many years to learn that skill.

I can tell you two things which can help you to communicate with animals without learning the gift. The first thing is to mean what you say. Look the animal directly in the eye when you communicate with it. If all else fails, you can use what you whites call 'Baby talk.'"

Very surprised, I asked, "What?"

Father replied, "I know it sounds crazy, my son, but animals communicate emotionally. And unless they are intent on killing you, they all love to hear baby talk."

I thought he might be crazy until 12 years later, in 1985,

when I was trying to wrangle a 9-10 foot rattler at my house in Topanga, California.

At this point the huge snake had struck out twice past my thigh and missed, luckily. I was trying to get it to go into a large trash can so that I could relocate it. I remembered Father's words from 12 years earlier, and I began talking baby talk to the huge serpent.

"Atsa' cutest widdle snake, he's the handsomest little guy. I wouldn't hurt him for anything. All I want him to do is go into the trash can so I can let him go again where it's safe, and the food and water are."

I know you won't believe this, but it's the truth. After those few sentences of baby talk, the buzzing slowed down to a click and the rattler slowly crawled into the trashcan, and I got him relocated.

And over the years I have yet to find an animal that does not respond to baby talk in one way or another, even raccoons. It seems to be a reassuring way to calm them down; just some more great wisdom from Father that has served me well throughout the years.

One day Father decided it was time for me to see his revered "Precious."

We walked from his camp for about 15 minutes to a tree covered area on top of a bluff, and there under the trees was a tarp covering what appeared to be something the size of a car.

Father turned to me and putting his hands on my shoulders he said, "Other than you, my son, only three other people have ever seen my Precious." I replied "I'm honored, Father."

He walked over and pulled off the tarp, revealing a 1957 Chevy four-door sedan almost completely covered with every kind of chrome accessory possible.

It looked like someone had taken a pristine 57' Chevy and ordered every exterior accessory from the JC Whitney catalog and stuck it on the thing. It must've had at least 30 rearview mirror sets of all styles all over it, going in both directions. Aiming both to the front and rear, it also had numerous hood ornaments, mud flaps, chrome skirts, etc., I might add.

I said, "Father, I had a car just like this, except mine was a two-door, and mine was green instead of blue, and mine had a Corvette motor. What kind of motor does yours have?"

I opened the hood to see an empty cavity. Stunned, I looked at Father and asked, "Father, where's the motor?" How did you get it here?"

Father replied, "My Precious does not require a motor, because she has nowhere to go. She is home. She has always been here. And she will always remain here.

To honor her, once every moon, I walk into Clinton or go to Kamloops, and trade antlers, and other things that I find, for another chrome jewel to adorn her beautiful body.

Once every three moons I clean her inside and out, and wax her top to bottom.

After all she is a beauty queen, not a beast of burden to be used for something as trivial as transportation."

I thought to myself, "Is this man crazy, or am I the crazy one?

He's been spot on with everything that he's taught me so for. So why question this now.

After all, what's more fun than a car show in the middle of nowhere. What a trip."

I stayed with him for eight more illuminating, and interesting days until a strange truck came rolling up to the camp and Brian jumped out.

He said that they had begun to worry about me again, and he came down to check on me.

He told me there were some new available good looking girls at the commune; and that they could actually use my help on a couple of their projects as they were a little short on manpower for a few weeks. It was pretty easy math for me; new available good-looking girls and a shortage in manpower.

I told Brian that I would be happy to help them, and that I couldn't leave with them now, but would be happy to head up there in a few hours.

Father came out of his lodge to see who had arrived.

Brian said, "Hello, Little Bear. How are you?"

Father replied, "The man who breaks horses. How are you my friend? And how is your friend the other man who breaks horses doing?"

I knew right away that he was referring to David.

Brian replied, "We are both well. Life is good. It's good to see you again Little Bear. I guess we'll see you later this afternoon, Bob."

Father waved and said, "It is good to see you again as well, man who breaks horses." Brian jumped back into the truck and he and the guy driving left.

Father asked, "So you must leave, my son?" "Yes, Father. They need some help at the commune. And they are my friends so I must go help them."

"That is true, my son. If they need your help, and they are your friends, then you must help them.

Will I see you again my son?" Father asked,

"I'm sure that you will, Father." I said, "But before I go, there are some things that I want you to have.

Extra things that I really have no use for that I believe you could use.

You were looking for tools when we met at the Clinton dump, right?"

"Yes, my son. I am always looking for tools." Father replied. I smiled and said. "Well, have I got some stuff for you?"

I opened up the toolboxes above and on either side of the wheel wells of the truck bed.

I had a lot of stuff in there that I thought I would need on the trip that I never had found a use for that were very heavy. I remember asking him, "Could you use a big vise?"

Father replied, "Yes, my son, thank you." I pulled the 45 pound iron vise out of the truck and half dropped it on to the ground.

Father said, "It is very heavy, isn't it, my son. That means that it must be very well made. It is too heavy to carry with me every time I move camp, so I will find a special place in the forest to put it, and I will keep it oiled and covered. And I will walk to it when I need to use it. Thank you, my son."

As he talked, I was rummaging through the toolboxes looking for other things heavy to give him. "You told me that you make your own arrowheads and knives. Do you have an anvil father?

Father replied, "No, I don't, my son, but your first gift is already too much." "Nonsense", I replied, "Besides, I was going to get rid of these things anyway, you see, I have no use for them Father. How about a pipe wrench, can you use a pipe wrench?"

"Yes, my son. But these gifts that you give me are way too valuable. How can I accept them?"

"Father," I said, "I told you that these things have no value to me. And the kindness that you have shown too me by accepting me into your home, and sharing your knowledge and wisdom, which I'm sure will change my life forever, and for the better is priceless. What else could you use?"
"Stop it." Father shouted, "No more. No more, my son. No more gifts please, my son." I asked, "What's the matter Father?"

What I had failed to realize, and was not aware of, is that when an Indian receives a gift he must repay the gift giver in-kind', and not in-kind in actual value, but in-kind in the items perceived value by him.

So that the conundrum now was that this stuff was all nothing but junk to me; heavy junk, which I needed to get rid of to lighten the load of the truck.

However to him these were all treasures, indispensable implements of survival, if you will. And now he was obligated to repay me in-kind with items of equal value.

He invited me into his lodge. He sat down on the small bearskin rug with head attached and the claws as well.

I sat across from him on a woven Indian rug, and Lazarus lay down next to me.

The first thing that he pulled out was a pair of beaded butterfly pattern leather Indian dancing wristlets with leather fringe. He asked me if I liked them.

I told him that I did, that they were very beautiful, and that they must have been very difficult to make.

He replied, "They're yours my son." I started to say, "But Father, this is too valuable".

He interrupted, "Be quiet, my son. What about this?"

He handed me a large Bowie knife in a beautiful leather beaded sheath. It had a beautiful antler handle with an abalone inlaid eye inset in the base of the antler handle. Engraved in the huge extremely sharp blade where the words "Arkansas Toothpick".

I started to object again, "Father, this is too much", when Father interrupted again. "Do you like this." he said as he reached behind him on the other side and pulled out the long ermine pouch and handed it to me. It was the softest fur that I had ever felt and beautiful in color.

I untied the end and opened it. I couldn't believe my eyes.

It was the hand carved silver and ivory ceremonial peace pipe that he always smoked from. The ivory appeared to be made from walrus tusks.

I had never seen it this close before. It was exquisitely carved with Native American drawings done in a form of Scrimshaw adorning it.

I loudly protested. "No Father. This is way too valuable. This isn't right. Take this back. I can't accept this. It's too valuable. Give me something less valuable; if you feel that you have to give me something;

I don't know. Give me that old bearskin rug with a bare spot on it." Father went "deer in headlights" on me.

He was speechless. He just sat there staring at me with wide eyes, and his mouth wide open.

In my LA, city boy, white man stupidity, I had inadvertently asked for his most prized possession;

His giveaway animal, the animal which gave its life for him, when he was a boy; he had fasted for many days on his vision quest to become a Brother of the Shield, until a small black bear laid down, and gave its life for him, so that he could become a Brother of the Shield.

He did not kill it; rather it surrendered its life, so that he might live.

So that when he sang it to the other side of the Great River, and took its name, and painted its likeness on his shield, and cosumed it's flesh, it became a constant reminder for him of the most significant event in his life.

It had been his prized possession for so long that he had worn a bare spot in the hide from sitting on it in the same spot for over 50 years.

And I had inadvertently just given this great man, who I respected and admired so much the greatest insult conceivable.

That is when I realized what I had done. And before I could apologize, and explain my blunder, his look of extreme shock, and amazement, suddenly changed to a broad grin, as he said to me in that raspy whisper of his. "You shall have them all, my son.

And all that I ask is that you take care of "Little Bear", and teach those that you meet when you go back South to the white world that you know, what I have taught you.

To stop hurting the Earth, stop killing each other, and all of the other creatures. And most importantly change your ways, and go back to nature before it's too late; because if you keep destroying the Great Mother Earth, eventually she will have to fight back. And when she does that will mean the end for all white men and all men of all colors, and almost all of the animals. I am talking about the end-of-life as we know it my son. So tell them, and get them to change their ways before it's too late."

I tried to get him to keep his giveaway animal, and the other priceless objects. But he forced me to take them.

So I told him that I would do my best to convince as many people as possible that his message was true.

I shook his hand. We embraced and patted each other on the back, and he petted Lazarus and Lazarus licked his hand.

I told him that I would see him soon. Lazarus and I jumped into the truck and we were on our way back to the commune. (Sadly the items that he gave me, except for the dancing wristlets, along with all of my 16 mm footage that I took on the trip were lost in the 1980 flood in Topanga, California, during which everything that was stored in my garage, and most of the garage itself were washed away.)

As we slowly drove away, I looked in the rearview mirror and waved what would turn out to be a final goodbye; and Lazarus looked back from the passenger door window and gave an anxious whimper, his way of saying goodbye to Father.

Good old Lazarus, he was always ahead of the curve. He knew what I would not realize until much later; that sadly this would be the last time that we would see Father.

It was nearly month before I got back down to his campsite, and he was gone. He had moved his lodge to another campsite. God only knows where.

Whenever I went into Clinton I would ask the guys at the auto parts store/garage/ gas station, if they had seen him? Usually the answer was no. But once they told me that I had just missed him. He had been in a few days earlier to trade some antlers, and arrow heads for some reflective mud flaps, obviously for his "Precious."

So I drove up to where he kept his" Precious" right away with Lazarus hoping that we might catch him there. But there was no sign of him.

I left him a note telling him to leave me a letter, or a map with directions with one of the gas station guys in Clinton telling me where he was, so that I could find him again.

I would check with them every time I went into town. That is, until it got too cold up there, and I headed back to Michael's in Vancouver. And then back home to LA.

I'm really sorry that I never got to spend more time with this amazing man who had such an influence on my life. He wised me up on so many things, and gave me so many gifts, both spiritual and otherwise.

I must say that I firmly believe that one day I will reunite with Lazarus and Father on the other side of the Great River, and Father and I will talk again about life and death.

And life will feel good again, even in death.

And I will be able to throw the stick for Lazarus again, and Lazarus will be able to bring the stick back to me again.

And then finally the circle will be complete, as in the great story of the Circle of Shields handed down from father to son for centuries by the Brothers of the Shield.

Chapter 22

Back to the House of Che for fun with Freddy the goat, comic book hero face painting on acid, and then back to Michael's--one step ahead of another crazy jealous boyfriend

I was still sad about leaving Father when Lazarus and I arrived at the commune that afternoon.

The first thing that I noticed upon arrival was that a new Che Guevara flag with him in black silhouette upon a white background had replaced the old torn and weathered red background version that I knew. Also a new flag adorned the second largest building on the compound. It was the Revolutionary war flag showing a picture of a segmented snake in a circle with the caption "Don't tread on me".

I immediately thought somebody's been to Vancouver.

By this point all of the dogs at the commune knew my truck, and me and Lazarus, because the barking was moderate, and all tails were wagging.

Lazarus and I jumped out of the truck into the middle of the throng of dogs, me petting and greeting as many as possible, Lazarus sniffing and wagging. It was K-9 old home week. I talked with a couple of the guys who told me that Brian and David were down on the backside of the property by the beaver pond building a sauna to use during the rapidly approaching winter.

The sauna design that they had in mind, was the kind where you sweat for as long as you can take it, and then jump into the freezing pond water. The guys said that it was supposed to be very healthy for you.

I replied, "It sounds like a quick trip to a bout with pneumonia to me."

Lazarus and I followed them down to the sauna construction site, and were welcomed by Brian and David.

David had a construction question for me. "Bob?" he asked, "We have to build this thing right up next to the water's edge. Would you build this like a regular log cabin, or in some other way?"

I replied, "Well, David, I'm no builder, but I did get a chance to see how they built a lot of the places down on the beach in

Marina Del Rey, and what I learned from that is that you need to get down to some form of bed rock if you want the side closest to the water to stay.

So I guess I would coat 4 posts with pine tar, or what have you, and then drive 2 of them vertically into the edge of the pond until they won't go any further, support them horizontally, and drive 2 more in away from the pond, connect all 4 posts horizontally, and build from there.

You can drive them in using that homemade crane that you use to move the logs for the log cabins. Just put a big rock or something heavy on the end of it, and lift it up, and then drop it down on to the top of the post." David replied, "That's a great idea, Bob. Glad you're back brother."

It was getting late, so they stopped work for the day, and we went back up to the main house.

There was a lot of activity, people cleaning, others making dinner, and still others setting the dinner tables.

The guys weren't kidding; I was introduced to three new single girls. They were all cute, but the prettiest girl was a dark-haired beauty with big dark eyebrows named, Marylee. And thinking about it over the years I've come to the conclusion that my infatuation with hairy women probably was greatly influenced by Marylee.

Now, don't get me wrong. In the 60s and 70s almost all women were hairy to some degree or another. In those days if you got a woman's panties off and she was shaved, you would probably be afraid that she was fighting a BAD case of the crabs, and be somewhat hesitant to fuck her.

I managed to sit across from Marylee during dinner, and we had a great conversation.

And after dinner, I and some of the other guys entertained everybody with music, both individually, and together.

I made up a song about the commune and Brian and David that was pretty funny and got a lot of laughs. And Marylee seemed to be suitably impressed.

Afterwards she and I went for a walk, got high, and wound up back in my camper.

This girl really had me turned on, I think, partly, because

Marylee was also the name of the first girl that I ever had a crush on at the age of seven.

As we kissed and I began to undress her, and myself, I was getting more and more excited.

I began to think as the foreplay progressed "Wow, this girl is a fox, beautiful face, beautiful breasts, great hips and legs."

And then as I pulled her panties down I thought, "Holy shit. That's the biggest Bush that I've ever seen in my life."

The problem was that while I was thinking the last thought I didn't realize, but I was also saying it out loud (probably from the shock of it all.)

I looked up at her to see her sexually stimulated smile slowly melt into a sad frown. A tear slowly ran down her cheek as she whimpered, "It's too much, isn't it. I know I should do something about it.

It's the family curse. My whole family is very hairy. Every time I do my legs and armpits I think that I should be doing something about my pussy as well, but I just don't know how to go about it by myself."

The whole time she was talking I was thinking about how I was going to dig myself out of this one.

And then I said, "No. You don't understand. I think it's cool.

She interrupted, "You don't think it's ugly? You don't think it's nasty? I had one guy who wouldn't even make love to me because he said it was nasty."

I replied, "Nasty? On the contrary, I think it's beautiful. It's just the biggest one that I've ever seen. But it's still beautiful, just like the rest of you."

As she wiped a tear from her eye, her spirits began to lift, and she said, "Really? You really think it's beautiful?"

As I pushed the hair aside revealing her vagina, and slowly leaned down toward it, I looked up at her and said, "Let me show you how beautiful I think it is."

As my tongue began to do its job, I heard her give out the first of many soft wet moans, and the foreplay was over.

The sex was great, and as I reached up to turn the kerosene lantern off, I saw Lazarus looking at me with an expression that seemed to say, "This shit is getting old. Where's my bitch, you asshole?"

I looked back at him as I slowly turned down the lantern and said, "Fuck you Laz. You have your fetching, you junkie. And, besides, you're fixed anyway."

Then with the lantern out I crawled back under the covers with Marylee who asked, "Who were you talking too?" I replied, "I was just talking to the dog. It's a long story."

She let out a little laugh, and we were back to making love, and then off to sleep.

We awoke the next morning to the loud clang of the breakfast, lunch and dinner steel triangle that hung on the porch of the main building, the reminder to everyone that breakfast was ready, and that if you weren't up, to get your asses up.

She and I got dressed. I let Lazarus out of the truck, and we went up to the main building for breakfast. Marylee and I sat at the first table with Brian and David and their families.

The subject of conversation was primarily the construction of the sauna, and whether or not to dig a deadfall pit on the path that the grizzlies always seemed to come in on during their destructive rampages into the compound. I pointed out that the idea seemed quite dangerous to me, and the idea was shelved for the time being.

David said that when he was in Vancouver he also picked up a bunch of acid, and suggested that some of us try it and that if it was good, a bunch of us could drop acid on Saturday and we could all paint our faces like comic book characters.

What fun. I forgot to mention that these folks had no television, and nothing for entertainment besides board games, musicians, and a four track tape player that until David had recently gone to Vancouver and purchased 20 used tapes, had only three tapes. Because a couple of the goats had gotten out of their corrals, a while back, and gotten into the main building and eaten all but three of the tapes, along with all of the food, etc.

Because that's all they had for entertainment, their main source of entertainment was comic books, which they purchased every time they went into Clinton. And even though the goats had eaten a lot of the comic books when they ate the tapes, they still had thousands of them to read.

So the idea was that everybody drops acid, and paints their face like a comic book character.

We worked on the sauna all that day, and at dinner that night it was decided that Brian, David, and I would drop the acid the following day to see how good it was.

I felt really honored. It was almost like I was one of the leaders of the commune as well.

The next morning when we got up Marylee told me that she would be close by, and if I had a bad trip she would be there to help me ride it out. So while everybody else had breakfast Brian and David and I dropped acid with some Red Zinger tea.

At the commune there were three goat corrals: one for the female goats and kids, or baby goats, one for the male goats, and one for Freddy.

Freddy was and inordinately large male Billy goat, with a large set of horns, he stood 56 inches at the withers, so that when someone my height of 5'10" stood in front of him, he was almost looking you right in the eyes. He was very heavy with huge strong shoulders, and according to David was a cross breed between a very large female goat, and a huge wild mountain goat, which accounted for his size, and somewhat narrow jaw; and of course a lot of his wildness! I might add that it took 10 guys and a bunch of rope to hold him long enough for Brian to take his measurements.

Freddy was big and strong, and had a real attitude, because he knew he was big and strong.

There were a number of people at the commune that refused to look Freddy in the eye.

All of the women and children, and most of the beta males that lived there gave Freddy's corral a wide berth.

And I must admit that he had hurt a few people.

Even Brian and David didn't like going into the corral with him unless he was tied up first.

The acid was butterfly windowpane. Tiny clear tabs with an almost microscopic outline of a butterfly on each clear square tab.

Just about the time that I was beginning to think that the stuff was no good, it started to come on.

It was definitely different than other acid I had had before. The psychedelic effects were definitely different.

Instead of everything melting, and a feeling of paranoia setting in, colors seemed to be heightened, and much more brilliant.

The only thing that I can compare it too is something a kin to being in a Michael Mann film, or a character on Miami Vice, if you know what I mean.

In other words reds were really red. And greens were really green. It was also accompanied by a kind of euphoria. A kind of 'All's right with the world', combined with I'm invincible, and I can do anything.

I've had these sensations numerous times on other kinds of acid since, and every time I usually did something very dangerous.

Brian said that he was going to go down and check on the construction. David smiled and said he was going to go and pick some flowers. And when I looked around the main room of the main building,

I was alone. So I thought to myself, "I'll take a walk."

Which I did, I walked out past a couple of the outbuildings to the corrals. One of the girls was milking the female goats in their corral.

And I sat down and leaned up against a tree opposite Freddy's corral.

When he saw me he ran over towards me stopping just short of the top corral rail, the large wooden triangle around his neck slapping against the rail making a loud crack.

As dust flew up around him he stared at me with steely eyes, and stamped his large right front hoof on the ground.

And staring back at him, and directly into his eyes I smiled and said, "Hey Freddy. How's it going buddy?"

Freddy seemed to stiffen, his stare as deliberate as ever, he let out a loud snort.

Still smiling I stood up, and began to walk toward him, still staring him directly in the eyes.

The closer I got, the more agitated Freddy became. But I continued forward, still smiling, undeterred, because after all, I was invincible. And, besides, Father had told me how to talk to animals. So obviously Freddy would understand that I meant him no harm, and that I came in peace.

This is one of those stories that while you're telling it you have to wonder why you're still here.

By the time I reached the corral, where Freddy's huge head

hung out over the top rail, he seemed to have calmed down a bit.

I spoke to him again, saying, "Wow. What a handsome guy you are. Breaking into baby talk I continued, "He's just the handsomest little guy. Yes he is. He dis da biggest old handsomest Billy goat dat der ever was."

I reached out to pet him, and he pulled his head away, and backed 10 or 12 feet back into the corral, away from the fence.

Continuing my baby talk, I crawled between the corral rails and walked towards him in the corral saying, "What's a matter, Freddy? I wouldn't hurt him for all the money in the world. He's such a good boy." Reaching out and touching both of his horns with my hands, I began to pet his horns in an upward stroking motion.

In the background I could hear people yelling, "Oh my God. What is he doing? Somebody get him out of there before he gets killed. Quick somebody find David or Brian, hurry."

I remember thinking, "I hope they're not worried about me? Freddy and I are fine; besides, I'm invincible."

I could hear the commotion, as more and more people began to gather at a distance circling the corral that contained me and Freddie.

The sporadic cries of impending doom that were springing forth from the crowd, coming from every direction, rising above the dull mumbles and whispers that filled the air. "My God, why isn't somebody doing something. Get that poor man out of there before he gets killed.

Where's Brian, or David? What are they going to do; they're tripping on acid too. Well, I'm getting get my gun."

While all of this was going on around me, I continued to talk to Freddie in a soft, low baby talk, soothing, and comforting; while I petted his face and muzzle.

I kissed his muzzle, and ducking under his long horns I grabbed him around the neck, and while still talking softly to him, gave him a long hug.

At this point I heard David's voice first saying, "Everybody quiet down, Now." His voice seemed to come closer, "Bob. Slowly, and calmly, back away from the goat." Then I heard Mary Lee say, "Listen to David, Bob, you're in danger!"

Irritated, I turned to David and Mary Lee, and replied, "David, Marylee; I've got this. Freddie and I are having a moment.

You people have all misjudged this goat. He doesn't want to hurt anybody. It's just that you all misunderstand him, and constantly seem to piss him off. And frankly right now, I know how he feels, because you're starting to really PISS ME OFF. Why don't all of you just go about your business and just leave me and Freddie alone? We're doing fine. We are actually having quite a conversation. I wish you could join us."

I went back to hugging Freddie.

David replied in a concerned and almost terrified voice, "Bob. Listen to me carefully. You don't know what you're doing. You are loaded on acid, and you're not thinking rationally right now. Do exactly what I tell you to do. Slowly back away from the goat."

Now extremely angry, I turned to David and yelled, "I don't know what I'm doing? Well we'll see about that right now won't we."

When I yelled at David, Freddie jumped a little, and the whole commune, including Mary Lee, let out a loud communal gasp in unison. Turning back to Freddie I petted him some more, and whispered into his ear, "Its okay Freddie. They just don't understand us. But we'll show them. Won't we, kid?"

Releasing my grasp on Freddie, but still petting his left cheek I turned to David and Mary Lee and said, "Watch this."

I put one hand on each of his horns, and pressing my forehead to his forehead I began to say loudly, "I love you, Freddie. And I know that you love me. And I promise that I will never, ever let anyone ever hurt you, because you're my friend."

I could hear the same loud communal gasp emanating from the crowd, interspersed with occasional cries, screams, and whimpers.

But Freddie and I were oblivious to such nonsense. We were, if you will, in the zone.

I learned later according to numerous onlookers, including Mary Lee, that the terrified crowd watched me communicating head to head with Freddie the goat for what seemed to be (for the crowd) an eternity, but turned out only to be around 1 minute or so.

After which I took both hands and rubbed the top of Freddie's head, kind of like you do with a big old shaggy dog when you're done playing with him.

After that I turned my back on Freddie and started to walk away from him. The loud communal gasp permeated the air once more.

Stopping, I turned and looked back at Freddie who remained standing where I had left him some eight to ten feet away. Looking at him I slapped the side of my thigh three or four times coaxing him to follow me saying, "Come on Freddie. Come on kid. Come on. You can do it.
"The crowd gasped again, even louder this time. I heard a scream. In my periphery I could see one of the women in the area where the scream came from fall to the ground. (She had fainted.)
That's when Freddie began to move. Not running, but not walking either.
I turned my eyes from Freddie to see one of the guys from the commune starting to raise a rifle.
I yelled at the guy with the rifle, "If you hurt this goat, I'll kill you." Freddie began to slow down a few feet before he reached me.
And when he reached me he slowly nuzzled my chest with his muzzle, and then a giant sandpapery tongue went into my beard and worked its way across my cheek.
I patted Freddie three or four times on the shoulder, and calmly walked over and stepped outside of the corral.

Once I was outside of the corral the whole commune let out a giant cheer, and began to applaud; which scared the hell out of both me and Freddie.
People ran up to me from all sides, as I walked away from the corral. Brian and David pushed their way to the front of the pack, with Mary Lee of course.
While Mary Lee hugged me; Brian started by asking, "What were you thinking Bob?"
David interrupted saying, "Screw that. We know what he was thinking. He's fucking loaded on acid. The real question is, how the hell did you do that Bob?
That goat has hurt a lot of people. And you go in with him for a few minutes loaded on acid, and the next thing you know you're hugging him, and he's following you around like a puppy dog. How the hell did you do that?"
I replied, "I learned some things from Father about

229

communicating with animals. And I don't know if it was the acid or what, but I can talk to Freddie. In fact I can tell you what he's thinking right now."

David asked sarcastically, "Oh yeah? Tell us Bob. What's Freddie thinking right now?"

I replied angrily back to David, "Do you mean other than the fact that you're an asshole, David?

He's thinking that he finally has a friend at this commune.

Think about it, David. I know that you guys didn't realize what you were doing at the time, but as far as Freddie's concerned, all that you have ever done is to bully him.

You see guys, fear, and paranoia are a powerful thing, and the stronger the fear, and the paranoia, the more we tend to overcompensate.

So every time that you brought half the guys from the commune to laso and restrain poor Freddie just to get in the corral with him, he began to hate you more and more.

Until after a while he became enraged any time he saw anyone.

I promised him that I would try to get through to at least one of you guys so that he will still have a friend here when I have to leave.

And he told me that he was fine with that.

One of the guys in the crowd said "Talking to goats? Sounds like the acid talking, to me." The crowd laughed in unison.

Angrily I shouted back at the Doubting Thomas, "You'll see when the acid wears off asshole, you'll all see."

Leaving Mary Lee, I pushed my way through the crowd over to the greenhouse that stood some 35 feet away from Freddie's corral. I went inside and yanked out four or five mature carrots from the planter boxes;

And making my way back through the crowd, and going past Mary Lee, Brian and David, and stepping through the corral rails, and into the corral. I walked over to Freddie who calmly walked to me, and began to feed him the carrots while saying loudly to the crowd, and looking directly at Brian and David,

"And by the way, another thing that just infuriates him is how you torture him by growing really tasty vegetables a few feet away from him, and then only feed him your left over garbage.

So it would be nice if every once in a while if you would feed him a few carrots, or radishes, or a tomato or two.

As I fed Freddie the carrots with one hand, and patted him on the neck with the other, he appeared to be smiling as he mowed through the carrots.

Brian took off his cowboy hat and scratched his head asking, "You learned all of that from Little Bear in a few weeks?" "I learned a whole lot more than that from "Father" or "Little Bear" as you call him."

From that day forward I was the only one at the commune who could freely go in and out of Freddie's corral.

Once when one of the other guys helped me bring some hay into Freddie's corral, and Freddie chased him out of the corral with a vengeance, scaring the hell out of the poor guy.

Then he calmly walked back to me and snuggled his head up underneath my arm as a sign of affection.

I worked with David and Freddie, and taught David some of the things that I had learned from Father over the next week or so. So that by the time that I had to leave the following Sunday David could go in and out of the corral and could pet Freddie.

I was happy to know that when I finally had to go, that I had kept my word to Freddie, and that he would have a friend at the commune after my departure. A few days later another small caravan of kids came through the commune heading east to Montréal, and, sadly, Marylee and a couple of the other girls went with them. But she had family in Montréal so I understood.

I had just about recuperated from the Freddie acid incident of four days earlier when Saturday rolled around.

And I knew that I was going to be in for it, when 20 or so of us met in the main building and Brian and David started handing out hits of acid, and people started picking through comic books and choosing the characters they wanted to be.

Taking face paint, they painted their faces to look like their respective chosen comic book character in front of the five or so mirrors pulled from every building in the commune.

It was decided that only half of the commune's members would participate. The other half was composed of children, and those who would watch the children, and those who would watch over and take care of the people on acid. It was a good plan.

As a big pot of Red Zinger tea brewed on one of the big iron cook stoves, people started dropping acid, and painting their faces.

A tall attractive woman walked through the doors of the main building where we all were.

She was the new neighbor who had moved in less than a 3 miles to the south just off of the logging road, and was rebuilding an old homesteaded house for the winter while living in it.

As a 'Howdy Neighbor' present she had brought two big jugs of homemade wine. One was blackberry, and one was elderberry.

This was when I learned that I can't personally combine alcohol. Red Zinger tea and acid.

I had dropped the acid about 35 min. before she arrived. And now I was searching through the comic books, while alternately drinking Red Zinger tea, and sampling glasses full of the two wines.

After about three or four glasses of wine and a couple of cups of tea, and leafing through comic books for about a half an hour, I was starting to feel the effects of the wine, the acid, the tea, and an empty stomach.

I picked out a comic book, and saw my character. I rummaged through the face paint picking out colors to match my character. I looked at the comic book cover and then called out the paint colors as I grabbed them.

Silver, I've got to have silver. And black, I need black, some red for the one eye, yeah, and blue. Don't forget the blue.

Grabbing the paints, and comic book, I ran over to the mirror in the corner, away from everyone else and began to apply the paints to my face; Re-creating the image on the cover of the comic book, with my face as the pallet. Using every ounce of artistic talent that lay within the confines of my acid and alcohol soaked brain.

After what seemed to be an eternity of painstaking toil and effort, suddenly, my task was complete.

I had become "Deathlok the Destroyer." I was so proud of myself. I turned to the group to show off my new face.

Everyone in the room gasped. I remember thinking to myself, "I must be getting good at freaking people out."

Brian, laughingly, said, "Jesus Christ Bob, "Deathlok the Destroyer?"

What the hell; have you fucking flipped out or something?"

David chimed in, "Yeah, Bob. Deathlok is a killer Cyborg. Are you trying to scare the shit out of everybody?"

Well, other than making a few of the small children cry when they saw my face, everything went fine until I began to peak about five hours later.

They told me that I really started coming on to the neighbor lady. And that she got fed up with me and left and drove home.

However, an hour or so later in my drug addled state of mind, somehow I decided that she had invited me over.

So I decided to fire up my truck and go see her, managing to knock down at least half a dozen small trees with my truck in the process.

And if that wasn't bad enough when I got too her house, I began to proclaim my love for her loudly, while pounding on her front door.

After she had screamed at me for four or five times to go away, she finally pulled a 30-30 lever action Winchester rifle on me, and told me to get off of her property, or she was going to kill me.

Luckily the gun was enough to persuade me that discretion is the better part of valor, so I left and made my way back to the commune, and fell asleep in my camper.

This sad story she angrily relayed to anyone who would listen at the commune the next morning, while I was still sleeping it off.

She also said that she was going to tell her old man when he got back home the next day, and that in her words, "He would probably finish the job for her when he got back".

About one o'clock that afternoon Brian and David woke me up, told me the story, and reminded me that a woman was more than a woman in the wilderness.

Then they told me that I should hit the road right away if I wanted to stay breathing. I thought to myself, "Wow. This is the second time that I have had to run for my life from the House of Che, because I got mixed up with the wrong woman."

Brian and David told me that the coast should be clear for me to come back in three weeks or so. Because her old man was gone for months at a time and only came back for a week at a time.

So I packed up my stuff, and Lazarus and I were off to Michael's, for another run at debauchery, good food, soft beds, hot showers, and sex, drugs and rock n' roll.

And seeing that by now I was starting to look like a scraggly version of "Grizzly Adams," I was ready for a big dose of Michael's place.

Besides, Michael's people could always clean me up real good. And it was going to be great to see Chartreuse again.

Chapter 23

Back to Michael's for some R&R, feeling spiritually rejuvenated, and physically depleted

Because I had to run away from the House of Che, just ahead of another angry and crazy boyfriend, I was ready for more of the free and easy, sexy, anything goes lifestyle of Michael's place.

I only saw a couple of hitchhikers on the way into Vancouver, and they looked a bit unsavory to say the least, so I didn't stop for them.

And instead Lazarus and I drove directly into Vancouver nonstop.

After a couple of stops along the way for gas, etc. we arrived at Michael's gates about eight o'clock that evening.

As usual, when I buzzed the intercom, an unfamiliar voice asked, "Who the fuck is it?"

I replied. "It's Hippie Bob. Are Michael, or Josh around?"

The reply came back, "Are you Cowboy Hippie Bob? Or Marina Del Rey Hippie Bob?"

To which I answered, "I'm Marina Del Rey Hippie Bob. I guess Michael still has Cowboy on the do not admit list, huh?"

The voice came back, "Are you sure you're Marina Del Rey Hippie Bob?"

Now getting very frustrated I replied angrily, "Enough of this bullshit! Just go get Michael, or Josh or anybody from the Flying Circus. They all know my voice. I'm tired of this third-degree crap."

The voice on the intercom came back much more subdued, and almost apologetic. "They're all gone out of town. They should be back in a couple of days."

Even more exasperated I asked, "Everybody? What about Chartreuse?"

The voice in the box asked, "Who?"

Now I was beginning to wonder where I was going to go if I couldn't get into Michael's place. I thought, "Maybe I can sleep in the camper on the beach?"

I tried one more time asking, "Is there anybody in there who has been staying with Michael for more than a month or two?"

The voice replied, "Jerry has."

I asked, "Do you mean Big Jerry?"

The voice replied, "Yeah Big Jerry."

I said, "Go get him. He knows me."

About 10 minutes later, Big Jerry let me in. Big Jerry as I mentioned before, was kind of a resident caretaker for Michael, watching the place while he was gone away on his trips. Taking care of the animals and fixing anything that broke around the place.

As Lazarus and I drove down the long cobblestone driveway, we only noticed a couple of peacocks and the small pony along the way.

However these animals were enough to get Lazarus all worked up. His tail wagging, he barked a few hello style barks.

There were only about half as many cars and trucks parked in the huge circular cobblestone driveway in front of the house as would normally be there.

The first thing that I did was to let Lazarus out of the truck for a walk on the grounds. After the walk Lazarus and I started up the front stairs.

As we did, four or five good-looking young kids in various states of undress (It was unusually warm at that time.) came running down the stairs towards us.

They were laughing, and smiling, and as they ran, all of their long hair flowed from side to side. Two of the girls were topless and their breasts bounced up and down as they navigated their way down the stairs. I remember thinking that a picture of that scene would make a great welcome mat for Michael's house.

As they ran down the stairs towards me all clean-shaven and innocent, looking beautiful and handsome and smelling of rosewater, and lilac oil; they stopped when they got in front of me, the girls still giggling, one of the young guys looked at me and said, "Far out man. You look like you've really been out in it.

You've got to promise to tell us some stories later, man."

I said that I would. "Right on. See you later." he said.

And with that they all continued down the stairs laughing and giggling. As Lazarus and I walked in the tall ornate leaded glass front doors,

I could see some of Lay Low Eddy's latest graffiti handiwork. One of them read, "If cops are the man? Are meter maids the woman?"

Another new example read, "Who the hell is Mojo Filger? And why won't he get out of my head?"

As I walked through the large mansion with my dog at my side I began to realize that this time I had been gone WAY too long. The only person that I recognized in the whole place was Jerry.

As we strolled I questioned Jerry about the whereabouts of all of the missing people.

It turns out that Michael had taken the entire Flying Circus and a few select newcomers on a trip to Montréal.

Josh had left Michael's place over a month earlier on one of his walk across Canada planting marijuana trips; which made me wonder why I hadn't seen him, or heard of him when I was at the House of Che, as he would normally stop there on his way east.

And according to Jerry, Chartreuse had not been back since she had joined a group of people headed to Montréal a few weeks after Josh and I had headed up to the House of Che roughly a month or so before.

I asked Big Jerry if there was a free room, and he replied, "Nothing's changed here, brother, just crash where you can. Good to see you again. I've gotta check on some things, check you later."

After looking around some, I noticed that there was only one bag in the green room. This room was called that because of its jungle motif, and of the all-encompassing jungle mural with exotic plants and animals.

I ran down to the camper. Grabbing, clothes, scissors, a razor, towels, etc., I locked up the camper and headed back upstairs with Lazarus.

I first took the scissors and cut as much of my beard off as possible. I also cut out what serious knots I could not comb out of my hair. Then I took the razor, shampoo, and conditioner, shaving cream, and curl relaxer and went into the bathroom with Lazarus.

First I shaved my face. Then I put Lazarus in the shower and bathed him. Afterwards I dried him off. And then opening the bathroom door I let him into the bedroom.

When I opened the door to let him out, I was shocked to see a very pretty young redhead standing in the bedroom.

I was standing in the doorway completely naked with a few shaving cuts and still scraggly hair. I quickly tried to cover my crotch with my hands.

The girl looked me up and down before I could cover myself and she started to giggle.

Embarrassed I said, "I'm really sorry. I didn't know anyone was there." Smiling she replied, "Don't worry about it. You know that we're all free spirits here. Besides, I like what I see so far, except the jury is still out on that hair." She began to laugh out loud.

I started moving to one side of the door to cover my exposed body.

I said, "My name is Bob."

Still smiling she replied "Oh I know exactly who you are. You're Hippie Bob. The good Hippie Bob. California Hippie Bob, your reputation precedes you.

Michael has regaled us with stories about you and Josh. My name is Amber.

When I heard that you were here, and I saw you bring your stuff into the green room, I moved Lina's stuff out to another room, so that we could have this room to ourselves.

You see, I want to get to know you better; I want to hear all of your stories, and explore that whole body of yours. So do something with that hair, and get cleaned up so that I can start exploring."

I have to admit that at first I was a little stunned.

I stood there staring at her for a few moments, speechless. As horny as I was, the first thought that entered my mind was, "Why did you ever leave this place, you Idiot."

However what I said to her was, "Just give me a few minutes. I'll be out as quick as I can."

She smiled with a sly grin, while petting Lazarus, and said "Okay."

I jumped in the shower, began shampooing my long curly hair. I had forgotten how filthy I was as I watched the dirt run down the drain.

After shampooing my hair twice, I poured the relaxer on my hair and let it soak, while I soaped my body down; as I began to soap my body down I began to notice a rapidly growing erection.

It seemed like thousands of conflicting thoughts were bouncing around in my head at one time.

Things like, "Am I ever going to get all the knots out of this hair? What am I going to do about this erection? If I walk out of the bathroom with an erection, she may think I'm a maniac pervert. Should I jerk off in the shower to get rid of the erection before I go out?

If I jerk off now, and then she wants to make love right away, will I be able to get it up, and if not, then what."

I was so filled with sexual tension and angst that I didn't know if my head, my penis, or my balls, would explode first.

I decided to concentrate on cleaning up, and thinking about nonsexual things. And hope that that would take care of the erection problem. 20 minutes later I was very clean; my long brown curly hair was un-matted and looked good. And after taking a leak, my erection was doable at quarter-mast.

I opened the door from the bathroom to the bedroom, and as the steam rushed past me out of the bathroom, for a moment I couldn't see anything.

And then as the steam dissipated I could see Amber lying on her side on one of the beds completely nude. And she looked good. The fly on my blue jeans started to bulge out as I rapidly went back into full erection.

With a somewhat disappointed look on her face Amber said, "I can't believe you; I wait patiently for almost a half an hour for you, completely naked, in my sexiest pose. And you come out of the bathroom with your clothes on?

However, you may just have saved yourself with that growing bulge in your pants." She laughingly said, "Now get those clothes off, and get into this bed; and I mean right now, Mister."

Over the years I have had occasion to take my clothes off very fast, many times in my life.

However I do believe to this day that that may have been some sort of record for me. I had my jeans, shirt, and shoes off in what seemed like a millisecond; and was on top of her, and inside of her.

I kissed her passionately, and then pulled back for a moment looking at her beautiful face and into her beautiful green eyes. I had only done about ten or twelve strokes, when she looked at me and let out a soft, wet, warm, moan.

At which point I had one of the most violent, electric, convulsive, orgasms of my entire life. And surprisingly she was jerking and convulsing right along with me.

And she let a loud scream.

And when she did I felt a rush of warm fluid fill her vagina. And it began squirting out around my penis in every direction.

A geyser like stream blasted into my face and mouth.

Immediately I thought, "What the hell. Did she just piss all over me?" I pulled out and more fluid gushed out as she continued to loudly moan.

Annoyed and a bit perplexed, I demanded, "Did you just piss all over me... Looking exhausted, she looked up at me and smiling she replied, "So obviously you've never been with a squirter before, have you?"

"What's a squirter?" I asked.

Seeming irritated she snapped back, "A squirter, dumbass. That wasn't piss. That was cum.

"Really, you're kidding?" I said

"You sure came a lot more than I did."

She started explaining it all to me. When she finished,

I said, "Wow. That's really cool, and kind of historic. You're my first squirter."

As I lay there draped half on, and half off of her body, I began to apologize, stacking the excuses one on top of the other, like one stacks cordwood. It'd been a little while since I had been with a woman, and she was so beautiful that I simply had no control, I said. And obviously I had never been with a squirter before. The excuses just kept pouring out of me until she stopped me. Putting her hand over my mouth, she said in a very consoling way; displaying what appeared to be wisdom beyond her years, "It's okay, baby. I understand. Besides, I thought it was really cool, too. I've done my share of balling. But I've never had a guy come inside of me like that, you were so powerful. And that's the fastest that any man has ever made me come. It just makes me dig you even more."

I thought to myself, "That was really sweet of her too say." We kissed some more. And fell asleep in each other's arms.

As I fell asleep I thought to myself, "It's good to be back at Michael's. It's good to be somewhere that I don't have to prove myself all of the time; where beautiful young women believe that I can do no wrong. And then I thought, "Why am I going back to LA, again?"

We slept through the night, and Lazarus woke me up early, wanting me to take him out for a walk.

I kissed Amber and told her where I was going, and took Lazarus for his walk.

It was freezing outside, I had forgotten that we were going into fall, and that winter would be closing in soon. So I got some socks and a jacket out of the truck, and we shortened the walk.

When we went back inside 10 or 12 of the 40 or so people were up, and the heat was on, so it was nice inside.

I went into the kitchen and made some toasted bagels and Lipton tea, put them on a tray, and Laz and I went back upstairs. I sat the toast and tea down on the night stand, and crawled back into bed with Amber. She immediately protested, "You're so cold.

"Is that food that I smell?" She asked in a soft sexy voice.

I replied as I kissed her on the neck, "Yes. I made toasted bagels, and tea, while I was downstairs."

She turned to face me saying "Oh. That's so sweet of you."

I gave her a long passionate kiss on the lips and said, "Let me get the tray. How do you want your tea? It's Lipton. Would you like cream and sugar?"

She replied, "Just hand me the tray. I can do it myself."

As she added the cream and sugar to both of our cups of tea, both of her beautiful soft breasts jiggled.

And as I watched them my penis began to rise again. As she handed me my cup of tea, she looked down and asked, "Is that what I think it is?

She reached under the covers grabbing my penis with her right hand, and stroking it a few times, she said, "You're so horny. I love it. Let's drink our tea, so it doesn't get cold, and then I'll take care of that little fella for ya."

We finished our tea and bagels, and then she jumped under the covers, and giving me head, she got me off in a few minutes.

As I sat there in bed leaning against the headboard, watching her head go up and down under the covers,

I remember thinking, "My God. This girl is amazing. Why did I ever leave this place? I mean, the time with Father was amazing as well. But this girl is something else. It's too bad that there aren't any female Brothers of the Shield, Sisters of the Shield if you will.

Wow. Imagine. A good looking Indian gal who could teach you everything about life, while fucking you, and sucking you, and doing it all at the same time. I know that I would stay up here for the rest of my life then."

That's when all thoughts left my body as she brought me to climax, and I began to flop around on the bed uncontrollably, like a Mexican jumping bean.

Later that day, Big Jerry announced that he had received a call from Michael in Montréal, and that they were staying another week.

He also announced that he needed more help with the chores. And he posted a list of chores for everyone.

He had been very considerate in drawing this list up; he had even put friends and couples together.

Amber and I were given a great job, the job of helping to feed the animals. This job was actually considered an honor. And we really enjoyed it, for the week that it was ours until Michael came back.

There were many memorable incidents that occurred while I was with Amber.

And I believe that she was one of only five or six women that I came in contact with on the entire trip, who, but for circumstances beyond our control, might still be with me to this day. The first lady of course was Chartreuse, the second was Amber, and the third was Marylee. The fourth would have been Kathleen; and the fifth Cassandra, and Lucy Lou sixth; however in their own way all the ladies that I was with on the trip were great, and, given the opportunity; I would settle down with anyone of them now! Still I have to say that Chartreuse will always own a special place in my heart, because she loved me so deeply, and unconditionally,

Going back to the historic incidents that occurred while I was with Amber; the first one of course was the squirter thing.

However the next incident occurred a few days later at around 2:30 in the morning.

Amber and I were out in the heated pool, naked, making out passionately, and getting ready to make love.

As I kissed her, I heard something in the bushes.

I opened my eyes, and looking past her while we still kissed, I thought I saw someone crouching in the bushes.

I stopped kissing her and told her to hang on for a minute, that I thought I saw someone in the bushes.

She turned and we both focused on that area. It was hard to see because of the steam rising off of the pool into the chilly early morning air. And that's when I recognized that old familiar face; it was Lay low Eddy.

I whispered to Amber, "It's Lay Low Eddy." And she replied, "Really, who's that?"

I said in a voice just loud enough for Eddie to hear me, but not loud enough to scare him off. "Eddie? Is that you, buddy? It's Hippie Bob. You remember me, right?" Eddie changed positions slightly, but did not reply right away.

I tried again. "Eddie? It's California Hippie Bob. You remember me. We met back at the beginning of summer. I really love the new rhymes, I noticed a couple of the new ones that you put up on my way into the house.

You know you really should start writing stuff down. I mean like on a notepad or something.

I think you could sell these, like in a book or something; and make your own coin. Hell Eddie, you might make enough coin to buy your own mansion. Come on guy. What do you need?"

Amber whispered in my ear, "Wow. You are really hard. Do you want me to see if I can get you off while you talk to Eddy?"

I replied "Sure. I guess?" I moved up onto the top step of the shallow end of the pool where we were. And she began blowing me.

Just then that weak little voice of Eddie's started crackling out of the bushes.

He asked, "Is there anybody else still up in the house?" I answered, "Yes, of course there is. This is Michael's place. You do remember where you are, right, Eddie? Why, what do you need?"

And an even more pathetic reply came back from Eddie, "It's really cold, and I'm really hungry. Do you think you could get me some food? And bring it out and leave it for me?"

"Sure." I replied, "What do you want to eat?"

Eddie asked, "What's in there?" By this time Amber was starting to really work on me. So I was having trouble concentrating. I replied, "Weeellll. There iiis aah Hamm. Annd some homemade breaddd, and cheeese. And some hooomme made potato salad."

Eddie interrupted asking, "Who made the potato salad?"

I replied now only moments away from climaxiing, I did!"

Eddie came back with, "What did you put in it? I replied while beginning to climax "Everything you put in potato salad, except I added mustard, and dill pickle juice. Ohhhhhh mmmmy Goodddd... Ahhhhhhhhh."

Eddie's screechy voice came back with. "Wow. That sounds like some amazing potato salad. Bring me a bunch of that.

And two thick sliced ham and cheese sandwiches on thick sliced homemade bread with mustard please. Thank you."

By now Amber having completed her task was up lying on top of me, with her head resting on my heaving chest. I kissed her on the forehead.

And replied to Eddie, "You got it guy. I saw a big thick down comforter in the front closet downstairs. Could you use that as well? Eddie replied. "That would be great." I continued, "I almost forgot. What do you want to drink? There's apple juice, orange juice, soda pop, or water.

Eddie said. "A jug of apple juice, and some water, would be great."

I replied, "Just give me 10 min. to put it all together, and I'll bring it out and put it all where you are now. Is that okay?" Eddie's squeaky crackling voice came back with, "Thanks, man. You are really cool, Bob. I mean it, thanks a lot."

I replied, "No problem, Eddie. And I'll go into town tomorrow, and buy you a couple of notepads, and some pens. So that you can write down your rhymes on one of them, and you can leave us notes on the other one, to tell us what you need whenever you can't get into the house."

Eddie replied, "Far out, man. Cosmic."

I looked down at Amber who was just starting to shiver, and said, "Let's run into the house, before we freeze our asses off." And that's what we did.

And I took Eddie everything that I had promised him, including the notebooks and pens the next day.

As Amber and I crawled under the covers with Lazarus sleeping at the foot of the bed, she looked into my eyes and said, "That was so cool, getting to see Lay Low Eddy, with you actually talking to him.

And that was so neat how you thought to bring him food, and the comforter and notepads, and pens and everything. I see why everybody likes you. You really are a nice guy."

I kissed her and said, "I'm not going to let a nice kid starve, and freeze to death, just because he's too shy. But that doesn't make me anybody special. That just makes me a human being.

Amber said, "Well. You're special to me. Do you want ta fuck before we go to sleep?" I replied softly, "No. I'm too tired.

Let's just cuddle and go to sleep. I do realize however that I owe you one in the morning.

So I'm going to try and wake you up by giving you some head for a change.

Besides, I want to experience what it's like to have you come while I'm giving you head. I want to see if I can take that tsunami of yours without my neck breaking." We fell asleep laughing in each other's arms.

Amber and I had a wonderful time over the next few weeks. She wasn't just very pretty, she was also very funny, and spunky, and gutsy as well.

Once when we were in Chinatown in Vancouver, in a Chinese restaurant, she kept trying to unzip my fly, claiming that she was going to blow me right there in public.

Every time that I would push her hand away, and zip my fly back up, and tell her to stop it.

She would say loudly, "Please. Please. Let me have it. I need your hard cock in my mouth. I want to taste that hot cum;" laughing the whole time, as I kept telling her to be quiet, while my face became redder, and redder from embarrassment.

I finally had to drag her out of the Chinese restaurant that we were in, because I saw the proprietor on the telephone, angrily trying to communicate with the cops using his broken Chinese accent.

She felt the whole thing was hilarious.

And I believe that that may have been the first time that I used the line, "Yes; the whole thing was very funny; at least it would have been right up until the arrest."

However, even with her craziness I was becoming very fond of her. This leads us up to the next historic Amber moment for me, which also leads us to the next chapter, Chapter 24 The return of Chartreuse and one of the greatest Ménages a trois of all time.

Chapter 24

The return of Chartreuse and one of the greatest "Ménages a trois" of all time

The weeks that I spent with Amber at Michael's were wonderful. One day we were leaning against the railing at the top of the large cascading staircase that led from the huge two story high entryway up to the numerous second-story bedrooms, which included Michael's master bedroom. It was nice and warm inside the mansion, and the dress code at Michael's had always been clothing optional. Amber and I were leaning up against the railing kissing, I was dressed in boxer shorts and Amber was dressed in nothing but panties. I might add that Michael's place is one of the only times that I have ever worn underwear in my life, as I have gone commando since the age of seven.

Amber always knew how to really turn me on, and as I pointed out in the last chapter, she really enjoyed having sex in front of other people.

As she had noticed two guys watching us intently from one of the bedrooms, she put her hand inside my boxer shorts and began to stroke me while we passionately French kissed.

I was starting to get quite an erection, when suddenly one of the two tall front entry doors flew open, and a large group of people fell through the front door, laughing uproariously.

And a flood of other people followed them, some of them stumbling in, and some of them walking; but everyone was laughing, and giggling, and whooping and hollering.

That's when everyone in the upstairs bedrooms came to the top of the stairs to see what was going on.

It was then that I noticed Michael in the middle of this large cluster of cackling humanity that filled the foyer; he was right in the middle of the group with a pretty girl under each arm.

Three or four of the kids at the top of the stairs screamed out, "Yeah, Michael's home."

Michael looked up at the kids, and yelled laughingly, "Thanks guys. It's good to be back."

He then turned his upward gaze to the right, seeing me and Amber arm in arm dressed in nothing but our underwear, and me with an erection that was sticking out through the flap in my boxers, as Amber continued to jerk me off.

Michael yelled out, "Bob, Amber, Hey everybody, that's Hippie Bob, and Amber. He's the good Hippie Bob, California Hippie Bob. And wait until you hear his stories."

I replied, "It's good to have you back, Michael, everybody has missed you. This place just isn't the same without you."

Michael replied, "It's good to be back, Bob; you see everybody, that's what I couldn't put my finger on, that's what's been bothering me for the last few weeks. Clothes, clothes, too many goddamned clothes.

You see that, everybody, that's why Bob is one of my favorite people. Here he is with Amber, out by the upstairs entry railing, half naked with a hard on.

That's the kind of thing I've been missing! By the way, I'm sorry for interrupting you two.

I wish we would've come in a few minutes later, and then all of you guys could really have seen something.

Okay, that's it. Everybody who wants to stay and party take your clothes off, now!

Those of you who don't, can go get in your cars, have a nice life, and get the fuck out."

Everyone began disrobing as they left the foyer walking down into the huge living room area. However there were still people coming through the front door asking things like, "Why is everyone taking their clothes off?" And others replying, "I think there's going to be some sort of orgy or something."

Michael started running upstairs, leaving a trail of clothes behind him.

As Amber and I looked down upon the ensuing mayhem of the communal striptease; there she was walking through the door, as pretty as ever, with a large grin on her face.

She gazed upon the clothes flying in every direction, and loudly laughing, she threw her arms in the air and yelled, "Now I know that we're really home again."

It was Chartreuse. I watched as her eyes left the unfolding melee downstairs and turned upwards to see Michael reaching the top of the stairs throwing his shirt onto the top stair and making his way toward his huge master bedroom.

As he ran behind me and Amber, Chartreuse stopped following Michael with her gaze, and fixed it upon us.

Her broad smile seemed to melt into a blank stare when she saw the two of us together.

When I saw this I smiled and yelled down to her, "Chartreuse, Chartreuse!"

I grabbed Amber by the hand, and pulling her behind me down the stairs toward Chartreuse I asked her, "Do you know Chartreuse? Was she here when you arrived?"

Amber blurted out half of an answer, "I don't think so," just before we met Chartreuse halfway down the stairs.

I let go of Amber's hand as Chartreuse and I almost collided in an embrace at the midpoint of the stairs. After a long kiss I said, "It's really good to see you."

Smiling and pulling back, she reached down and grabbed a hold of my penis which was now sticking a little more than halfway out of my boxers at full attention and said, "You must be really glad to see me," as she began to laugh.

An apparently slightly perturbed Amber loudly proclaimed, "Oh no; that's all my doing."

And then she put out her hand as if to shake hands, and she continued, "Hi, I'm Amber; nice to meet you."

Chartreuse released her grip on my penis, and shook hands with Amber, replying with a very sly look, "Chartreuse. Very nice to know you."

By now you could cut the sexual tension with a knife. So I quickly said, "Let's go upstairs to the bedroom so we can get all caught up!"

Chartreuse pulled her dress off up over her head, saying, "Sounds good to me."

And as the three of us started up the stairs she took off her bra and dropped it over the railing, and smiling at Amber she said, "When in Rome?"

By the time we walked into the green room Chartreuse was pulling her panties off, and was now completely nude.

And seeing that, Amber took her panties off, and I was trying to figure out what to do while making small talk.

Amber and I sat down on one of the queen-size beds, and Chartreuse sat across from us on the other one.

I asked Chartreuse, "So did you meet up with Michael and

his entourage in Montréal?"

I was doing my dead level best to look her directly in the eyes, as she was sitting right across from me with her legs spread and her elbows on her knees, with both hands under her chin as we talked.

She replied, "Yes. I'm sure that you probably heard that I left here some weeks earlier for Montréal with a group of kids that were headed that way.

And if we hadn't have run into Mick and Dave at one of the concerts, we might have missed them all together.

But as you know, Bob, once you get on the Michael train, there is no getting off, because it's a runaway train that makes no stops. So here I am back in Vancouver again, at Michael's house.

However I must admit there are much worse trains that you could get stuck on. But, boy, am I tired."

And with that she laid back upon the bed leaving me nothing to focus on but her beautiful breasts, as well as her two spread legs which led my eyes back to the inescapable focal point of her gaping pink vagina surrounded by her dark hairy bush.

All of my hard work focusing on her eyes and trying to focus solely on the conversation went right out the window.

My semi hard erection was now standing straight up, and hard enough that it seemed like I could crack walnuts with it.

However I still attempted to continue the conversation asking, "Did you have fun in Montréal?"

Amber reached over and grabbed my erection and I jumped a little, because it was so sensitive by this point.

Amber interjected before Chartreuse could answer my question, saying, "Sorry to interrupt, you guys continue catching up, but there is something I need to do right now."

I replied, "Okay babe."

And Chartreuse, lying back on the bed still staring at the ceiling, said, "Sure, that's cool."

As Chartreuse began to answer my question about her trip to Montréal, Amber knelt down in front of me, and spreading my legs, she pulled my entire package out of my boxers and began giving me head.

I don't know if you'll believe this or not, but I was so worked up by this point that each stroke of her warm lips and mouth were extremely exhilarating while being somewhat painful.

I mean that, here I was staring at Chartreuse's beautiful body and inviting vagina while Amber gave me head. All the while I was still trying to remain composed, and listen to Chartreuse's story. The only thing that I can kind of compare it to is being involved in the greatest ménage a trois ever while in the middle of Church services on Sunday morning.

Chartreuse continued on blindly with her story unaware of what was going on right across from her.

Amber got maybe six or seven strokes in, and then I had one of the top 10 most powerful orgasms of my life.

Right in midsentence, I screamed out over Chartreuse's story, "Oh fuck, oh shit, ahhhh."

I opened my eyes just in time to see Chartreuse rise up from the bed staring at me still uncontrollably jerking from the orgasm, while Amber continued bobbing and sucking to keep me spasming while Chartreuse looked on.

And apparently Amber did a good job of ramming her point home. That point was, "Bob is mine. So back off, bitch!"

Seeing this, Chartreuse grabbed her panties and jumped up off of the bed, and giving me an angry stare, started storming out of the room.

Pleadingly I said, "Chartreuse. Don't go. I really want to hear about your trip. I'm sorry."

As Chartreuse neared the bedroom door on her way out Amber raised her head and loudly said, "Hey. Where are you going? I was just trying to get him off so that he could focus on your story. Why are you mad? Hell, he was staring at your pussy the whole time that I blew him."

As Chartreuse left the bedroom slamming the door behind her, Amber looked up at me with a quizzical look and asked, "What's her problem?"

Sadly I looked down at her and said, "We used to be an item, a few months back."

Amber replied, "Oh. Why didn't you tell me? I mean if I would've known, we could've both gotten you off. Still, there was no reason for her to storm out of here like that."

I was still a little sad, because I didn't want to hurt Chartreuse. I leaned down and kissed Amber on the forehead. I picked her up and sat her on my left knee and kissing her again, I said, "You know how much I care about you, right?"

Looking deep into my eyes, Amber replied, "Of course I do."

I went on, "Well I care just as much for Chartreuse. And the last thing that I wanted do was hurt her. I'm sorry that I never had the time to explain what was going on to you. That was my fault. I was hoping that you might pick up from our interaction on the staircase, that Chartreuse and I were very close at one time, I'm sorry about that."

Amber looked deep into my eyes, and gave me a very soft kiss. And in a very soft consoling voice she said, "That's okay baby. I'm going to make this right. I don't know if it's going to be tonight, or tomorrow night. But very soon I'm going to see to it that the three of us are like three peas in a pod. And things for all three of us will be better than ever. You just leave everything to Amber, sweetheart. Trust me."

I replied skeptically, "Oh yeah. How the hell are you going to do that?"

Amber leaned over and whispered into my ear, "I'm a witchy woman, baby. And there isn't a man or a woman on this planet that I can't seduce."

She giggled softly and gently nibbled my ear lobe, and grabbing my head with both hands, she laid a big wet kiss on my forehead.

Laughing loudly, she announced, "Come on. Let's go downstairs and get something to eat, I'm starving. Besides, I'll bet you that there's a full-blown orgy going on in the living room by now. And if I know Michael, he's probably filming it."

I quipped, "If I know Michael, he's in the middle of the orgy, filming the orgy, while he has someone else filming him, fucking, while filming the orgy."

Amber let out a loud laugh, jumped up from the bed, and pulling me from the bed, she smiled and said, "Well, come on then, before we miss it all."

And so, boxers and panties in hand we danced naked down the stairs to see what new debauchery awaited us.

Soon Amber would be showing me how seductive her witchy ways could be, and still, to this day, every time that I hear the Eagles song, "Witchy Woman," I think of Amber, my Witchy Woman.

By the time we got downstairs, the whole place seemed to be in some sort of bizarre chaos.

People were scurrying about in various states of undress which was not unusual for Michael's place, but rather than having fun, they all appeared to be on some sort of mission.

Two naked guys were moving a couch from one room to another, while a girl dressed in only panties was carrying a lamp in another direction.

Amber and I stood at the bottom of the stairs watching these curious goings-on until I finally looked at her and asked, "What the hell is this? Let's go into the living room, if there's anything really happening, it'll most likely be happening in there."

We somewhat apprehensively walked into the huge living room. Apparently the orgy had started. 15 or 20 people were getting it on in one corner of the huge living room, while Michael filmed it all with one of his early Sony U-Matic camcorders.

Amber asked, "Should we go jump in the pile?" I replied, "Not right now. I'm worried about Chartreuse, and, besides, I want to see you work this witchy woman magic that you've been bragging about so much."

Amber gave me a nudge, and smiling she said, "Okay smartass. But when she falls in love with me, don't say I didn't warn you."

She chuckled, and started walking rapidly ahead of me into the other room.

Stunned and confused, I stumbled behind her asking, "Whoa. Whoa. What was that? I thought that the idea was for all three of us to fall in love?"

Abruptly she stopped; and turned on a dime, walking back just as fast toward me.

And when we met she looked me in the eye with one of the few looks that I've ever seen in my life that displayed both whimsy and disgust at the same time, saying, "Men. You're all the same, more is always better, two-ways, three-ways, four-ways, five-ways, a ménage a trois'. So I tell you that I'm going to seduce your ex-girlfriend so that you can experience your ultimate ménage a trois fantasy. But are you content with that? Noooo!

Being a typical man, you have to have your ultimate ménage a trois fantasy forever, when all the time deep down you know the truth, and that is that you could only handle that ultimate ménage a trois fantasy of two beautiful women attached to your cock 24/7 for no more than a few weeks, before you'd be looking for greener pastures."

She reached up and putting a hand on either side of my face she pulled my head down to her, and looking me directly in the eyes, she sternly said, "Don't try to play director. Don't get weird, or jealous. Just sit back and shut the fuck up. And watch me work my magic. If you can do that, I promise you some of the best sex that you've ever had in your life.

If you can't, or if you feel the need to be controlling, or weird, or whatever, I promise you that I will still seduce Chartreuse. The difference will be, that instead of you, me, and Chartreuse making love for weeks, maybe months, it will be me and Chartreuse making love, and we will be making love in whatever room you're in, and wherever you are, until we make you so crazy that you will tuck your tail between your legs, and hightail it back up to that commune of yours.

And you have my word on that, Mister." Then she gave me a long passionate kiss, and asked softly, "Is that clear?"

I snapped to attention in military fashion, and saluting her I replied," Yes ma'am, you have full authority ma'am. Your wish is my command ma'am. I am only a lowly private in the witchy woman army ma'am."

Laughing she said, "There's nothing sexier than a compliant man.: And then displaying a comically contrived startled look she blurted out, "Oh my God. I think I'm wet. Yes, I am wet, very wet indeed! Seeing a macho mountain man pretending to be compliant and subservient has literally turned my vagina into a rain forest, wow."

Pretending to act annoyed, I said, "Okay that's enough of that shit! Let's go find Chartreuse, so that I can pretend to be compliant and subservient for both of you."

We only had to scour six or seven rooms before we found Chartreuse, sitting by herself in one of the downstairs pantries. We could both tell that she had been crying.

Amber ran over to her, with me right behind.

Amber asked softly, "What's the matter, darlin'?"

Choking up Chartreuse snapped, "I don't want to talk about

it."

Then I asked, "What's the matter?"

That's when Chartreuse screamed at me, "I said, I don't want to talk about it. Just get out!"

I started to talk again, "But."

Chartreuse interrupted me, screaming, "Get out! Get out! Geeet Oooout!"

At this point Amber waved me out of the room.

I left. However I only went around the corner so that I could hear how Amber was going to seduce Chartreuse.

It took Amber a little less than an hour to do her stuff. I didn't have a watch on, however this is my best guess as to the timing of the whole witchy woman routine.

Around 10 minutes spent consoling her. Another 10 minutes explaining to her that Amber and I were not boyfriend and girlfriend, and reminding her about how Michael's place was a 24-hour free love zone.

10 to 15 more minutes telling Chartreuse how I talked about her all the time, and how sad I was when I came back to Michael's to see her, only to find out that she had gone to Montréal.

Another seven or 10 minutes with Amber pointing out that even though she was the one blowing me, I had never come that hard for her before, and that was because the whole time that she was blowing me I was staring at Chartreuses' naked body and specifically her beautiful vagina.

The last 10 or 12 minutes were spent telling Chartreuse how beautiful she was, and how she, Amber would give anything to have Chartreuse's beautiful face, great breasts, high cheekbones, soft creamy skin, black curly hair, and beautiful pussy.

During the same time period she was doing some sort of exotic show and tell, with a mirror.

I could hear her saying things like, "Look how pretty your eyes are compared to mine. Look at your beautiful skin compared to mine with the freckles. That's the curse of the redhead. Look at the shape of your breasts and nipples compared to mine, they're so much nicer.

Take your panties off for a second. You look at my pussy and then look at yours. You see mine's a little crooked. But yours is gorgeous. It's absolutely perfect, my God, woman. You could have any man or woman that you wanted.

This isn't still that old stuff about Michael dumping you for another girl six months ago, or so, is it? Oh my God. It is, isn't it?

Upstairs you must've felt like all of a sudden Bob was dumping you. Oh baby, noooo, Bob still loves you. I think in his own way he loves me too, but certainly not as much as he loves you.

Our whole deal is strictly based upon convenience. You know, love the one you're with.

Personally, I enjoy sleeping with women as much as I do men. The most important thing for me is that I really need to feel a kinship with the person."

That was the last word that I heard out of Amber.

I could hear movement and some heavy breathing. And when I couldn't take it anymore, I snuck a quick peek around the corner.

Amber had made her move. She and Chartreuse were kissing heavily while fingering each other. Both of them had their eyes closed so I continued watching.

Amber broke the kiss and pulled back, opening her eyes, so I leaned back behind the door jamb so that I couldn't be seen.

However, when I heard the slurping and moaning, I just had to peek again.

And sure enough, there was Amber on her knees with her face buried in Chartreuses' vagina.

And she was really getting after it, like a starved wolf set loose in a meat locker.

Chartreuse was leaning back, legs spread wide, and her eyes seemed to be rolling back in her head, as her moans grew louder, and louder.

I couldn't take it, and began jerking off while I continued to watch them.

And then, as if she had eyes in the back of her head, Amber turned and looked at me.

I tried to hide behind the door jamb again, but before I could, Amber was motioning me into the room.

She said, "Good. You're hard, put your cock in her mouth."

Chartreuse continued to squirm with pleasure. Her eyes still rolled back in her head as Amber continued to finger her.

As I moved toward Chartreuse's mouth with my penis,

Amber said softly to Chartreuse, "Here he is baby, the man you love, the man who loves you, so put his cock in your mouth, and show him how much you love him. And he and I will show you how much we both love you."

I don't think that I was in Chartreuses' mouth for more than 15 or 20 seconds before I came, screaming," Oh God. Yes. Yes."

And then, not 10 seconds after I came, both Chartreuse and Amber came simultaneously. How did I know this, you ask?

Because Chartreuse rapidly convulsed while screaming out, and pressing Amber's face into her vagina with both hands.

At the same time Amber, while also convulsing, squirted so hard that it sounded like somebody tipped over a 5 gallon bucket of water onto the floor. Immediately afterward the three of us collapsed into a pile on the floor of the huge pantry. But that's when all three of us heard Michael yell, "Cut. Print. That's a wrap, everybody."

The whole pantry and the hallway outside erupted into loud raucous laughter, and applause. The three of us looked up to see Michael and another other guy turning off their camcorders, with the pantry and hallway behind them filled with laughing and talking onlookers.

Angrily, I yelled at Michael and the rest, "Jesus Christ Michael. Can't anybody have an intimate moment around here without you shoving a camera up their ass? Fuck!"

As everyone began leaving the hallway, and Michael and the other guy put down their camcorders, and began to leave the pantry, Michael laughed loudly and replied, "Come on Bob. Lighten up. It's all in good fun. Besides, you know the rule. Everyone has to take one for the team around here every once in a while; and anyway, you are always talking about repaying me in some way for my kindness, right? Well. You just did. Because I guarantee you that I will be beating off to this footage for years."

And with that, what was left of the entire voyeur's peanut gallery broke into uproarious laughter once more.

A few minutes later the two girls and I were upstairs in the shower, and then the three of us climbed in bed together, while Laz curled up in his usual spot, and the party continued to rage downstairs.

Chartreuse and Amber fell asleep quickly with me in the middle and one lady on each arm.

I stared at the ceiling for a few minutes thinking to myself, "Am I dead, because this sure seems like heaven."

As I finally fell asleep, dozing off into a sex filled dreamland, there is no way that I could've known that we had only scratched the surface of the sex filled, drug crazed events that lay ahead at Michael's.

But for now I was content to have a warm, soft, beautiful woman that I cared about, and loved on either side of me, in a big soft warm bed.

The last cognitive thought that went through my mind before I went into total dreamland was, "Fuck the wilderness."

Chapter 25

I finally meet Elias Mobius Rex, the Great Methaqualone Marathon and orgy. Cassandra and Kat arrive on the scene while Amber and Chartreuse wear me out

Lazarus woke me up early the next morning crying to go out.

I crawled out from between Amber and Chartreuse got dressed and took Lazarus downstairs for a walk. It was cold outside with just a hint of a snow flurry.

Lazarus really had to go both one and two, but he made quick work of it, as it was so cold that he was shivering.

Then I grabbed my pipe and the bag of Alaskan Thunder Fuck weed from the truck, and we both ran back inside.

It was nice and warm in Michael's mansion and I remember thinking to myself that it must cost him a fortune to heat the place in the winter, and to cool it in the summer.

I also remember thinking about how amazing it was that his front doors were always unlocked, and half the time in the summer they stayed wide open a lot of the time.

Yet he had never been robbed, or burglarized, or anything.

About the closest thing to that, that I ever heard about was that from time to time some of the animals like the zebra or the goats when he had them, had wandered into the place at night and wrought havoc in the kitchen, and elsewhere.

By the time I got upstairs, and back to the green room, Chartreuse and Amber had moved together under the covers and were cuddling sound asleep.

I took off my clothes and jumped under the covers with them, snuggling up to the two of them draping my arms and legs over Amber and putting one of my hands and feet on one of Chartreuses' breasts and feet, respectively.

Immediately both ladies began to scream out in protest. "That's too cold. You're freezing. You're like a piece of ice. Stop it. Let go!"

Laughing, I began to touch both ladies all over their bodies with my cold hands and feet, until they both jumped out of bed.

And angrily they both shouted at me, "What's the matter with you? What are you, crazy? I was having a great dream and you were in it, asshole."

As they screamed and gestured angrily at me, all that I could think of was how beautiful they both were, and how sexy their beautiful breasts looked as they jiggled and bounced up and down with each exaggerated gyration.

Laughingly I apologized and pointed out how beautiful they both looked and how horny they made me by just watching them bounce around while angrily chastising me.

Chartreuse said smiling, but still feigning anger. "Well. Don't do that again. So we made you horny, huh?"

Amber, now smiling as well, clapped her hands together and squealed, "Yeahhhh."

Then both ladies jumped back into bed with me and began rubbing my body all over, especially my hands and feet to warm me up.

Chartreuse and I kissed while Amber went down on me, and after a while the ladies changed places. Eventually, both ladies went down on me under the covers.

I remember looking down at the covers that rolled back and forth. Sometimes almost resembling ocean waves and other times looking like two small animals in a bag.

As they brought me closer and closer to climax my head rolled back, and I gazed upon the ceiling with its hand-painted clouds, and partial rain forest canopy, and thought to myself, "I wonder if I could talk Michael into letting me stay here forever."

And with that thought my eyes closed. I let out a groan and with a series of protracted convulsive thrusts I was off on another orgasmic ecstasy ride, and after getting both ladies off, we all jumped into the shower, which was always fun in and of itself.

We all got completely dressed, which was uncommon at Michael's. But after such great sex and the shower, it just felt right; for some reason.

The place was just starting to stir and the smell of food was rising up from the kitchen downstairs.

I took a deep breath, sampling the food laden air and announced loudly, "It must be Sunday""

"Why do you say that?" Amber asked.

"Because Michael is back, and I smell Eggs Benedict, and

Kona coffee brewing. And Michael always has Eggs Benedict on thick sliced French toast with fresh fruit and whipped topping, fresh squeezed orange juice and champagne Mimosas, and Kona coffee Sunday mornings, along with everybody else, of course. It's quite a production, along with most other meals in this place."

Chartreuse agreed saying, "That's right; so what are we waiting for? I'm starving."

The three of us and Lazarus, tail wagging, raced downstairs to the kitchen.

As we strolled into the large kitchen, we noticed 15 or 20 people in the living room already eating and drinking. Larry, one of the many resident chefs that came and went at Michael's place, was cooking away with the help of Big Jerry, and four or five others who were thick slicing bread, whipping eggs, cutting fruit, making orange juice, and the like.

Between people like us watching, and grabbing food as soon as it was cooked, and those who were feverishly making it, the huge kitchen was almost full.

That's when Michael strolled into the kitchen with a girl under each arm. And with a big smile on his face. He loudly announced, "Is that Eggs Benny I smell?"

Under his left arm was one of the most beautiful blondes that I have ever seen.

She was truly stunning, and she was wearing the ceremonial see through Teddy that everyone knew designated her as Michael's latest conquest, and most likely his newest girlfriend.

He went on, "You guys all met Cassandra and Kat last night, right?"

Cassandra was the beautiful blonde and Kat was her friend, who apparently was along for the ride, and quite cute in her own right.

At first I thought I was the only one, until I looked around the room and noticed every guy in the kitchen was staring at Cassandra, including Larry, who only stopped staring when he noticed that the eggs were burning.

I couldn't believe it. It had only been 45 min. or so since I had gotten off and this girl was so gorgeous, that I was starting to get hard again. As the bulge in my jeans began to grow I looked away, however as I looked around the room.

It appeared that every guy in the room was not only staring at Cassandra's face and body, but they were also all in various states of arousal. The most obvious one being Jimmy who was cutting fruit in the nude and was stiff as a board.

Michael was grinning from ear to ear. There is nothing that Michael loved more than being with the girl that every other guy wanted.

Amber looked around the room and nudging Chartreuse she said loudly enough so that everyone could hear, "Wouldn't you love to get a whole room full of guys hard like that, by just showing them what you've got?"

Chartreuse replied, "I've done that before. Now, I'm just happy to get Bob hard and play with you, but I must say that is impressive. We just got Bob off a little while ago, and now look at him, after just a few minutes of checking that out, he's as hard as a rock again." Then everyone in the room laughed at her comments.

Michael broadly smiled and announced to the group his reply to Amber and Chartreuse's comments, "What can I say, ladies? It's good to be me."

Everyone laughed again, and we all went back to cooking and getting fed.

We all grabbed our food and went into the gigantic living room, and the news was on. Michael had the first rear projection big-screen TV that I had ever seen, because they had just come out, and were very expensive.

The girls and I were eating and drinking Champagne. Lazarus was in heaven running around the room garnering various scraps of bacon and eggs, and French toast, etc. from everyone in the huge room.

I noticed Michael dressed as usual, in nothing but an open robe, get up and head for the Sony U-Matic player next to the big screen.

He grabbed a tape from his robe pocket and shoved it into the machine and then scurried back to his two waiting ladies and his breakfast. As he sat down suddenly the newscast was replaced with a video of my three-way with Amber and Chartreuse from the night before.

The entire room burst into a loud cheer, which was accompanied by even louder applause.

Michael screamed over the applause, "Author, author. Encore, encore."

As others in the room took up the chant, Amber yelled over the crowd into my ear, "Do you want me to get you off while we watch the video?"

I looked at her like she was insane and replied, "No thanks. Michael just killed my hardon."

I yelled to the two ladies over the loud chanting, "Let's all stand up, and give them a bow. That's the only way that we're going to get them to shut up."

And that's what we did. We smiled and stood up and bowed and sat back down, however the chant of "Encore. Encore." continued, as I shook my head NO, and attempted to wave the crowd off.

Suddenly Michael yelled out, "What, no encore?" And the room slowly grew silent.

Thinking impulsively, I replied "Michael. For Christ's sake, I just got off a few minutes ago. Let me at least eat my breakfast and recharge a little. I need protein. I'm out of sperm for Christ's sake. My balls are like BBs. I'm just a man, not a sperm squirting lawn sprinkler."

For a few seconds you could hear a pin drop.

And then Michael began to laugh louder and harder than I had ever heard him laugh before. And the entire room followed suit.

He jumped up and ran over to me. He reached down and grabbed my right wrist, and holding my right arm up in the air.

He loudly announced, "Ladies and gentlemen, my hero, California Hippie Bob, a man who doesn't mince words. Who always tells it like it is a man who is fearless, and yet is one of the funniest S. O. B.'s that I have ever met in my life."

And with that he motioned for me to stand up. And I did.

He went on, "A man who I am proud to call my friend."

Smiling, He turned and gave me a big hug. The whole room stood up and began to applaud.

I was in complete and utter shock as he hugged me. I could feel his junk rubbing against my leg, and I was thinking about how glad I was that I had put on my jeans.

However as the applause died down, and it started to get quiet, I felt that I needed to say something. So I announced loudly, "Thanks, Michael. That means a lot to me."

Michael began to laugh loudly again. And then turning to the crowd he continued; "I was just fucking with you Bob, you dumb ass."

He broke into loud laughter again, and putting his arm around me, he began to laugh loudly while jumping up and down, his robe and genitalia flailing in all directions, and the entire room broke into raucous laughter again, and I must admit that I was laughing right along with everyone else.

Michael shook my hand, we hugged, and he walked back over to Cassandra and Kat.

And as he continued with his breakfast, I heard him say to Cassandra while pointing at the big-screen. "Watch this. This is one of the hottest three ways that I've ever filmed, and this just happened last night, you know, you were both there. Do you two know what I think makes this scene so hot, it's obvious that all three participants really care about each other, and that translates into great sex!"

Michael continued to stare at the screen, making comments like, "Look at the intensity. Look at Chartreuse's eyes. She almost appears to be in a state of Nirvana."

Cassandra turned and looking over her shoulder gave me a big long sexy smile.

As she slowly turned her gaze back toward the big-screen I noticed that virtually every other guy in the room who had been staring at her was now looking at me in amazement.

That's when Amber leaned over to Chartreuse and said, "Did you see that? We're going to have to keep our eyes on that one." Chartreuse agreed. And even as played out as I was, I began to get hard again.

Michael continued loading his porn's greatest hits from over the years, critiquing each video as only Michael could.

I told the girls that I was going to go upstairs and take a nap, the food and champagne had made me sleepy.

I thought that I would give Lazarus a quick walk before my nap as judging from the size of his belly, he had about 3 pounds of food scraps in him, and must need to take a crap.

When I opened the front door, there, walking up the front steps was Josh with another guy. Lazarus ran down to them wagging his tail and whimpering.

Josh leaned down and petted Lazarus, I said, "Josh. How are you I was beginning to worry about you, and who is your friend?"

Josh replied, "Bob. This is Elias Mobius Rex; I know you've heard me talk about him." "Yes, very nice to meet you, I've heard so much about you from Josh." I replied.

He was a strange looking little man with long scraggly dishwater blonde hair, thick glasses, and mismatched clothing; kind of a cross between Alfred E. Newman of Mad Magazine fame, and a mad scientist.

"Come on in, you guys, its cold outside. "Josh". I queried, "I still can't understand how you walk around in this kind of weather with nothing but sandals and a robe on?

You guys go on in; Michael and everybody are in the living room. I'm going to walk Lazarus, and then we're going to catch up. See you in a few."

I gave Lazarus a good walk, which he obviously really needed, and we went back inside.

By the time we got back inside everyone was still hugging Josh, and shaking Elias's hand. It was good to have someone else be the center of attention for a change.

As I was tired anyway, I decided to leave them to their moment, and go back to my original plan of taking a nap.

And so while everyone ate, and drank, and caught up. I and Lazarus went upstairs and fell asleep.

Some hours later I was awakened by the girls and Josh, the two sweet melodic voices of my dreams softly announced, "Wake up sleepyhead. Get up, time to wake up and join the party."

But then suddenly the soft, sweet, melodic voices were replaced with Josh's loud harsh voice declaring, "Come on. Get up. What do you want to do, sleep your whole damn life away?"

And with that I was awake.

Josh and the girls told me that Michael had decided to have a big party. And Josh told me that Elias Mobius Rex had brought along a pint of pure methaqualone with him.

So of course I asked, "What the hell is methaqualone?"

I guess it's about here that I should explain that methaqualone was the main ingredient in Quaaludes, a drug that would play an important part in my life a few years later in Venice, CA, but that's the next book.

Josh replied, "Oh, you're going to love this stuff. It takes away all of your inhibitions."

I asked, "What exactly do you mean by that?"

And Josh replied, "It makes anyone who takes it at least 10 times looser, and sexually wilder, than Amber is on her wildest day."

And with an amazed look Amber and I replied almost in unison, Amber saying, "Far out." And me saying," Holy shit."

Josh smiled saying, "So lash down the cargo, and batten down the hatches.

Put on your helmets. And tighten your seat belts, kiddies, because it could be a wild and bumpy ride; but it is guaranteed to be another amazing ride.

And best of all, everybody is getting laid, guaranteed, and that's good for me, because I'm way overdue."

We all laughed, and headed downstairs, filled with anticipation combined with a little trepidation about what lay ahead for us on Michael's newest roller coaster sex ride to hell.

But, what the fuck, you only live once, right.

And, besides, I knew that Cassandra was going to be there, and she had just given me that come fuck me smile at breakfast.

I began thinking, "Oh my God, what if I get to make love to that girl tonight? And then Michael gets mad at me and won't let me stay here anymore? Well then,

I guess I can always hide out with Lay Low Eddy, and sneak around the place like he does. Because the way things are going I sure as hell don't want to leave here, ever.

By the time we got downstairs to the party, it was starting to ramp up.

There were roughly 30 people in the living room, five or six of them were dancing to music that played on the huge stereo set up, while Michael's homemade pornos ran on the big-screen without sound.

We walked into the kitchen, there was a huge spread of food of all kinds on the counters and tables in the kitchen, and in the hallway, and against the wall in the living room along with lots of iced Champagne, and beer, and wine.

Everyone was drinking what was supposedly a Champagne punch in a giant punch bowl, with a ladle and plastic cups on the counter in the kitchen.

Josh said, "Let's all have some punch." So we all began to fill cups with the punch and drink it. It was actually very tasty with just the slightest hint of an aftertaste. After I had finished a cup of the punch,

Josh told me, "Well, you said you wanted to know what methaqualone was like? Now you'll find out.

My eyes widened. "What do you mean?" I asked.

Josh replied, "Elias put a quarter of a pint in this batch of punch."

Frightened I asked, "Is that a lot?"

"No. Calm down Bob. It's all been scientifically calculated. What do you think we are, insane? It's just the right amount for everybody to have a really good time."

I noticed over Josh's shoulder, that Big Jerry had a big smile on his face. When I leaned around Josh, I could see what the big smile was all about. I walked around the huge center island in the kitchen to see an amazing sight.

Big Jerry who was not a very handsome man, and who I had never seemed to get any action to speak of at Michael's, was smiling because a quite attractive, well-dressed middle-aged woman that I had never seen before, was on her knees aggressively blowing him, while apparently playing with herself.

"No wonder he was smiling." I said, "Who the hell is the woman who's blowing Jerry?" I asked.

Josh chuckled and replied, "Oh her? She's the caterer. I think she was saying that she's married with kids. Amazing punch, huh?"

I asked, "When did she have any punch?"

Josh replied, "I saw her drinking a cup just before we came upstairs to get you."

I replied, "Wow. That's amazing."

That's when Josh replied, "And the night is still young my friend. The night is still young, and on that note."

Josh put down his empty cup, and walking over to the caterer he pulled up his robe and exposing his genitals, he grabbed her left hand and put it on his penis, and she began stroking him and blowing him too.

By this time I was in sheer amazement, and was starting to feel quite horny myself, and beginning to get hard.

The girls started giggling and grabbed me by the hand and dragged me into the living room while stripping. By the time that we got to the other side of the huge living room, they had both left a trail of clothes from the kitchen to the tapestry couches on the other side of the room.

They began pulling my clothes off fast. Once they had my clothes off, they pushed me down onto one of the couches.

They slowly worked their way down my body, kissing and licking their way to my crotch.

As they both worked on me I took my gaze from them, and began to look around the room. I couldn't believe my eyes; more people began to fill the living room.

Everyone was either naked, or getting naked fast, clothes were flying off of people like roof tiles in a tornado.

I had witnessed smaller orgies at Michael's before, but nothing like this.

There were three ways, four ways, four guys and one girl, and what appeared to be a rapidly growing, nine person daisy chain, guy on girl of course.

I caught sight of Michael, now nude, with his camcorder of course, moving slowly through the heaving, moaning sea of flesh with Cassandra and Kat in tow.

Cassandra was trying to kiss Michael's neck, while Kat appeared to be trying to jerk him off.

But he kept moving constantly, and panning his camera, only stopping briefly to capture the most lurid scenes for his future viewing pleasure.

He wore a broad grin as he continued to video the landscape. However, because of all of the movement, both Cassandra and Kat were having trouble trying keep up with him, much less please him, and he didn't seem to be interested in what they were trying to do for him, anyway.

So it wasn't long before their attempts at pleasing Michael seemed to become almost mechanical, and smiles rapidly melted slowly into frowns.

Cassandra began looking around the room and her eyes met mine. Slowly her frown became a smile again, and I saw her lean down and whisper in Kat's ear. Kat looked over my way and began to smile as well. They both left Michael to his filming and began walking toward me, and Amber and Chartreuse were so concentrated on me, that they didn't even notice.

Cassandra and Kat sat down on the couch on either side of me. Cassandra whispered into my right ear, "May we join you?"

"Certainly, you may." I replied, "However, it seems to me that the two of you have been ignored for a while, and deserve some attention as well."

I gave Cassandra a long sensuous kiss and then leaned down and began sucking on her left nipple.

I then began playing with her vagina with my right hand, and turned my head toward Kat, and giving her a long sensuous kiss, I leaned down and sucked on her right nipple and began playing with her vagina with my left hand.

By this point the entire room seemed to have reached, "the point of no return." That is the point in a sexual encounter, whether it be between two people, or 200 people having sex at the same time; where the overwhelming desire to achieve orgasm is being countered by the overwhelming desire to have that feeling of ecstasy that one achieves pre-orgasm last forever.

It was at this moment that I finally realized what Josh had been talking about when he had referred to the "orgy smell."

As people moaned loudly, women screamed out in orgasmic pleasure and men loudly grunted or verbalized their orgasms.

That is when I could smell a slight pungent odor, it was almost imperceptible, and yet it was there.

My focus was drawn back to the ladies when I heard Amber say, "What the hell is this?"

I looked down to see Amber and Chartreuse glaring up at me.

Thinking fast I said, "This, my dears, is an orgy, and from what you've told me you both know all about orgies, and Michael was so busy videoing the festivities that he was ignoring these two ladies. So they came over here, and I invited them to join us. However, I would actually prefer to be kissing you two, so do you gals want to change places?"

Cassandra said meekly, "Okay. That's cool."

Kat nodded in acceptance.

So I stretched my arms out to Chartreuse and Amber, smiling

and saying. "Come on up here, ladies. Let's make out."

They both took my hands and changed places with Cassandra and Kat. I was amazed, and couldn't believe that they went for it.

Cassandra went down on me first, and I could only watch for a split second or I know that I would've come instantly. I focused on kissing Amber and Chartreuse.

However, it was obvious when she handed off my penis to Kat, who to my surprise was even better at oral sex, that I didn't have long before my orgasm was going off, maybe only a few seconds.

I pulled away and looking straight ahead. I said, "Excuse me, ladies."

Standing up, I said to Cassandra and Kat, "Open up, ladies."

They both opened their mouths and leaned their heads back and I shared one of the largest orgasms of my life with the two them.

Amber announced loudly, "What a gyp, where's ours?"

And then jumping off of the couch, she began sucking on me proclaiming, "We deserve some of that. After all, we did most of the work."

I noticed the camera lights turning off. And I also noticed that Michael had been filming the whole thing.

I remember thinking, "Oh my God. I've fucked up now."

With a sad look I said, "Sorry Michael."

Smiling at me, Michael replied, "Nonsense Bob, this is an orgy, and the girls have to have their fun too. Besides, in less than 24 hours, you've managed to make your way into my greatest three-way, four-way and now my first greatest five-way tape, and my greatest cum shots video as well. Hell, man, you're rapidly becoming a legend around here. Keep up the good work. Now, I've got to go over and capture that growing daisy chain in the corner. That looks hot."

Michael turned his camcorder back on and started wandering away toward the daisy chain.

I put out my hands and helped Cassandra and Kat to their fee, and then I helped Amber and Chartreuse up from the couch, and asked them all if they would like to retire upstairs to the green room where we could all have some privacy. Luckily for me, they all said yes. So we grabbed an ice bucket with two bottles of champagne and five champagne flutes and some snacks, and headed upstairs.

When we got upstairs to the bedroom, I locked the door and put Lazarus into the bathroom.

It became apparent very rapidly that all of the girls except Kat were bisexual, and Kat was a fast learner, at least once "witchy woman" Amber got her hands on her, that is.

The ladies came numerous times that night, and I came once more myself inside of Kat while she was going down on Amber, and Cassandra was going down on Chartreuse.

I could only get away with it at that moment, because both Amber and Chartreuse were too occupied having their own orgasms to notice what I was doing.

When everyone was finished having orgasms, we were all spent. It was decided (mostly by Amber) that she and Chartreuse and I would share the one queen-size bed, and Cassandra and Kat would sleep in the other.

About six or seven a.m., I had to pee really bad from all of the champagne, so I got up and went into the bathroom to take a leak. Lazarus to his credit had not crapped or peed on the bathroom floor but was in desperate need of an immediate walk.

I put on my clothes and jacket and took him outside for a good walk. It was cold and there was about an inch of snow on the ground. He was running around like he was on a hot plate, shivering and peeing, shivering and crapping, it was truly a sight to behold.

When we went back upstairs I pulled down some towels and put them on the floor in the bathroom for him and closed the door.

When I began to take my clothes off to go back to bed, I began to survey the room. Amber and Chartreuse were cuddling together under the covers like the night before, with the covers almost over their heads, and Cassandra and Kat were sleeping apart facing away from each other on either side of their bed.

Immediately the small devil that plagued me throughout what I refer to as my quote unquote "Dog years," hopped up on my right shoulder!

He whispered in my right ear, "Now's your chance to do what you've really wanted to do all along, fuck Cassandra. But you don't want to do it in here, because if Amber and Chartreuse hear you, and wake up while you're fucking her, they'll throw a shit fit.

So go find an empty bedroom, you stupid asshole, before it's too late.

So that's what I did. I couldn't find an empty bedroom. What I did find two doors down, was an empty walk-in closet with three comforters conveniently stored in it. I put two on the floor to lie on and had the other one to cover us.

I crept past the two beds full of people sleeping in the room, and back to our room. I knelt down beside Cassandra, and putting my hand over her mouth. I shook her a little bit.

She started to say something, as her eyes slowly opened, however I muffled her speech with my hand while putting my finger to my lips and quietly shushing her.

I whispered in her ear, "Do you want to come with me and have some fun? It'll be sexy, dangerous, and exciting."

With my hand still over her mouth she nodded her head up and down in approval.

Then I whispered in her ear again, "Get up real slowly, and quietly, so that you don't wake anybody up."

And she did so, as I took off all of my clothes quietly. And then naked as jaybirds we crept down the hall and into the walk-in closet closing the door quietly behind us.

When she lay down upon the two maroon colored comforters, I had to take a moment. I stood over her, looking down upon her.

Cassandra looked up at me and whispered, "What are you doing? What are you waiting for?"

I replied, "I'm sorry. It's just that you're so beautiful. It's like you're perfect. For a moment there, it was like I was drinking in your beauty with my eyes."

Smiling, Cassandra replied, "I think that may be the sweetest thing that any man has ever said to me. Now get down here and make love to me. Ever since I had you in my mouth, I've been dreaming about what it will feel like to have you inside of me. And I can't wait anymore. So get down here."

She was incredible. Beautiful, soft, tender and very loving; and on top of all of that we came simultaneously.

It was at that moment that I realized I had now reached a new plateau at Michael's.

I had not only managed my way into four of his best of sex

videos, and managed a five way with four of the most beautiful women in the house.

I had actually stolen the super pretty new girl right out from under his nose. And she liked me better than Michael, with all of his millions.

We kissed for a long time and then fell asleep in the pile of comforters.

Something woke me up, and I checked my watch, and it was 8:30 a.m., so I woke her up, and we made our way back to our room, and crawled back into our designated beds with no one the wiser.

As I started to fall asleep again, I remember thinking, "There must be some way that I can talk Michael into letting me stay here permanently; however that may be a little harder now that I snagged Cassandra away from him.

Oh well, tomorrow is another day, of sex, drugs, and rock 'n roll, and debauchery.

And so ended the great methaqualone marathon orgy of 1973; little did I know that within a couple of weeks I would be back up at the House of Che for one last time, before coming back to Michael's, and then south to LA, forever.

Something that was so unimaginable to me at that point in time; that I would have laughed at anyone who had even suggested such a thought.

But like the old adage goes, "The only thing certain in life is uncertainty."

Chapter 26

Trying to keep four women happy and satisfied for a few weeks, and then back to the House of Che for one last time

I was really enjoying sharing a bedroom with four beautiful women. Cassandra, Kat, Amber, and Chartreuse appeared to be enjoying my company is much as I was enjoying theirs.

As beautiful and sexy as Cassandra was, and as innocently sexy as Kat was, and as wildly over-the-top crazy and sexy as Amber was, I felt myself spiritually growing closer and closer to Chartreuse.

I had started using Chartreuse's given name again. And she really seemed to enjoy me calling her Darla again.

It was really great having four lovely women being jealous when it came to me, not amongst themselves, but when women other than the four of them that were staying at Michael's would approach me, or even flirt with me, and anyone of my fearsome foursome (as I started referring to the group) would see it, the shit would hit the proverbial fan.

I remember Michael saying to me, "How do you do it Bob? Your own personal constant five-way with four beautiful women for weeks now, and no fighting, and all five of you are always happy.

You have to tell me what your secret is.

I mean, I've never been able to keep the same four women in my bedroom for longer than a day or two. And then they're always at each other's throats."

I replied, "I don't know if there is any real secret to it Michael?

I know that it must help that my ladies are all bi-sexual. And that we are all equals in every way.

And even though the other three ladies know that I love them all equally dearly, we all know that there's a little more of a spiritual bond between Darla and me."

Seeming somewhat befuddled Michael asked, "Who the hell is Darla? Jesus Bob. Have you got a fifth girl in there with you now?

Fuck, man. Are we going to have to find you a bigger

bedroom or something? You are rapidly becoming my fucking fulltime hero."

Looking very puzzled at Michael, I said, "Michael? You don't remember that Chartreuse's real name is Darla?"

"It is?" Michael replied, "Oh. Yeah, that's right. You mean she prefers Darla to Chartreuse?" Again, looking puzzled,

I told Michael, "For her it's a kind of a term of endearment. Do you understand?"

Michael scratched his beard with his right hand, his eyes gazing toward the ceiling, and then looking back into my eyes he said, "Oh. I get it. You've created your own pack. You are the alpha male, Chartreuse is the alpha female and the other three ladies are the betas. But you all enjoy each other's company and like to talk, and most importantly your interaction with them is not simply sexual, right?

In other words it's like a slumber party in there, and you're the boss chick with the dick. Right!

Very nice man, very clever Bob; so in essence, the secret is making the ladies your friends so they all know that you love them equally, so that eliminates the jealousy thing.

And then you make them buddies so they don't feel like sexual objects, very nice man, very clever. You know Bob; over these last few days you've made me realize that I have been drastically underestimating you for way too long. WAY TOO LONG."

Flustered, I replied, "God dammit, Michael. You still don't get it. It's not a gimmick. I really love all four of these women. I really enjoy their company. I tell stories to them, and they tell me stories, we all tell each other lots of stories. I play guitar and we sing songs together; did you know all four of them have really nice singing voices? In other words, Michael, I'm not pretending to do anything to keep them all happy and in line so that I can simply fuck them.

There is no secret! All that you have to do is learn to enjoy women for who they really are, which is way, way more than simply a sex object. If you can truly do that, not only will you have less trouble with the women in your life, but you will be able to grow spiritually by leaps and bounds".

"What you really need, Michael is to spend a month with

Father; you know; Little Bear the Brother of the Shield that taught me so much.

The real problem with that is, that I don't think either one of you would enjoy the experience.

And I am positive that you would never last long enough with Father to learn the things that you really need to learn.

But on a brighter note, you can start looking at women differently on your own, change is always good, so just do it."

Michael laughed and gave me a big hug, we smiled and shook hands and I went back upstairs to my ladies.

My time with the fearsome foursome ended about a week later when Cassandra and Kat decided to head north with a couple of handsome young guys that came through Michael's in a van.

And then there were three.

And about a week later a guy came to Michael's with a message from Brian and David for Josh.

The message said that they really needed as many guys as he could round up to help them finish a couple of more structures and the sauna for the winter.

Naturally Amber and Chartreuse wanted to go, but it was starting to get really cold and snowy. And deep down in my heart I knew they weren't really ready for that.

Chartreuse was adamant about going. And she threw a tearful tantrum when I said the last and final NO!

Amber was fine with it, of course, because she was a very strong young lady, sadly she was much stronger than Chartreuse, when it came to matters of the heart.

As Josh and I and Lazarus, and two young guys from Michael's that I barely knew (It's been so long that I can't even remember their names) headed towards the Fraser River Valley and the House of Che. I remember thinking, "I know that I must hurt Chartreuse every time that I leave her behind; and I know that one day I may have to leave her behind forever." And then I thought, "What's wrong with me, why can't I seem to settle down?

Is it because, (like when I was a child) I would stand up in the car seat so that I could see everything, everything that was new and different and I would do this with great excitement, until I was finally so tired that my body would have to sleep. Is that it? I can't settle down because I always have to see what's over the next horizon?" I thought about it during the whole trip up to the House of Che from Vancouver.

Josh kept commenting, "Wow man, you sure are quiet, are you all right?"

By the time we reached the House of Che just after dark we were greeted by the loud chorus of 100 or so barking dogs.

I was so depressed that after greeting everyone, I just ate a little something, fed and walked Laz, and went to bed in the camper.

To add to my depression when we had stopped for gas in Clinton on the way up, the guys at the station said that Father had not been in, in a while, and hadn't left me any messages!

The next morning Lazarus and I were up early, as was the rest of the commune.

During breakfast Brian and David showed us rough sketches that they had drawn up of the new buildings; and what would be needed to finish the sauna by the pond.

The four of us each joined different groups appointed to accomplish different tasks to achieve the proposed projects.

I joined a group cutting and constructing the log cabins, because of my chain saw experience, learned from fighting wildfires.

Josh worked on the completion of the sauna, and the two young guys that came up with us joined two other groups. That's always the way that Brian and David liked to do it. And I must admit it worked very well.

Before I did anything else, I decided to check on Freddy the goat, I was curious to see if he would still recognize me after this long.

But he ran over too me as soon as he spotted me. I hugged him, and went into the grain storage building, and brought him some oats, and some lay mash mixed in a bucket, and Freddy was in Hog Heaven.

I stayed with him, petting him until Brian yelled," Fuck that goat; we've got work to do! You can spoon with him after work!"

I replied, Screw you Brian, the way that I understand it I am a volunteer!"

Brian replied," Well volunteer your ass over here and get too work, goat boy!"

I came back with, "Touché, Brian, I am a Capricorn, after all!" We both laughed.

It was very cold, and one of the girls from the commune put together a little coat and some booties for Lazarus.

Brian pulled me aside and told me that he thought she liked me.

She didn't hold a candle, looks wise; to any of the fearsome foursome however, she wasn't ugly either.

And she had a very attractive quality about her, a bosomy Rubenesque type body, with rosy cheeks blue eyes and curly brown hair, and a small gold ring in her nose.

She had a cool hippie name, "Blossom."

And within 5 min. of beginning my conversation with her, I knew that she had a kind heart and was very bright and funny, and that she was going to be my companion and lover for my stay at the House of Che at least.

She was very kind to Lazarus, bringing him scraps, throwing the stick for him, and petting him a lot; and that made me like her even more.

And she turned out to be quite a lover and showered me with attention as much as she did Lazarus, if not more so.

However, about three days into my stay, I must admit she was starting to wear me out. Work hard all day, and then eat, and then Fuck all night, began to wear me out quickly.

However the really great thing was that Blossom was also very understanding, saying things like, "We can just go to sleep and cuddle if you want, honey."

She liked to call me honey. However, I don't think she ever knew, or understood how calling me honey scared the living shit out of me.

As the work went on week after week it began to get colder and colder, until the first blizzard came during the night, one night.

I recall Lazarus waking me up early in the morning to go out, and when I tried to open the camper shell door, which opened outward and upward, it wouldn't open. As hard as I tried I couldn't open it.

And the tailgate wouldn't open out either. And then I looked out one of the side windows to see what was going on, and both of the windows were solid white with snow.

I said, "Holy shit. We're fucked!"

When I said that, Blossom woke up asking, "What's going on?"

I looked at her, and trying to act calm I said, "Now don't panic. But I think that blizzard that came in last night has covered us completely with snow."

Lazarus barked a few times, and then scrambled through the crawlspace between the camper shell and the cab of the truck. He began to bark rapidly at the driver's side window.

I looked through the crawlspace and sure enough I could see daylight, 6 inches or so at the top of the driver's side window.

As I told Lazarus to quiet down, I thought to myself, "Damn, that's a smart dog; he's saved my life again.

That trip to the SPCA, three years ago is the best trip I ever made. I commended Lazarus saying, "Good boy, good boy, Lazarus." And then I grabbed a milk bone and tossed it to him through the crawlspace.

Now the problem was that there was no way that I could get through that crawlspace with all of my cold weather clothes on.

So while Blossom looked on, I stripped down completely, and started to try to squeeze my body through the small aluminum crawlspace.

I pulled back initially because my skin was sticking to the frozen aluminum. The opening was way larger than I needed; I just stuck to it where ever I touched it. Luckily we had some cooking oil inside the camper and I made it through with the cooking oil smeared over my shivering body on the second attempt. Blossom started handing me my clothes through the crawlspace, and a towel to wipe the oil off.

My teeth were chattering and I was shivering when I finally got fully dressed with boots, gloves parka, etc. I jerked on the window crank and finally got it to start to lower. I began to pull snow into the truck because there was no way to push it out away from inside the truck.

I finally got enough snow out of the way so that I could exit the vehicle, and Lazarus was right behind me. I told Blossom to see if she could get the wood burning stove in the camper going and that

I would get some people to help dig her out. And she replied, "Okay honey." I cringed as I turned to see how the rest of the commune buildings had fared.

Everyone in the main building had made their way out of the windows on the second story, and they were in the process of digging out others in the single-story outbuildings, some of which had snow up to, and over the roof line. Other buildings were completely covered with snow.

The entire commune was filled with an air of emergency; combined with panic. Luckily all of the animals, including Freddy were fine, having been brought inside during the storm.

Freddy had the luxury of being in his own small building, because of his reputation!

All of the dogs were crammed into the main room of the main building, and everyone else was on the second story.

As I noticed more people being pulled out of the outbuildings and the crew of rescuers grew exponentially, I realized that we were going to be all right.

I turned back to the truck and saw smoke start to rise out of the small chimney that came out of the top of the camper shell. For some reason, this site sealed the deal for me.

Still to this day I don't know why I said it, but I leaned in the window and said to Blossom, "I'm going to get help, honey." Cringing right after I said it.

And Blossom replied "Okay, dear." And that reply and that blizzard sealed another deal, for me anyway.

The pond was frozen over. But the guys got enough snow down and broke through the ice and fired up the recently completed sauna, and during that night everyone in the commune took turns spending 15 or 20 min. in the superheated sauna and then diving into the frozen water of the pond.

This experience was described by Brian and David as quote unquote, "Better than sex."

However, I would describe it as worse than being sucked into a jet engine at full throttle on acid, or maybe being skinned alive and dropped into a pit of molten lava.

You see when my superheated body hit the ice water, I literally thought that my heart was going to jump out of my chest, and I couldn't breathe at all for around 20 seconds.

As they pulled me out of the frozen pond and dragged me inside to the warmth of the sauna, I made up my mind.

I was done with blizzards, I was done with saunas, I was done with the House of Che,

I was done with Blossom, and most importantly, at least for the winter of 73-74 and except for a trip back to Vancouver and the luxury and opulence of Michael's place, I was done with Canada.

All that my mind could think of, and all that my body craved, was the warmth and the sunny beaches of Marina Del Rey, and California.

The whole commune got together the next day, and we dug, and plowed our way up to the logging road just about the time that the logging companies' snowplow came through.

I went back to my truck, packed up my stuff, told Blossom and everyone else that I was headed back to California. Blossom and I did a tearful goodbye, and I managed not to cringe when with tears running down her cheek, Blossom gave me a long kiss and said, " I'll miss you honey."

And with that and a big hug from everyone at the House of Che, Josh (who decided to go back with me), Lazarus, and I headed back to Michael's place.

I'm still convinced to this day that Josh, who walked from one end of Canada to the other every few years, wearing nothing but sandals and a robe actually got the crap scared out of him by that blizzard, and all of a sudden Michael's, and actually any form of heat and any place to live that wouldn't kill you, was looking pretty DAMN good to him.

All the way back to Michael's I was thinking about Chartreuse, and if she was still there and if so did I have the balls to make her my girlfriend and take her with me?

Or would my wanderlust and my general lust, over power what I knew was best for me, once again, or more importantly would the little head start to think for the bighead again, causing me to just stay and fuck my life away at Michael's.

    Whatever I decided, and whatever happened, I knew one thing for sure. Like the rest of this trip; it was certainly going to be interesting.

Chapter 27

Back to Michael's for one last time. My first time sleep raping with Chartreuse, and then back to LA with a broken dog, broken rib, and a broken truck.

The two kids from Michael's place that went up to the House of Che with us decided to stay there and help the commune with the digging out process.

The drive back to Vancouver from the House of Che was very slow and tedious.

Luckily Josh was along to spell me with the driving.

The snow was heavy and we followed snowplows most of the way.

By the time we got to Michael's they were just finishing clearing the snow from the long driveway and the normally closed huge front gates were open.

We only noticed one new face, a young kid already going by the nick name "Tex," he claimed to be from Amarillo.

We parked the truck, and Josh went inside, while I walked Lazarus before going in.

It was so funny watching him running around the parking area, which he had been trained was off-limits for going to the bathroom in the summer, but which was now surrounded by a four foot wall of snow that surrounded the huge circular driveway, he looked at me with a befuddled look, and then jumped over the four foot wall of snow and stuck in the three foot drift of snow behind it. Going deeper into the snow drift the harder he tried to get out.

I finally had to go in after him, to rescue him. And then, after coaxing him for a while to go to the bathroom where I had trained him not to go earlier, he finally went, and I cleaned it up.

As Laz and I walked through the huge front doors and into Michael's I was shocked to see people fully clothed and other than some soft conversation in the distance, the mansion was totally silent.

No loud rock 'n roll music? No naked people having sex everywhere? Was this the wrong house?

I walked into the kitchen where I heard Josh's voice.

Josh was talking to Michael, who immediately ran up to me yelling, "Bob'O, Bob'O, my hero. Marina Del Rey, California

Hippie Bob." While excitedly hugging me he said, "We've all missed you and Josh, Bob. We've missed you a lot."

I replied, "We've missed you too, brother. You have no idea."

Michael pulled back and looking at me. He said. "Oh my God, every time you go up to that commune you come back all scruffy and dirty, and looking like a mountain man.

We are going to have to get you cleaned up again." I asked Michael if Chartreuse was still there.

He replied, "Yeah, she's here, she's upstairs.

But since you've been gone she's moved into the white room with Terri, Cassie, and Steve and I think that she and Steve seem to be kind of an item, if you know what I mean?"

My mind went into overdrive, filled with dueling emotions.

Half of my emotions were filled with rage and jealousy that she was with another guy so soon; and the other half of my emotions were filled with relief and closure bathed in the realization that I wouldn't have to wrestle with whether or not to ask her to be my girlfriend, and take her back to LA.

At that point in time I thought I still might have a girlfriend living in Marina Del Rey; a girl who I needed to stay with at least initially upon arrival in Los Angeles; at least until I could find somewhere else to live. I must've been wearing a blank stare and thinking about all of this for a while, because I heard Michael say, "Bob, Hello, Bob, Oh good, you're back. Where'd you go buddy?

You weren't thinking about Chartreuse were you?"

I said, "No. I'm happy for her, at least if he's a good guy?"

Michael replied, "You know Steve? You remember him? He's a great guy. If somebody comes here and they are and asshole Big Jerry and a couple of the other big guys just launch them off the property. I'm sure that she'll want to see you. Do you want to go up to the white room and say hello?"

I replied, "Okay."

And up the stairs Lazarus and I went, the bedroom door was closed so I knocked quietly two or three soft knocks,

I waited about 20 or 30 seconds and then Lazarus and I started back downstairs.

Suddenly I heard that soft voice come from behind the bedroom door, "Who's there? Who is it?"

I scurried back to the door with Lazarus and replied, "It's Bob. You know, California Hippie", my sentence was interrupted as Chartreuse dressed in nothing but panties threw open the bedroom door leaped into my arms and interrupted my sentence with a big kiss.

I almost went down to the floor when she wrapped her legs around my waist while kissing me; she was kissing me all over my dirty bearded face.

And then she pulled back and looked into my eyes saying, "Oh baby, I've missed you so much. Why were you gone so long? Well, you're back now and that's all that matters." And then she went back to kissing me on the lips as she released the grip that her legs had on my hips and put her feet back onto the floor pulling my head down slightly.

That's when out of the corner of my eye I saw a sleepy looking Steve, scratching his head coming out of the bedroom door.

He extended his hand, and said, "Good to have you back, Bob.

She's all yours. All she ever does is talk about you, anyway. Sometimes she even yells out your name when she's coming." He yawned and continued, "And after a while that shit gets old. Well I am going downstairs to get some breakfast. I smell food."

Chartreuse said, "Bye, Steve. It was fun."

And then looking back at me, she said, "What did they do to you up there? First, we have to cut that bird's nest of a beard off. And then, give you a long cream rinse and shampoo in a long hot shower. And then were going to feed you and pamper you, maybe a massage?

Oh, I forgot about sex. Are you horny? You want to fuck right now? Or do all the cleaning, feeding and pampering first? Would you like me to have a few of the other girls join us? Three or four of the new girls that I've told about you want to fuck you really bad."

I interrupted her, "Whoa. Whoa. Slow down. You've been right about everything I want to do so far, and in the right order, except the horny part. The trip down through the snow was a nightmare. And I'm exhausted. So how about I get all cleaned up, shave the beard, and then we go downstairs and eat. And then you and I can come back up here, I'll make up Lazarus's old bed for him in the corner, you give me a quick massage, and we go to sleep cuddling. How does that sound?" She replied, "That's cool. But after the massage, if you want me to get you off with a quick blow job to help you sleep I could get into that."

I kissed her on the forehead saying, "That's really sweet. But at this point unnecessary. It's like this, the cleaning up in the shower will wake me up some, but the food is going to make me very sleepy as I am very tired. We may wind up even skipping the massage. So I just want to clean up and eat something and go to bed if that's okay?"

Kissing me again, she said, "Of course it's okay. You're back, and we're together, that's all that matters."

I shaved my beard with her help, and we climbed into the shower together and she helped wash and rinse my long scraggly curly hair. And as the heat was on in Michael's mansion we strolled downstairs in our underwear.

As we walked downstairs the smell of fresh baked bread, and bacon and eggs permeated the air.

Lazarus ran ahead of us down the stairs and into the kitchen in search of his usual tricks for treats routine. Most everyone at Michael's knew Lazarus, and there was a kitchen routine that Lazarus did when we were guests at Michael's.

Whoever was cooking in the kitchen would throw pieces of meat in the air, and Lazarus would run and catch the food in his mouth.

No matter how difficult the throw somehow Lazarus would manage to catch the piece of food.

I remind you that Lazarus was a fetch junkie, and if you will, an extreme athlete.

More than once I had come down the stairs at Michael's to see everyone gathered around the kitchen *ooing, aahing*, and cheering, only to push my way through the crowd to see Lazarus making some amazing leap to catch a piece of ham in midair in the kitchen.

And more than once I had put a halt to the shenanigans exclaiming, "I don't want a fat dog, and I don't want an injured dog."

And then I would pick up Lazarus and carry him out of the kitchen, to the boos, and hisses emanating from the gathered crowd.

Along with the negative messages that the gathered crowd

would blurt out, like, "You're a downer, dude.

And that Lazarus is far out, man. Or hey, man. I'll bet if you gave your dog acid he could fly like fucking Superman, man."

We had a great breakfast and we went back upstairs, I made Lazarus his bed in the corner.

Chartreuse took off her clothes and we climbed into bed together in fetal position, with my chest against her back my left arm under her neck, and my right arm around her breasts.

I was so tired that I immediately dropped off to sleep and began to dream.

I dreamt that it was summer, and that I was walking along a trail in the woods with Father, and that unexpectedly Father had stopped, and he began to chant, as he chanted, he lifted his left arm pointing up the trail, and there I saw a beautiful naked girl sitting on a rock beckoning too me.

Father motioned me forward and as I walked closer towards her, I realized that it was Chartreuse on the rock beckoning too me, and as I got closer she spread her legs and smiling she spread the lips of her vagina. and when I reached her, I dropped to my knees and begin to devour her vagina like it was a slice of cold watermelon, and I had just walked out of the desert, licking, and sucking as she screamed and moaned in ecstasy.

In the dream she was coming so hard, that I had to fight the massive current of cum to reconnect my lips with her vagina. As the flood of multiple orgasms subsided, I pulled my pants down and penetrated her. Pounding her like a jackhammer until I groaned with my own loud orgasm, and then her moans became louder and louder.

And finally her screams became so loud that I actually woke up and realized that I was covered in sweat, as was she, we were both out of breath and both still jerking violently

I'll never forget what I said, and she said as I looked into her eyes. I said while still out of breath, "Oh my God. That wasn't a dream. That really happened.

And she replied, also still out of breath, "Oh baby. That was the greatest sex that I have ever had in my life, period. I love you baby. I was shocked and didn't reply right away.

And before I could, some guy shouted, "Yeah, right on dude, right on."

Applause erupted in the middle of him saying right on, and I turned to look behind me to see a room filled with people that both Chartreuse and I had been oblivious too.

Michael ran out of the partially clad group of onlookers consisting of people cheering, applauding, and a few, both men and women, who were continuing to masturbate and achieve climax like the ones who were cheering and applauding had apparently already done.

Michael ran up to me, screaming over the crowd, and sitting down on the edge of the bed. "You never cease to amaze me man. You two not only woke up the entire house, you proceeded to get the entire house off, single-handedly, and I mean that literally, in the sense that for the most part everybody, male and female watching you were jerking off.

One of the guys in the crowd moaned and came into his cupped left hand. Michael smiled and screamed, pointing at the guy, "See. See what I mean. That was me and a lot of others over the last 20 min. or so."

Michael got off of the bed stood up, and motioned the crowd to quiet down, which they did.

Michael announced, "The legend continues. The prodigal son returns. Marina Del Rey, California Hippie Bob." Some people started to clap, however I shouted over the beginnings of applause saying, "Great. Thanks everybody. We appreciate it. Now, can you all please get the fuck out of the bedroom and continue your jerk off festival elsewhere, so that we can have a private moment together alone, please."

Michael began to motion people out of the room, and the throng of gathered masturbating voyeurs began to retreat out of the bedroom with Michael motioning with his arms to round up any stragglers as he herded them like horny sheep out of the bedroom door.

He was the last one out of the door and as he closed the door. He said softly, "Sorry Bob. Sorry Chartreuse. But that was fucking legendary. Oh shit! I forgot my fucking camera; goddammit!"

As he finally pulled his head back and softly shut the door.

Without warning Lazarus barked. I yelled at Lazarus, "You've got to be kidding me, how you bark. Now you're a watchdog. You let the whole house sneak in and watch us having sex; and then when everyone leaves and the door closes, you bark? I've got to get out a here. Michael's place has even turned my dog into a pervert."

Chartreuse began to laugh uncontrollably, and I started to laugh with her, so Lazarus's spirits seemed to lift a bit because he realized that he was out of the doghouse.

A few days later I overheard someone refer to me as Hippie Bob the Sleep Raper which pissed me off at first, however when women that I had wanted to sleep with at Michael's started dragging me into closets, bedrooms, and once even all the way out to the loft of Michael's barn to have sex with me, I started to enjoy the moniker.

It seems that Chartreuse had spread the word to everyone that would listen at Michael's, about how great the sex had been, and especially the way that I went down on her. And how we were both sound asleep when I started going down on her, making it that much more exciting.

At Michael's, without my knowledge, I had become the King of cunnilingus, the Don Juan of dreamland. The point is, with everyone in the house throwing hundreds of monikers at the wall, the one that stuck was "The Sleep Raper."

I was not real happy with the moniker itself, but I must admit that it was really special to be the one guy in this mansion, (with 35 to 40 different, constantly changing mostly good-looking women,) who virtually all of them wanted to fuck or suck without anyone else knowing.

It was exciting, sexy, and the more that the rumors flew of this girl doing me in the closet, or that girl doing me in the barn, the more impressed Michael became.

And best of all Chartreuse didn't care because we spent every night together, like boyfriend and girlfriend.

And, besides, she had the guy that every other woman in the place wanted.

I have to admit that during my entire life, while I was in the music business, doing comedy, etc. That this is the one time in my life that I truly felt like a Rock Star, with the exception of a couple of times a few years later during my Quaalude days.

But as they say, with most fame comes tragedy, as was the

case with me. You see all the women loved me and Michael thought I was great. I was starting to get a lot of dirty looks from the guys, and I don't just mean boyfriends, sure they were mad, but there were even more guys that were not as upset that I had slept with their girlfriend, but were really pissed off that I had been dragged into a closet, or a pantry, and ravished by a woman that they had the hots for, and who had rejected them, even during some of the orgies.

After a few weeks of Rock Star bliss, it became readily apparent that I needed to get out of Dodge before I met a gruesome, untimely and apparently accidental death.

Josh had heard some talk, and agreed with my assessment of the situation. I recollect sitting in the pantry early in the morning with Josh discussing what my options were, and why this was happening again.

I remember nervously asking Josh, "I don't understand it? Why do I constantly have to run away from some commune, always just ahead of some angry, jealous, bloodthirsty, revenge filled husband or boyfriend.

And now I've got multiple ones running me out of Michael's place.

Josh being Josh, calmly replied, "This isn't rocket science Bob. You can't keep fucking other guys' women, without expecting a few negative consequences.

If you want to keep doing that kind of shit, then next time come back as a dog." He got a good laugh out of me with that one. We both came to the conclusion that I needed to be heading back to LA, ASAP.

Now the Chartreuse dilemma presented itself again.

Josh chimed in, "You tell me that you barely have enough money left to get you back to Marina Del Rey, and your old girlfriend.

Who you haven't written or spoken to this whole time; and yet you hope that she will let you stay with her in your old place on the beach? But it's obvious that your chances of her letting you stay there with a new girlfriend are zero. So you gotta ask yourself, how much do you love Chartreuse? Can you start over again in LA with Chartreuse? If things get tough in LA will Chartreuse stick with you?"

I interrupted him saying, "Stop. Stop. I get it. I get it. I can't take anyone back to LA with me. I might still be welcomed with open arms by Shelley. And then again, she probably has a roommate, and may have a boyfriend by now. So I gotta head back South alone."

Later that morning I went upstairs, woke up Chartreuse and gave her the bad news.

There was a lot of crying. I got slapped a couple of times. I kept trying to tell her that as soon as I was established in LA that I would contact her and get her a plane ticket down to LA, so we could live together.

However, she wasn't buying any of it. I was just another bastard who had broken her heart again.

I walked out of the bedroom crying, leaving her crying on the bed. It was one of the lowest moments ever in my life, in a few hours I had gone from rock star, to reprobate.

I told Michael my reasons for leaving and that I would miss him, and the place, and everyone. I asked him if he could gather everyone inside and out of the place, into the living room downstairs in half an hour; and he said he would.

I couldn't believe it. He actually teared up a little and said, "That's the thing about legends they're here one minute, and then they're gone the next. But trust me, Bob, you won't last in LA. You said it yourself; you came up here in the first place because LA was driving you crazy, literally. So I know you'll be back soon.

That's why I'm only going to say, so long, Bob. Because I know you'll be back soon, and the minute that you push that intercom button on the front gates and announce your arrival, I am going to start planning the biggest God damn orgy that this place has ever seen, even if I have to spike the neighborhood water supply with methaqualone to do it."

We both laughed and he gave me a big hug with his open robe pressing his partial hard- on against my leg which was as awkward and disquieting as ever, but I always let it slide, because it was just Michael being Michael.

I went back to the white room to gather my stuff and Lazarus. I tried to talk to Chartreuse again. I even called her Darla, her real name, and when I did, she swung around, and in a fit of rage, tears streaming down her face.

She loudly announced, "Don't you call me Darla. You don't have the right to call me Darla. In fact you don't have the right to even speak to me at all. Just go about doing what you do best. Pack up your shit, and run. Run to the next girl that you're going to romance and screw and make her fall in love with you, and then break her heart, and leave her behind, like an old discarded tire on the side of the road. Go do what you do best. Just get out of my sight, you son of a bitch. Get out! Get out!"

She stormed into the bathroom and slammed the door.

I rapidly finished packing, and leaving all of the stuff I had in the bathroom. Lazarus and I made our way down stairs and out to the truck.

I gave Lazarus a quick walk and put him in the camper shell.

I walked back into Michael's for the last time down the long hallway and into the giant living room where everyone but Chartreuse was gathered.

Michael announced my entrance to his gathered flock saying, "Here he is folks. Marina del Rey, California Hippie Bob. He's here to wish is all a fond ado, for he is on his way back to Marina Del Rey to give it one more try. But we all know he'll be back soon because he'll miss us, the sex, the food, the booze, the drugs; oh hell, he's going to miss it all too much, right."

At this point the entire group of 60 or 70 people filling the living room shouted in unison, "You're fuckin' right he is, Michael."

The whole group, led by Josh and Michael ran over to me, taking turns giving me hugs and shaking my hand. This all took around 15 or 20 minutes, at which point Josh announced to the group that he was going with me down to the ferry across to the states.

As I walked to the front door, women running up and kissing me, and guys shaking my hand and patting me on the back, my mind was spinning.

Was I doing the right thing? Should I stay?

I mean, after all, I've got a really good thing here. And with only a little under 500 bucks in my pocket, I could be screwed by the time I hit LA.

It's so easy living here, and after all, I do have real feelings for Chartreuse and she loves me. All of these emotions ran through my mind as I continued to walk to the truck.

Josh climbed into the passenger side, and I opened the door to the driver side, turned and waved to the 20 or so people who were dressed for the cold weather out front and they waved back. And just before I climbed into the truck, I looked up at the second story hallway window to see Chartreuse standing there crying.

I climbed into the truck put the key in the ignition turned the key and a starter turned over and over and the damn thing wouldn't start. I let off of the ignition and looked angrily at Josh, who started laughing his ass off.

He stopped laughing long enough to say, "Well. You better try it again if you don't want to go from legend, to anti-climactic lummox Bob."

I tried starting it up again. This time it sputtered a little bit.

And the third time was the charm. I pumped the gas pedal a few times and it started right up.

As we drove away I looked in my review mirror to see Chartreuse running away from the second story hallway window, probably to go cry in her room.

We stopped inside the gates, and while they slowly opened, and Josh prattled on, giving me directions to the ferry,

I turned my face away from him, and looking out of my window I quickly wiped the tear from my left cheek so that he couldn't see it.

All the way across Vancouver to the ferry I kept thinking, "What are you doing. Are you insane? You've got a good thing here. You don't know what's waiting for you in LA, probably nothing. You've got no money. Your truck's acting up. Your dog's hurt.

I forgot to mention that that morning one of the guys was throwing a piece of food for Lazarus, and he slid into the wall very hard, and now Lazarus had a pronounced limp.

Before I knew it (with all of this going on in my mind), Josh yelled out, "Slow down. We're here. Pull over there behind the line of cars, and park.

See the ferry there? We have a half an hour before they start loading. You are in line now, so let's go over to that grassy area and give Lazarus a walk while we say our goodbyes, brother."

We walked and talked, and smoked a joint while Lazarus did his business; and then little Josh put his arms around my midsection and then lifting me off the ground, he squeezed me so tight that the air went out of me; and I heard something pop. I let out a scream!

He put me down immediately, and asked, "What happened?"

I answered, "I can't breathe, and I'm in a lot of pain. Did you hear that loud pop?"

He asked, "Where does it hurt?" He started feeling around my chest area; and when he touched a new swollen area on my right side. I let out another scream.

He said, "I'm so sorry, man. I think I broke your rib just hugging you goodbye.

You're not leaving today. We've got to get you back to Michael's and before that to a clinic."

I shouted, "The clinic, yes; but Michael's, no. I can't go back there, no way."

Josh said, "There's another ferry out of here in three hours. We'll go get you patched up at the clinic and back here in time to go across on that one." And that's what we did.

Josh drove us to the clinic, and they took x-rays, determined it wasn't a major fracture, cinched and taped me up real good, gave me a bunch of pills for pain and inflammation, etc. I was worried about the cost with my limited funds. Until Josh reminded me that it was all free.

We made it back to the ferry in time, and said our goodbyes.

I drove onto the ferry as Lazarus barked his last goodbye out the passenger side window to Josh.

We made it through customs fine, because it was the good old days. So they never found the weed that I had stashed inside of my binoculars.

We gassed up in Washington; and since I filled the extra tank as well, we didn't have to stop for gas again until Roseburg, Oregon.

As we were gassing up again in Roseburg it was really getting dark and looking like a big storm was coming, and sure enough as soon as we got back onto the highway, here came the rain.

Lazarus and I had only gone a few miles down the highway in the pouring rain, when I saw what appeared to be a young woman holding a baby, hitchhiking in the pouring rain.

I immediately pulled over, and put Lazarus into the camper and opened the passenger side door.

The rain was pouring down and she was soaking wet, she climbed up into the cab of the truck, and her baby was crying.

I turned up the heat in the cab and pulled a small blanket from between the two seats, and handed it to her to wrap around her and her baby.

I asked, "Where you headed?"

She replied, "Where ever you are."

This startled me a little. I asked her what she meant by that.

She explained that her old man had beaten her up again, and that when he drank he could get real mean. She said that she really needed some place to stay, at least for the night or if she could find the right person for a week or a month, or even the rest of her life.

I thought to myself, "Wow, I really feel sorry for this girl. She's so desperate."

I told her that she could spend the night in the camper with me, and that I could drop her off the next day wherever she wanted, but that I was heading to LA, and that when I got there I was going to have to live for a while with my old girlfriend. She told me that she understood, and that, that was fine.

I gave her one of my furniture business cards which had the Driftwood address on it in the Marina, and I told her that she could write me at that address, if things got really bad.

But that I wouldn't be at that address long, but my mail would be forwarded to wherever I was living when I moved.

She thanked me, and we pulled off the highway onto a road that looked promising for campsites.

As the rain was letting up and it was starting to get dark, I found a nice secluded open area that was a perfect place to spend the night. It was about 300 feet off of the road.

I let Lazarus out, opened up the tailgate, and propped up the camper shell door, and got the wood stove in the camper going with dried wood that I carried in the storage compartments on the side of the truck.

I asked her if she was hungry and she said, "Yes, some food would be very nice." I asked her if soup and sandwiches would be okay and she replied that she was a vegetarian, but that she was so hungry that anything would do. I told her that she was in luck, because I had two lettuce, tomato and avocado sandwiches, and that I was making lentil soup, and she said, "Oh goody, my favorite."

Just then, Lazarus ran up with a stick. She was sitting on the end of the tailgate and had set her baby, who was now sleeping wrapped in the blanket that I gave her, inside on the floor of the camper.

I told Lazarus that I couldn't throw the stick for him. I was busy making dinner.

So she said, "Oh, I'll throw the stick for him." And she did over and over, while I was cooking dinner.

I thought to myself, "I like this chick. She's cool, and cute, in a Rubenesque sort of way. Pretty face, too bad about that small scar on her cheek, probably a gift from her asshole of a boyfriend. I wish I had time to drive her home, and walk up to the son of a bitch and kick the shit out of him, or put a hole in him with my Enfield if he comes out with a gun." I told her that the food was ready, and that I had water or white wine to drink with dinner, her choice.

She replied, "What a gentleman. White wine for me please. Thank you very much."

She washed up after throwing the stick for Lazarus and we had a nice meal with wine, and I asked her if she wanted to smoke a joint? She replied, "Yes please."

As we both sat on the tailgate passing a joint back and forth, without warning she reached back and picked up her baby who was starting to stir. She popped out a very nice-looking breast and put her baby's mouth up to it and it began to suckle. After the baby finished feeding and we finished the joint she asked, "Do you mind if I change his diaper?"

I replied, "Go right ahead, I'll give my dog a quick walk." Lazarus and I were back in a few minutes. And she had the baby all changed and had disposed of the old diaper.

I said, "There's only the one bed on the floor but the sheets are clean and the top blanket comes off to reveal a bottom blanket which is clean, I can crank the stove up for you, and leave more wood for you to add to the stove during the night; so you shouldn't need more than two blankets and I can sleep in the passenger seat up front, and my dog can sleep in the driver's seat.

She looked at me with a puzzled expression, and she asked, "You're kidding, right? If it's easier your dog can sleep up front, if he'll be comfortable up there? But you and I are sleeping in the bed. My baby shouldn't start crying. I can put him over by the stove to keep him warm.

The real question is, would you like me to give you some head before we fuck?"

I smiled and replied, "I think that if you really want to do it right now, about all that I can handle is some head. I've got a cracked rib."

She smiled, asking, "If I really want to? Mister, you are a handsome man. And you are a gentleman. That's a rare combination around these parts. And I don't know where you're coming from, but wherever it is, you were getting chased and screwed by a lot of good looking women."

Now she had piqued my curiosity. I came back with, "Oh yeah? And how do you know all of that?"

"Every human has a certain gift," she said, "With some people its vision, others have a heightened sense of hearing, and having a heightened sense of smell is my gift. You see, even if you shower every day, which I can tell you do normally, there are places on your body where odors linger. Do you remember when I hugged you when we first got here?"

I replied, "Yeah".

She said, "I could smell the remnants of at least nine different women's perfume coming from your inner ear. I could smell three others in your hair over the Lilac shampoo that you shampooed with last. I can also tell that you don't wash your clothes nearly as often as you do your body, because there are the slight remnants of at least five women's vaginal fluid on your undershirt, and over 10 women's vaginal fluid, along with your cum, on your pants around your fly. This tells me two things about you.

One, you like to go down on women as much as you like them to go down on you, which is also a rare trait in a man around these parts.

And two, you have been having a lot of wild sneaky dangerous sex with a lot of good-looking women who were ravishing you.

You are literally drenched in sex. You've got me so horny just smelling you, that I could crack walnuts with my clit.

So if anyone's getting a mercy fuck here, it's me."

I asked her, "How do you know that the women were good looking?"

She replied, "That's simple. She perfumes were expensive, and vaginal fluids smelled young and innocent, I have been with a beautiful young girl or two before myself, and I know what they smell like."

She pulled off her top to expose two really lovely breasts, and she rapidly shimmied out of her tie-dye skirt and panties to expose a much tighter body than I had thought that she would have had, along with a great hairy pussy.

"You've seen mine, so it's time to show me what you've got; please?" she asked, almost desperately.

I took my shirt off exposing the bandages and tape that held my ribs in place.

She gasped and said "Oh baby. You do have a cracked rib. That's okay. I'll be very gentle. But keep going."

I pulled off my jeans, exposing my cock and balls.

And she shouted, "I love it, a free flyin' man, and such a handsome cock." She said, "Now leave your boots on, and put your dog up in the front, and then come back here and I'll take your boots, and socks off, and then you just get into the truck and lay down on your back and I'll take care of everything else. Oh my God, you've got me so horny. Just look."

She pointed down at her hairy pussy and pressed the hair down on either side of her clit, which was one of the biggest ones that I had ever seen. Her clit appeared to be erect, standing at roughly a 15 degree angle above her body.

I had never seen anything like that before, and I've never seen anything like that since.

She asked, "Have you ever seen a female hard-on before? I haven't had one in over eight years; not since my first time. That's what you are doing to me."

I climbed up into the truck. She closed everything up and added some firewood to the stove, and began having her way with me while I lay on my back.

I must admit that she was very good at everything sexually.

First she would give me just amazing head, and I would come, and then she would massage me for a half hour or so and we would kiss, etc., and then she would start jerking me off, and giving me head to get me hard again.

And then she would gently mount me going up and down on me while barely touching my body, and looking up at her while she did that felt so good, and was so erotic, that I would come again.

This went on virtually all night; including her gently sitting on my face a couple of times so that I could taste her.

By the next morning, after the three-week rock star routine at Michael's and then running into this chick, if it had been an option at that moment, I would have joined a monastery, just to get some R&R. Real R&R, that is.

In the morning after breakfast, she was really pitching me on the idea of taking her with me to LA. But I knew that there was no way that I could take her. The only thing worse than showing up at Shelley's with Chartreuse in tow would be showing up at Shelley's with a little hippie chick with a baby.

I drove her back to Roseburg to a friend's house, who was supposedly married to a cop, where she would go for safe haven when her boyfriend was on the warpath, as she put it.

We drove around the block once so she could make sure that her boyfriends' truck wasn't there.

Deep down I was hoping he would be there because even if I couldn't take him with my cracked rib I could sure as shit put a hole in his ass with my Enfield rifle.

But luckily for him, he wasn't, so she gave me a kiss, and said that she would write to me, and I dropped her off, and headed back South, on the highway.

It's funny how I can remember so many of the people's names from so long ago, some of whom I had a much shorter encounter with than her. All I can remember is that her name was something like flora, or fauna, or something like that.

The rest of the trip down to Los Angeles was fairly uneventful.

When I stopped that night on the beach, I walked Lazarus, and then slept in my clothes. Lazarus woke me up at seven and I let him out and watched him from inside the camper with the tailgate down and as soon as he did his business, I called him back in, closed the camper backup, and went back to sleep until late afternoon, when all of a sudden there was a tapping on the camper shell door, and Lazarus began to bark.

I asked who was there, and the reply came back, "California Highway Patrol Sir. Can you open the door please?"

I replied, "Yes sir, right away. The camper shell door opens out, and then up, sir, can you please stand back a little? I wouldn't want it to hit you."

I opened up the camper shell door and said, "How can I help you, officer?"

He was a very young neatly dressed Highway Patrol officer. He replied, "Well sir, there really is no infraction here. We do allow parking on this part of the beach. However, you see the tide is coming in, and it looked like this vehicle was unattended and I just wanted to make sure nobody was sleeping in here so I could have it towed. Because we've had people go to sleep in their vehicles overnight down here on the beach and get swept out to sea when the tide comes in. So if you could just move your vehicle off the beach, you would be doing us both a big favor."

I replied, "Thank you, officer, for your kindness, your alertness, and saving my life, my dog's life, and my vehicle."

He replied, "You're quite welcome, sir. You have a nice day."

My comeback was, "Thanks to you, officer, I'm quite sure I will." We shook hands. Lazarus and I climbed into the cab and we were on our way South again.

We stopped for a minute in Point Arena, California. But my lady friend was not at home, and after the experience there on the way up, I certainly wasn't going to camp anywhere near there. So we continued straight through to Santa Barbara only stopping when we needed to eat, get gas, or go to the bathroom; which because I was drinking coffee, added to mine and Lazarus's ideal bathroom schedule.

I recall that when I pulled off of PCH, and started driving down Pacific Avenue through Santa Monica and then Venice, on the way too Marina Del Rey. That they were working on Pacific

Avenue and that all of the little beach houses seemed like shacks, and I thought to myself, "I don't remember this place being so dirty and filled with all of these shacks!"

We finally turned onto Driftwood Ave., and drove up and parked kitty-corner from my old house. I thought to myself, "That's where I used to live, in that tiny little cracker box? Wow."

I looked over at Lazarus and said, "Maybe we should've stayed at Michael's!"

I pulled my wallet out and checked my money;

I had $52.00 left, a broken dog, a broken rib, and a broken truck. I forgot to mention that the overdrive went out again in Malibu; luckily I only needed it above 55 MPH.

I was about to find out if my broken dog, and me with my broken rib, were going to have to live in my broken truck or not.

I put the money back in my wallet and put the wallet in my coveralls and looked at Lazarus again and said, "This was a big gamble buddy. I hope that I haven't screwed this up for both of us Lazarus. But it's been one hell of a ride hasn't it?"

Lazarus barked an exuberant yes. "Now, you wait here, and I'll be right back. I promise." I said.

I got out of the truck and began to walk across Driftwood Ave to knock on Shelley's front door and find out whether I would be welcomed as a long-lost lover, and adventurer returned from the road, or shunned as the asshole who left and never wrote, or called, and then showed up over a year later unannounced, injured, and broke.

I only walked halfway across Driftwood, when suddenly I turned around and walked back to the truck. I had just realized that it was only about 6:30 AM, so I decided to take Lazarus for a walk on the beach, and to sit and watch the waves for a while before knocking on Shelley's door and learning my fate.

Lazarus was very happy about the new turn of events. I believe that he had been really excited about getting back to LA. He immediately found an old worn-out ball for me to throw for him.

I sat there around 40 feet from the water's edge throwing the ball for Lazarus, while reminiscing about the funny, magical, spiritually enlightening, sex filled journey that Lazarus and I had just returned from.

Many questions flooded my mind as I watched Lazarus retrieve the ball, and listened to the constant pounding of the surf against the sand, and the repetitive ebb and flow of the ocean, which I thought to myself, seemed to mimic the Yin and Yang of life.

I remember thinking to myself, "I can't believe that I only came to the beach in all three of those years that I lived down here to play volleyball, or follow some girl to try to get her back to my house for sex.

I never once came here just to reflect about whom I was, and where my life was going, or anything deep, and meaningful.

Wow. I really learned a lot on this trip! Klaus was right when he told me that I needed to get out of LA, because it was killing me. It was."

And now I was back in the belly of the beast that had once almost killed me. Had the lessons leaned on the journey been sufficient to allow me to survive the beast this time?

As the waves crashed, and the ball flew and was retrieved over and over again, the answer slowly came.

Josh, Holy Alex, and Father had all taught me that the city was not the real world, but the surreal world.

This knowledge would help me to deal with city life on its own terms.

All three of them in their own way had helped me to grow spiritually, and be more in tune with all living things, and most importantly they taught me that nothing is ever really what it really appears to be.

Michael in his own inimitable way had taught me that no matter whatever you are doing in life, if you're not enjoying yourself immensely, you should start doing something else, immediately.

Brian and David had taught me that there is no such thing as impossible; and that to them ridiculously impossible meant doable, just impossible meant no problem, and extremely difficult meant why are we even discussing this? An attitude that would serve me well, I was soon to realize in my rapid comeback over the next five years.

My hour and a half or so of reflection about the trip and how amazing it all had been, and how much I had experienced and learned, filled me with confidence; the confidence that I needed to react coolly and calmly when I knocked on Shelley's door, no matter what reaction I received from Shelley.

Lazarus and I went back to the truck. I dried him off with a towel, and put him in the cab of the truck, telling him, "Wish us luck, buddy, we're both going to need it." I walked back across Driftwood, Avenue, to knock on Shelley's door and see what kind of welcome I was going to get.

My heart was pounding with anticipation as I climbed the front steps of the little house. It was after 8 a.m., and I knew that she should be up by now.

But if you want to find out what happened when I knocked on that door, you'll have to read my next book, "Lude Beach," which describes the next outrageous "sex, drugs and rock 'n roll" adventures, which took place in Venice, California, over the next five years, from 1974 through 1979.

Me, Roomate Richard and Lazarus

www.ingramcontent.com/pod-product-compliance
Lightning Source LLC
Chambersburg PA
CBHW061632040426
42446CB00010B/1378